Nineteenth-Century American Fiction on Screen

The process of translating works of literature to the silver screen is a rich field of study for both students and scholars of literature and cinema. The fourteen essays collected here provide an up-to-date survey of the important films based on, or inspired by, nineteenth-century American fiction, from James Fenimore Cooper's *The Last of the Mohicans* to Owen Wister's *The Virginian*. Several of the major works of the American canon are examined, notably *The Scarlet Letter, Moby-Dick*, and *Sister Carrie*. The starting point of each essay is the literary text itself, the focus then moving on to describe specific aspects of the adaptation process, including details of production and reception. Written in a lively and accessible style, the book includes production stills and full filmographies. With its companion volume on twentieth-century fiction, this study offers a comprehensive account of the rich tradition of American literature on screen.

R. BARTON PALMER holds Ph.D. degrees from Yale University (medieval studies) and New York University (cinema studies) and has published widely in those two fields. He is Calhoun Lemon Professor of English at Clemson University, directs the Film Studies Program at Clemson, and is the Director of the South Carolina Film Institute.

Nineteenth-Century American Fiction on Screen

Edited by

R. Barton Palmer

CAMBRIDGE
UNIVERSITY PRESS

CAMBRIDGE UNIVERSITY PRESS
Cambridge, New York, Melbourne, Madrid, Cape Town, Singapore, São Paulo

Cambridge University Press
The Edinburgh Building, Cambridge CB2 2RU, UK

Published in the United States of America by Cambridge University Press,
New York

www.cambridge.org
Information on this title: www.cambridge.org/9780521603164

© Cambridge University Press 2007

First published 2007

Printed in the United Kingdom at the University Press, Cambridge

A catalogue record for this book is available from the British Library

ISBN 978-0-521-84221-1 hardback
ISBN 978-0-521-60316-4 paperback

Contents

vi   Contents

Illustrations

Notes on contributors

MARTIN BARKER is Professor of Film and Television Studies at the University of Wales, Aberystwyth. He has researched and written extensively within the fields of media and cultural studies, including *The New Racism* (1981), *Comics, Ideology, Power, and the Critics* (1989), *A Haunt of Fears: The Strange History of the British Horror Comics Campaign* (1992), *From Antz to Titanic: Reinventing Film Analysis* (2000), (with Jane Arthurs and Ramaswami Harindranath) *The Crash Controversy* (2001), (edited with Julian Petley) *Ill Effects: The Media-Violence Debate* (2001), and (with Kate Brooks) *Knowing Audiences: Judge Dredd, its Friends, Fans, and Foes* (2003). He served as the director of the international audience research project on the reception of *The Lord of the Rings*.

STEPHEN C. BRENNAN is Professor of English at Louisiana State University in Shreveport. He has published numerous articles on Theodore Dreiser in such journals as *Studies in American Fiction* and *American Realism* and is currently co-editor of *Dreiser Studies*. He is at work on a study of Dreiser's short fiction.

DEBORAH CARTMELL is Head of the Graduate Centre in Humanities and Principal Lecturer in English at De Montfort University, UK. She is an editor of the newly formed journal *Shakespeare*, co-editor of the Film/Fiction series, *Adaptations: From Text to Screen, Screen to Text* (1999), author of *Interpreting Shakespeare on Screen* (2000), and *Talking Shakespeare* (2001). She is currently editing *The Cambridge Companion to Literature on Screen* and working on *Literature on Screen: An Overview*.

MICHAEL DUNNE is Professor of English at Middle Tennessee State University, where he specializes in American literature. Among his books are *Hawthorne's Narrative Strategies* (1995), *Intertextual Encounters in American Fiction, Film, and Popular Culture* (2001), and *American Film Musical Themes and Forms* (2003).

JANET HUGHES, a painter and printmaker, has tutored for twelve years in the School of English, Film, and Theatre at Victoria University, Wellington, New Zealand, before and after completing her Ph.D. She now works as an editor for the New Zealand Parliament. Her principal research interest is poetry of the modernist era. *Stairdancing*, a collection of her poetry and prints, was recently published.

DAVID LAVERY is Professor of English at Middle Tennessee State University and the author of more than ninety published essays and reviews; he is also the author/editor/co-editor of ten books, including *Full of Secrets: Critical Approaches to Twin Peaks* (1995) and *Reading* The Sopranos: *Hit TV from HBO* (2006). He co-edits the e-journal *Slayage: The Online International Journal of* Buffy *Studies* and is one of the founding editors of the new journal *Critical Studies in Television: Scholarly Studies of Small Screen Fictions*.

JAKOB LOTHE is Professor of English Literature at the University of Oslo. His books include *Conrad's Narrative Method* (1991) and *Narrative in Fiction and Film* (2000). He has also edited and co-edited several volumes, including *The Art of Brevity* (2004) and *European and Nordic Modernisms* (2005). In 2005–2006 he served as the leader of a research project entitled "Narrative Theory and Analysis" at the Centre of Advanced Study, Oslo.

HARRIET MARGOLIS teaches film at Victoria University, Wellington, New Zealand. She is the author of essays on film, literature, and feminism published in such international journals as *Poetics Today*, *Semiotica*, *Para*Doxa*, *Cinema Journal*, and the *Quarterly Review of Film and Video*. Author of *The Cinema Ideal* (1988), she is the editor of *Jane Campion's The Piano* (1989) and co-editor of *Studying the Event Film: The Lord of the Rings* (in preparation).

DOUGLAS McFARLAND is Associate Professor of English and Comparative Literature at Oglethorpe University in Atlanta, Georgia. He has published studies of Rabelais, Montaigne, and Spenser, and is currently working on a book-length study of Peter Bogdanovich.

BRIAN McFARLANE is an Honorary Associate Professor at the School of Literary, Visual and Performance Studies, Monash University, Melbourne. His most recent books include *Novel to Film: An Introduction to the Theory of Adaptation* (1996), *Lance Comfort* (2000), and *The Encyclopedia of British Film* (2006).

R. BARTON PALMER is Calhoun Lemon Professor of Literature at Clemson University, where he directs the Film Studies and

International Culture program. Among his recent books on film are *Joel and Ethan Coen* (2004), (with David Boyd) *After Hitchcock: Imitation/Influence/Intertextuality* (2006), *Hollywood's Dark Cinema: The American Film Noir* (second revised edition, 2007), and (with Robert Bray) *Hollywood's Tennessee: Tennessee Williams on Screen* (2007). With Linda Badley, he directs the *Traditions in World Cinema* series.

MARCIA PENTZ-HARRIS is a lecturer in Management Communication at the University of Virginia's McIntire School of Commerce. Her current project combines literary, business, and dramatic interests and has a working title of "The Business of Building Men: Performing Commercial Masculinity in Popular Nineteenth-Century American Fiction and Drama." She has presented papers including "Dogs and Rude Mechanicals: Performing Manliness in Aiken's *Uncle Tom's Cabin*," "Housebreaking Your Man: Women Constructing Men in *The Lamplighter* and *The Hidden Hand*," and "'Is There a Doctor in the House?' Containing Female Physicians in Howells, Holmes, Jewett, and Phelps." She also presents annually with the Association for Business Communication and works as a consultant in public speaking and management communication, while researching for her Ph.D. in American Literature at the University of Virginia.

STEPHEN RAILTON teaches American literature at the University of Virginia. His most recent book is *Fenimore Cooper: A Study of His Life and Imagination* (1978). Among his other books are *Authorship and Audience: Literary Performance in the American Renaissance* (1992) and *Mark Twain: A Short Introduction* (2003). Since 1966, much of his work has been involved with exploring the uses of electronic technology in teaching and research.

ROGER SABIN lectures in Cultural Studies at Central Saint Martins College of Art and Design, University of the Arts, London. He is the author of several books, including *Adult Comics: An Introduction* (1993) and *Comics, Comix, and Graphic Novels* (2001).

LINDA SEGER is a script consultant and teaches screenwriting seminars around the world. She is the author of nine books, seven of which are on screenwriting, including *Making a Good Script Great* (1984), *Creating Unforgettable Characters* (1990), and *Advanced Screenwriting* (2003). She has also written *The Art of Adaptation: Turning Fact and Fiction into Film*.

JUDY SIMONS is Professor of English and Pro Vice-Chancellor at De Montfort University, UK. Her books include *Diaries and Journals of*

Literary Women from Fanny Burney to Virginia Woolf (1990), *What Katy Read: Feminist Re-readings of Classic Stories for Girls* (1995), and (with Rick Rylance) *Literature in Context* (2001). Her essay on Louisa May Alcott is published in *The Autobiographical Impulse*, edited by Maria Teresa Chialante. She is currently working on a scholarly edition of the letters of Rosamond Lehmann.

TONY WILLIAMS is Professor and Area Head of Film Studies in the Department of English at Southern Illinois University at Carbondale. He has contributed frequently to *The Jack London Newsletter*, is the author of *Jack London: The Movies* (1992), and *Body and Soul: The Cinematic Vision of Robert Aldrich* (2004), co-edited *Jack London's* The Sea Wolf: *A Screenplay by Robert Rossen* (1998), and co-edited *Horror International* (2005).

PAUL WOOLF is a Ph.D. candidate at the University of Birmingham, UK. His thesis examines depictions of Anglo-American love affairs and marriages in nineteenth-century fiction. Since completing Masters thesis about detective stories, he has written conference papers and journal articles on Arthur Conan Doyle, Anna Katharine Green, Wilkie Collins, and the television series *24*. He spent five years between undergraduate and postgraduate study originating, developing, and making television documentaries for major British broadcasters, an occupation that he now continues part-time.

Acknowledgments

The idea for this volume, and its companion, emerged from discussions with Dr. Linda Bree, senior editor at Cambridge University Press, that followed our serendipitous meeting at the Medieval Institute. I have benefited greatly not only from Linda's continuing interest and sound advice on sundry matters, but also from the comments of several anonymous readers, all of whom made very useful criticisms and suggestions. A larger, if more indirect, debt is owed to Jim Naremore of Indiana University and Bob Stam of New York University, whose stimulating work on film/literature adaptation has provided this volume with a theoretical program of sorts. The Calhoun Lemon foundation at Clemson University provided necessary research funds for completing this project, while graduate assistants John Longo and Kevin Manus ably assisted with copyediting the manuscript.

Introduction

R. Barton Palmer

Since the early days of the commercial cinema, many, perhaps most, important works of literary fiction have found a subsequent life on the screen, extending their reach and influence. Filmmakers, in turn, have enjoyed the economic and critical benefits of recycling what the industry knows as "presold properties." No doubt, this complex intersection has deeply marked both arts. Keith Cohen, for example, has persuasively argued that cinematic narrative exerted a decisive influence on the shift in novelistic aesthetics from "telling" to "showing," providing new depth of meaning to the old maxim *ut pictura poiesis*.[1] Film theorists, in turn, most notably Sergei Eisenstein, have emphasized the formative influence on cinematic storytelling of the classic realist novel, whose techniques and themes, adapted by D. W. Griffith and others, made possible a filmic art of extended narrative. Modern fictional form has been shaped by filmic elements such as montage, shifting point of view, and close attention to visual texture. An enabling condition of this constant and mutually fruitful exchange has been the unconventional conventionality of both art forms, their generic receptivity to outside influence. As Robert Stam puts it, "both the novel and the fiction film are *summas* by their very nature. Their essence is to have no essence, to be open to all cultural forms."[2]

Screen adaptations provide ideal critical sites not only for examining in detail how literary fiction is accommodated to cinematic form, but also for tracing the history of the symbiotic relationship of the two arts and the multifarious and ever-shifting connections between the commercial institutions responsible for their production. Until recently, however, neoromantic assumptions about the preeminent value of the source text have discouraged a thorough analysis of the complex negotiations (financial, authorial, commercial, legal, formal, generic, performative, etc.) that bring adaptations into being and deeply affect their reception. Traditionalist aesthetic considerations have also foreclosed discussion of the place of adaptations within the history of the cinema. For this latter is a critical task that requires the identification

1

and analysis of contextual issues that have little, if anything, to do with the source. In sum, the notion of "faithfulness" as the sole criterion of worth positions the adaptation disadvantageously, as only a secondary version of an honored work from another art form. An exclusive view of the adaptation as a replication closes off its discussion not only *per se*, but also *in se*. From the exclusive point of view of the source, an adaptation can only reflect value, for it does not result from the originary, creative process that produced its model. Traditional adaptation studies thus strive to estimate the value of what, by its nature, can possess no value of its own.

For this reason, it is not surprising that literary scholars have too often understood adaptations as only more or less irrelevant, if occasionally interesting, copies, as mere supplements to the literary source. From this perspective, the importance of adaptations is quite limited to the fact that they make their sources more available, extending the influence of literary masterpieces. Film scholars, in turn, have often viewed with suspicion and distaste the dependence of the screen adaptation on a novelistic pretext, seeing "literary" cinema as a less than genuine form of film art. The "grand theory" developed during the past three decades has emphasized the description and analysis of various aspects of cine-matic specificity; grand theory, however, has not for the most part concerned itself with the intersemiotic relationships that generate and define the formal features of film adaptations. A nascent discipline, eager to establish its independence, perhaps could not afford such tolerance and breadth of critical vision. An approach that postulated films as in some sense secondary, especially as derivative versions of valued literary texts, would enact in microcosmic form the institutional bondage of film to literature. It would also reinforce the notion that the cinema was a parasitic art form, dependent on prior literary creation. Providing popu-lar abridgements of literary masterpieces (to make the obvious point) hardly argued for the cultural importance of what Gilbert Seldes terms the seventh of "the lively arts." Studying filmic adaptation ran counter to the new theorizing about the cinema in the 1970s – not to mention the academic respectability and independence for which such work impli-citly campaigned. For literary and film scholars alike, adaptation studies encountered disfavor on both intellectual and institutional grounds.

During the past five years, however, the increasing popularity in cinema studies of what is usually termed "middle level theory" has turned the attention of scholars back toward the analysis of, and limited *in parvo* theorizing about, the material history of films and filmmaking, including the cinema's relationship with literature. A key role in this development has been the increasing institutional presence of cultural studies (or, in its more politically self-conscious British form, cultural materialism). Now recognized as a legitimate academic specialty, cultural studies ignores the formal and institutional boundaries between film and literature, even as it provides fertile ground for working on their interconnections. As Stam has recently remarked, "From a cultural studies perspective, adaptation forms part of a flattened out and newly egalitarian spectrum of cultural production. Within a comprehensively textualized world of images and simulations, adaptation becomes just another text, forming part of a broad discursive continuum."[3] From this point of view, treating a film as an "adaptation" is a matter of critical politics as well as of facts, the result of a decision to privilege one form of connection or influence over any number of others.

Other recent developments in postmodern theory have made it possible for literary and film scholars alike to take a more nuanced and positive look at film adaptations. There is no doubt, in fact, that the field has been thriving, with a number of important theoretical works published during the past decade. In particular, intertextuality theory and Bakhtinian dialogics now hold prominent positions in literary and film studies. Intertextuality contests the received notion of closed and self-sufficient "works," their borders impermeable to influence, their structures unwelcoming of alien forms. As an archly postmodernist critical protocol, intertextuality provides an ideal theoretical basis from which can proceed an account of the shared identity of the literary source and its cinematic reflex. Any consideration of filmic adaptation means speaking of one text while speaking of another. Adaptation is by definition intertextual, or transtextual, to use Gérard Genette's more precise and inclusive taxonomic concept of textual relations. A peculiar doubleness characterizes the adaptation. For it is a presence that stands for and signifies the absence of the source-text. An adaptation refers to two texts with the same identity that are not the same. Such forms of permeable and shared textuality can be accounted for only by critical approaches that focus on interrelations of different sorts, including the (dis)connections between literary and cinematic contexts.

In film studies the decline of grand theory has enabled the field to take the direction that theorist Dudley Andrew has long advocated: a "sociological turn" toward the consideration of the institutional and contextual pressures that condition the process of adaptation and define what role the adaptation comes to play in the history of the cinema. Critical studies of literary/film relations are beginning to focus on "how adaptation serves the cinema," as Andrew puts it; and this new direction of inquiry has the added advantage of shedding light on how the literary source is affected by becoming part of an intertextual, intersemiotic, interinstitutional series.[4] Robert Stam provides an anatomy of source/ adaptation relationships; these are surprisingly varied: "One way to look at adaptation is to see it as a matter of a source novel's hypotext being transformed by a complex series of operations: selection, amplification, concretization, actualization, critique, extrapolation, analogization, popularization, and reculturalization."[5]

Comparing the source and adaptation draws attention to the specific negotiations of various kinds involved in the process of transformation. Consideration can then be given to the role the resulting film comes to play within the cinema. The foundational premise of the approaches taken by the contributors to this volume has been that adaptations possess a value in themselves, apart from the ways in which they might be judged as (in)accurate replications of literary originals. Because it is sometimes a goal that guides those responsible for the adaptation process, faithfulness has found a place in the analyses collected here more as an aspect of context rather than a criterion of value. The fact (more often, the promise) of fidelity in some sense can also figure rhetorically in the contextualization of the film, most notably as a feature promoted by the marketing campaign. But very often it plays no crucial role in the transformation process and merits less critical attention than more relevant issues.

Undeniably, adaptations constitute an important area of modern cultural production, making them worthy and appropriate objects of study. But how to organize that study? Seeing a text as an adaptation means invoking its relations to two distinct but interconnected cultural series and its insertion within two divergent institutional series; adaptations become the analytical objects of two separate but not dissimilar disciplines in which topical, author-oriented, genre, and period forms of organization predominate. Film/literature adaptation courses are becoming increasingly prominent in university curricula, and they are usually housed within English or literature departments, where they are often organized, following the most common disciplinary paradigm, in terms of literary period. That practice has been followed in this volume and its companion, *Twentieth-Century American Fiction on Screen*. Although by no means the only interesting or pedagogically useful way in which adaptations might be studied, organization of the source-texts by period has the not inconsiderable virtue of offering literature teachers a familiar body of fiction with which to work. Additionally, this approach focuses narrowly on a selected stretch of literary history, permitting the analysis of how movements, themes, and dominant formal features have undergone "cinematicization." In treating American fiction of the nineteenth century, this collection marshals a broad sweep of expert opinion, literary and cinematic, on an equally broad field of texts.

Nineteenth-Century American Fiction on Screen has been conceived to fill the need for an up-to-date survey of the important films made from these texts, with the book's unity deriving in the first instance from the literary and cultural connections among the various sources. The fourteen essays collected here, all written expressly for this volume, each address the adaptation (occasionally adaptations) of single literary texts, though discussion, where relevant, also ranges over screen versions of other works by the same author, other releases by the same director, or films that are otherwise relevant. This book has a focus that provides a ready organization for courses in adaptation, with readings and viewings easily coordinated with the essays. Despite their singular emphasis, the essays also open up discussion into broader areas of importance. Although the scheme adopted here is in the first instance literary, the different essays are also deeply cinematic, addressing specific aspects of the adaptation process, including details of production where relevant and usually seeking to define the role that the film came to play within the history of the American cinema. Some contributors discuss the intersemiotic aspects of transferring a narrative from one medium to another, while others consider in depth the problems of authorship, an important question whenever the work of a valued author becomes part of the oeuvre of an important director or when the contributions of a screenwriter prove significant and defining.

In various ways and from different critical perspectives, the essays address questions of genre, sexuality/gender, ideology, censorship, politics, the representation of minority groups, and so forth. A major focus is the role of relevant contexts (institutional, aesthetic, commercial, legal, etc.) in determining the shape of the final product. No overly programmatic scheme, however, has been imposed on the contributors, who owe disciplinary loyalty to either cinema studies or literature. The aim instead has been to assemble a volume characterized by both a useful unity and a thought-provoking variety. *Nineteenth-Century American Fiction on Screen* addresses the needs of both literature/film students and those readers more generally, perhaps informally, interested in the fascinating phenomenon of adaptation. The volume exemplifies the varied fictional traditions of the period, from the Christian sentimental novel (*Ben-Hur, Little Women, Uncle Tom's Cabin*), to tales of mystery and romance (*The Last of the Mohicans, Moby-Dick, Murders in the Rue Morgue, The Scarlet Letter*), and, finally, realist and naturalist modes of writing (*Daisy Miller, The Europeans, The Portrait of a Lady, The Red Badge of Courage, The Sea Wolf, Sister Carrie, The Virginian*).

Much thought has gone into the selection of novels (or short fiction in the case of Poe) and films. In planning *Twentieth-Century American Fiction on Screen*, the extensive corpus of cinematic material provided a good deal of choice, but that proved not to be the case with films adapted from the fiction of the previous century. My starting point was a review of all commercial American adaptations of nineteenth-century American fiction from the sound era, roughly 1930 to the present. Silent films were rejected as being, in general, too difficult to obtain for classroom use, though some are included when there are multiple adaptations of the same source (e.g., the two versions, one silent and one sound, of Lew Wallace's *Ben-Hur*) or when the silent film is arguably the most interesting version and is available for classroom use (e.g., *Uncle Tom's Cabin*). After surveying the authors actually filmed by Hollywood, I discovered that a number of major figures, most prominently Washington Irving and almost all women novelists of the period (Louisa May Alcott and Harriet Beecher Stowe are the prominent exceptions) had never or rarely (and then generally unsatisfactorily) been adapted for the screen. Because it has been so dedicated to marketing modernity, broadly conceived, Hollywood production offers only a narrow view of nineteenth-century literature. Hollywood's most extensive engagement with nineteenth-century politics and culture is in fact through an essentially twentieth-century form: the western, for many decades the film genre most popular with American audiences, precisely because of the attractive version of nineteenth-century life and values that it celebrated. In the chapter devoted to Owen Wister's *The Virginian*, the emergence and flourishing of the western are taken up in detail.

As it happens, the nineteenth-century novelists whose fiction has been screened are almost all *major* in the sense that they have been and remain the subject of substantial critical work. Hollywood's taste, reflecting in some sense popular opinion, surprisingly coincides closely with the canon of valued texts that emerged during the institutionalization of American literature as a scholarly discipline in the first decades of the twentieth century. The table of contents obviously reflects academic opinion of the fiction in this period. So there are three chapters devoted to the works of Henry James, a central literary figure who also happens to be one of the most adapted of American nineteenth-century writers in the sound era. For the purposes of this volume, James has been counted as "American," though, naturally, his national affiliation, if it can be said to be in fact singular, is disputable.

The writers whose work is discussed here continue to find a readership. Their works, in other words, remain in print. They are also nearly all what we would now term "high cultural": Louisa May Alcott, James

Fenimore Cooper, Stephen Crane, Theodore Dreiser, Henry James, Herman Melville, Edgar Allan Poe, and Harriet Beecher Stowe. I have also included two writers, Lew Wallace and Owen Wister, who might be described as popular novelists with substantial historical, but arguably literary, importance as well. In the final analysis, of course, both the criteria used and the particular choices made are subjective, in the sense that they are based, first, on my knowledge of and experience with literary and film study and, second, on my appraisal of what material would appeal to scholarly and general readers, yet also prove useful in the classroom.

I do not know, of course, any more than anyone else, how to decide *objectively* what works, literary or cinematic, should be thought *major*. Among other prominent rankings, the American Film Institute has compiled a list of the "100 Best American Films." A number of the films I have selected, but by no means all, are on this list. If there is a comparable list for nineteenth-century American novels and short fiction, I am not familiar with it, but most of the literary texts chosen for this volume would likely be on it. But then even if such a list did exist, its authoritative value would be dubious. The canon of literary study remains very much in dispute and can hardly be said to be fixed or stable, as scholars such as Paul Lauter have shown.[6]

In planning this book, the status of both authors and works was in fact a preliminary condition. That I considered them *major* was a necessary, but not sufficient reason for inclusion. Another important purpose of this volume is to exemplify different aspects of the *process* of adaptation. In making the selections from among major works by major authors, I have picked formally and culturally interesting adaptations, by which I mean those that can be shown to have served the cinema in some significant or revealing fashion. For example, the fictional text might offer technical challenges (e.g., how do you film a novel with prominent antirealist elements such as *Moby-Dick*?) or the context of the adaptation might be interesting from the viewpoint of Hollywood history (e.g., in the case of *Uncle Tom's Cabin*, Hollywood's problematic engagement during the 1920s with racial politics). The film might constitute an important part of a director's oeuvre, with the source thus inserted into two expressive series, one literary and the other cinematic. As the contributors to this volume demonstrate with skill and insight, these films all hold interests that, while determined to some degree by their status as adaptations, also derive from their insertion within the history of Hollywood and the larger cultural role that the movies played in twentieth-century America, which was in part, as it remains, furthering the reach of honored, significant, and popular literary texts.

NOTES

1. Keith Cohen, *Film and Fiction: The Dynamics of Exchange* (New Haven: Yale University Press, 1979). See also his *Writing in a Film Age: Essays by Contemporary Novelists* (Niwot, CO: University Press of Colorado, 1991).
2. Robert Stam, "Beyond Fidelity: The Dialogics of Adaptation," in James Naremore, ed., *Film Adaptation* (New Brunswick, NJ: Rutgers University Press, 2000), p. 61.
3. Robert Stam, "Introduction," in Robert Stam and Alessandra Raengo, *Literature and Film: A Guide to the Theory and Practice of Film Adaptation* (Oxford: Blackwell, 2004), pp. 9–10.
4. Dudley J. Andrew, "Adaptation," in Naremore, ed., *Film Adaptation*, p. 35.
5. Stam, "Beyond Fidelity," p. 68.
6. See especially Paul Lauter, *Canons and Contexts* (Oxford: Oxford University Press, 1991).

1   A very American fable: the making of a *Mohicans* adaptation

Martin Barker and Roger Sabin

In 1936 the second major screen version of James Fenimore Cooper's (1789–1851) *The Last of the Mohicans* was released by a small outfit, Reliance Pictures, through United Artists. The film did very well at the box offices, and made a star of its lead male, Randolph Scott. Curiously absent from histories of 1930s Hollywood cinema,[1] it has been fondly remembered by many viewers, and still plays on television quite regularly. It also provided the basis for Michael Mann's 1992 remake; Mann credits the screenplay by Philip Dunne as a prime source for his own ideas. In 1997 we published a book about the long and extensive history of adaptations of *Mohicans*, across the media of film, television, animation, and comic books.[2] We tried to set the 1936 film in its production and cultural contexts. And in one important respect we got it wrong. This essay recounts what we discovered when an opportunity came subsequently to do further research in the archives.[3] A very telling story emerges, which has implications far beyond this particular film.

Cooper's novel was originally published in 1826. More than any other, it made his name as an "American author." Not the first, it was undoubtedly the best-known of his "Leatherstocking" tales which tell the life of Nathaniel Bumppo, or Hawkeye, the frontiersman who fictionally patrolled the forests of the North East – and who encountered the real circumstances of the French and English wars for control of America. *The Last of the Mohicans* is the story most directly concerned with that encounter, tying Hawkeye into the real historical circumstances of the siege, surrender, and massacre at Fort William Henry in 1757. The core of the narrative is the friendship between Hawkeye and his two Mohican friends Chingachgook and his son Uncas – the last two of this people whom Cooper writes as the *ur*-tribe of the Delawares – and their efforts to save the two daughters of the English Colonel Munro from the villainous intentions of the Huron Magua. In the novel the younger girl, Alice, dies with Uncas, who has fallen in love with her, leaving Cora to depart America with Major Duncan Heyward, the stiff British officer who has been changed by his encounters with the wilderness. Hawkeye returns to the wilderness, with the grieving Chingachgook.

One of the central themes of our book was that this story, so well known for its evocative title (but much less well known in detail), had the peculiar virtue of being almost infinitely adaptable. Its themes of wilderness, the origins of "America," the interrelations of race and sexes, could therefore be made to resonate with the particular concerns and tensions of each successive moment when it was reworked. In the case of the 1936 adaptation, we could point to a large number of changes. Much of the violence of the original story was toned down. Little of the original dialogue survived; instead, characters talked as though they were straight out of a family adventure movie. The characters of Alice and Cora were for some reason reversed, and the surviving Alice ends up with Hawkeye. But it was hard to say which counted as major, or minor, alterations. Some did look significant. For example, we pointed to the visual diminution of the "wilderness" into parkland. This connected with inserted dialogue in which Hawkeye becomes the mythic voice of a new conception of the frontier: as a land waiting to be developed into towns, cities. As an expression of the will during the Depression to industrialize the countryside in order to save the collapsing rural economies, this made and still makes sense.

We were particularly struck by one major narrative alteration. In the released version the narrative is topped and tailed by episodes not found in the novel. The story opens in Europe with a grandiloquent scene in St. James's Palace where George II is listening to his ministers debating the worth of trying to save America, and is persuaded by the prime minister to see it as the "raw materials of an Empire," to be tamed and exploited for England's purposes. But having embroidered this theme of a conflict between the interests of the English and the colonials, in which Hawkeye must take the side of the latter and face rough "English justice," the film solves this with an ending in which Hawkeye is forgiven, becomes a scout for the English, and of course gets the girl. Trying to make sense of this, we borrowed a claim from Dan Georgakas, that at this point Hollywood may have been responding to a quiet request by Franklin D. Roosevelt to make films which would challenge America's dominant isolationism.[4] Films showing that Europe and America share common interests could have been valuable – especially in the light of the increasing saber-rattling in Germany, Italy, and Spain.

On reflection, we came to doubt this account, for a number of reasons. Above all, it depends on the possibility that Roosevelt foresaw the coming European war. The temptation to see him in this way may be part of an attractive mythologization on which David Culbert has recently commented. Culbert lists a series of fallacies, including the idea that "Roosevelt is superhuman. He saw World War II coming, did everything in his power to stop it, but was thwarted by an isolationist Congress at home. Documents published in the last decade indicate that Roosevelt gave comparatively little attention to foreign affairs before 1939 . . . and had himself urged passage of the first Neutrality Act in 1935."[5]

This Neutrality Act required that America not align itself with either side in any European conflicts, and it was renewed and extended by further Acts in 1936 and 1937 – which again, Roosevelt signed without overt protest. These Acts suited American armaments manufacturers, who could now sell to whoever could pay. They also suited those within American politics who saw potential in totalitarian regimes such as that of Mussolini, who in 1935 had mounted an all-out invasion of Abyssinia, or those opposed on principle to the Republicans fighting Franco in Spain.

Roosevelt's personal position is debatable. Faced with a threat of filibustering over his New Deal legislation, he put his name to the Neutrality Act – and kept his own counsel as to the real needs of American politics and economy. Edgar Robinson, another historian, argues that "It is true that in the closing hours of the Presidential campaign of 1936, Franklin Roosevelt had warned the American people that in a world of war and rumors of war, the United States might not be able to maintain neutrality, non-involvement and at the same time a proper defense of American interests."[6] But even Robinson, a sympathetic historian, can only point to such small gestures.

Less sympathetic judgments saw Roosevelt as at best drifting, at worst displaying cowardice in the face of emergent fascism.[7] The already weak League of Nations was further weakened, and the message to Hitler, Mussolini, and Franco among others was pretty unequivocal – the American political leadership saw no role for itself in Europe. In fact, the Neutrality Act was weak – it forbade only arms and munitions; it said nothing about raw materials. Despite supposed neutrality, American exports to Italy of raw materials, including oil, steel, and copper, mounted across 1935–37.

In this situation the evidence to support the claim that Roosevelt sought Hollywood's help to combat isolationism would have to be strong. In fact, it is desperately weak. If there is a problem with relying on an image of a forward-looking Roosevelt urging ideological warfare on his isolationist opponents, there are even bigger problems with the supposed source of the story of his request to the studios: Jack Warner. It is hard to track down the exact source of the claim (it is not evident in his autobiography), but regardless of this, Warner is known as a self-aggrandizer, and an unreliable source.[8]

Several books have told the story of Warner Brothers' famous anti-fascist films.[9] These histories show that the great period of antifascist filmmaking, culminating in *Mission to Moscow* (1943), in fact began later than 1936. Michael Birdwell in particular makes clear that Warner was by no means the major impulse in their making – it was his brother Harry, who was no friend to Roosevelt. It was Jack who appears to have invented the story of the Warners agent supposedly murdered in Germany – who may in fact never have existed.

If there is no sure evidence of a company the size of Warner Brothers being enticed by the President, what of Reliance Pictures, source of *The Last of the Mohicans*? Tino Balio's business history of United Artists tells the story of the creation of Reliance. Joseph Schenk had joined United Artists in 1924, and it was his business acumen that rescued the company from an early demise. Reliance was one of Schenk's attempts to increase the output of films. In 1931 he attempted to persuade United Artists' Board to invest in independent producers, in order to increase the flow of product, but received mixed responses. Faced with embarrassment after this, he put his personal money in with Harry Goetz and Edward B. Small, only withdrawing when, in 1933, an alternative source – the banker William Phillips – came in.[10] It is just very unlikely that a company as small, incidental, even accidental as Reliance should be courted by the President. And that is before we consider the political views of Edward B. Small, as we shall see later.

Realizing the problems with our too-easy original explanation, our only recourse was to go back to the film's production history. What might be revealed by surviving archival materials? Friends and colleagues helped us to obtain some valuable sources. But crucially, we found large amounts of useful materials in three archives: at the Academy of Motion Picture Arts and Sciences, in the United Artists archive in Madison, Wisconsin, and most importantly in the library of the University of Southern California.[11] In the last we found – among other vital materials – eleven different, dated versions of the film, as variously pitch, script outline, or screenplay. Through analyzing and interpreting these, alongside their relations to other materials that we found, we offer here a picture of the *most probable* version of what prompted and guided the making of this version of *Mohicans*. What we did *not* find was any document even hinting at any underpinning political motives or interests in the making of the film.

The questions that in the end we found most profitable, when examining the scripts, were these. What alterations in the narrative sequence are made, between versions? What is the resultant scope and generic placement of the narrative? What traits and tendencies do characters embody? And what kinds of motivation are ascribed to different characters? Three names – John Balderston, Philip Dunne, and Ralph Block – are directly associated with the versions. However, we know (from a good deal of evidence) that the film's producer, Small – the one among the three founders of Reliance who took responsibility for production – read every version, and commented on them, probably from a number of angles (among these, their financial implications, and their audience potential). Balderston's name appears not only alone on the opening four versions and with Dunne's on the fifth (to which the evidence says he did contribute), it also appears on the tenth and eleventh – and on the credits to the film itself. However, we are reasonably sure that Balderston left the production long before these late versions, and that Dunne may have put Balderston's name on these because he was trying to reintroduce some elements from those early versions. Here, then, is an account of the phases in these script versions.

Phase One – John Balderston's "epic" proposal[12]

More than a year before the film would appear, Small [12]took a preliminary decision that the next big film that Reliance would produce after *The Count of Monte Cristo* (1934) would be a revisiting after fifteen years of Cooper's *Mohicans*. At this time, Balderston was on the writing staff at Reliance and he was asked to write a first pitch for the film. Balderston had begun his working life as a journalist. During World War I, he had been a war correspondent for the McClure newspaper group, and he then attained some success as a playwright, novelist, and scriptwriter (best known for his fantasy and adventure writing). He was known to his colleagues as a man of wide interests, and "liberal" views (we must be cautious of this term since it has a changing meaning). It should not surprise us, therefore, that Balderston's pitch for the film, embodied in a quite remarkable document, proposes to make it a geopolitical epic film, opening in the two opposed courts of France and England, and extending Cooper's narrative to take in the conquest of Quebec ("[I]f at first glance it seems far-fetched, you will find after we work out a treatment that what Hawkeye does is plausible, in character, and you and the audience will wonder why Cooper didn't think of it himself" [1:5]).

Balderston's pitch (March 7, 1935) begins with an explanation of his use of the term "epic" as "something more than a story about people fighting, loving, hating" (1:1). To be epic, a picture has to deal with "vaster themes . . . of general and permanent historical significance" (1:1). Balderston lists a number of films which he feels achieve this: alongside *Birth of a Nation* (1915; mentioned without any qualms about its racial attitudes), *All Quiet on the Western Front* (1930) and *Cavalcade* (1933) are the English-centered *Lives of the Bengal Lancer* (1934) and *Clive of India* (1934). All are stories in which human conflicts, often involving wildly unbalanced forces, are fought out bravely, and can be seen as changing the world. *Mohicans* is in this class, potentially. "Great armies battle in Europe, but our war is a side-show to London and Paris" (1:4). Balderston then retells the main thrust of the narrative, in terms that accentuate the conflict of mighty forces – but he covers his odds, by explaining how this can be filmed without impossible expense. What is interesting is that despite the title of the book, this approach makes the question of the Mohicans an "Indian sub-plot" (1:7), good for the film because it offers a "dramatic and tragic element" (1:9). He goes on: "Great pictures on this theme will be made, for it is a great theme, the conquest of one race by another" (1:11).

Balderston followed this with a nineteen-page outline (March 14, 1935), plotting the film's proposed scenes. This, as promised, opens in the French and English courts, with the French king under the thumb of a selfish, prima donna-ish La Pompadour, while the English king – albeit unwillingly – is persuaded to send extra troops to secure America. The most striking element about this outline is the strong contrasting of modes of behaving established for the English and the colonials, cap-tured in a scene where Munro's army, moving to Fort William Henry, is ambushed. The film, Balderston declared, "should show enough of this fight to show the difference between British and American methods of fighting" (2:7). Munro is outraged when he sees the colonials adopting Indian tactics and getting behind trees – he orders his men to stand and fight properly (a version of this survives to Balderston's fourth script attempt, where he has Munro declare: "This American mode of fighting will destroy the reputation of his Majesty's army! I'd rather lose a battle, than win it so!" [3:31]). What Balderston wanted was a demonstration of a *conflict between ways of seeing the world*. And what Hawkeye embodied for him was, very much, innocence. He describes him early on in this fashion:

Hawkeye, in his early thirties, nurtured and bred in the forests, trapper and hunter in peace-time, scout and Indian hunter in war, is ill-at-ease in the settlements which he visits as seldom as possible. In his face is the innocence and purity of a man never into contact with civilization; there is about him, when we get to know him, a beauty of spirit and charming simplicity, that is strangely matched with his efficiency as an Indian fighter. (2:6)

That character is at odds with the mannered civilities of Europe. So, when he and Cora find themselves attracted to each other, "it is so hard for the sophisticated Cora to understand this simple, wilderness mind; we observe, too, Hawkeye's fascination and wonder at this beautiful, vital creature, he who has never seen women other than squaws and slatterns around the trading posts" (2:8). Hawkeye even sees himself as "illiterate," therefore an impossible figure for Cora, a "great London lady" (2:15), to be attracted to. Balderston plays on this "innocence" in Hawkeye throughout; it allows him not even to be offended by an attempt by Heyward to bribe him to stay away from Cora – Hawkeye simply does not understand the appeal of money. And Balderston's Hawkeye displays an unvarnished willingness to give his life at the stake to save the women, because that is clearly what a "man" does – because once having given his word, "No Indian would take a white man's word, in war or peace, were it known that the Long Rifle had broken his faith. You'd have me shame my color, or my friends?" (2:132, retained in several subsequent versions).

Narratively, much of the action of the story follows Cooper's books quite closely, up to the point where Hawkeye shoots Magua after the deaths of Alice and Uncas, and Tamenund and Chingachgook mourn their loss. But a coda takes us to Quebec, where Munro is reunited with Cora, whom he had thought dead. Here Hawkeye uses his woodcraft skills to aid the assault on the Heights of Abraham, after which "we play the historical scene of the deaths of Wolfe and Montcalm." The film closes with Cora having realized that their worlds are incompatible and, reconciled with Heyward, preparing to return to Europe, while Hawkeye and Chingachgook "turn away back to the wilderness where they belong."

The third (151-page) version, again from Balderston, is largely a script enactment of this outline, with some small but important changes: for example, when Hawkeye, provoked by Cora asking if he does not find the Indian girls "lithe like gazelles, warm and passionate," replies sternly, "I'll not deny that some of our color comport themselves so. But I have never let myself forget that I am a man without a cross of blood" (3:69). This racial politics is a taken-for-granted in this, and the next version, where it becomes even more delineated and indeed twentieth century, when Balderston substitutes this sentence: "Never have I let myself forget, with the women, that I'm a man of pure white blood" (4:56).

Balderston's fourth revised screenplay (April 23, 1935) makes small but significant changes, whose origin and motivation we can only surmise. Both his third and fourth versions share a changed ending. Cora and Hawkeye acknowledge their love for each other, but recognize that their lives, their cultures are just too different. In heightened words they declare the impossibility of it all – most strongly in the fourth version. Cora knows that if she took Hawkeye back to try to live in London he would die.

HAWKEYE: "Aye, you'd not do that to me, because you love me. How then could I do the same to you? No, Cora, 'tis a star-crossed love, with a gulf between us as broad and deep as that tween that boy who never spoke his love, but who kissed the ground where your sister's feet trod, and who died for her."

CORA: "It's wrong, Leatherstocking. It's life, we can't fight it, but it's wrong."

HAWKEYE: "Your face will be with me, wakin' or sleepin', while life lasts, and the sweet thoughts of that night I thought to have been my last on earth."

CORA: (repeats his words with a pledge of her own): "While life lasts." FADE OUT. (4:131)

This version of the ending seals the sense throughout Balderston's versions of the script that this is to be a film about people living through events larger than themselves, caught up in epic battles which sweep them along – to the creation of "America." It is notable that this fourth version includes the death of not just Uncas, but also Chingachgook – who is made to die at the siege of Quebec. Thus is Hawkeye left to inherit the American earth, without even a vestige of the nonwhite races to concern him.

Phase Two – Philip Dunne's heroic individuals

Philip Dunne is by far the best known of those writers who worked on the script. It is Dunne's account in his autobiography *Take Two: A Life in Movies and Politics* (1980) that has come nearest to being the "official" account of what happened on the film. He has left behind a reputation as a "liberal." We will show reasons to qualify this – or at least to press the meaning of "liberalism" into an uncomfortable context. Younger than Balderston, Dunne had only recently come to work for Small, who had taken him on partly out of admiration for his father, the well-known humorist Finley P. Dunne. Small would later say of Dunne that he had a wonderful eye for a dramatic scene, but not yet a sense of overall narrative shape and thrust. His contribution initially comes in the form of a new main storyline (April 30, 1935) and then a full 151-page screenplay (June 14, 1935). There are some clear continuities with Balderston's work and approach. For instance, describing the initial scene in his storyline, Dunne writes of Munro: "Munro is confident enough to have his daughters with him. This confidence, and a stubborn adherence to the rules of war as fought on the open battlefields of Europe, are characteristic of the brave, bull-headed British officers" (5:1).

But it is not just these individual characteristics that are changing in Dunne's hands, it is now a sense precisely that these *are* "individuals" in a special way. Perhaps because he came to this as a writer of fiction (as against Balderston's journalistic background), Dunne tells his story *through individuals and what drives them*. The storyline is remarkable for just how strongly *motivated* every action by every individual is. In just one example, notice how situations and reasoning and emotional responses all combine to make a move inevitable:

Now the deaths of the unfortunate Alice and the last of the Mohicans serve a purpose. They bring Hawkeye and Cora close together. United by a common sorrow, they face the almost impossible task of working their way to civilisation. To go south is impossible – with a woman. The revengeful Mingoes are there. Their only chance is to go north – through hostile country, but where they will not be expected – and so win through to Quebec, and attempt to join Wolfe's besieging force.   (5:8–9)

When Dunne spelt out his storyline as a full 151-page screenplay, the shift in the sense and direction of the "epicness" becomes more apparent. The narrative is to be prefigured by a rolling caption:

"1757: Europe shakes as great armies of all nations clash in the world encircling Seven Years' War. The war leaps the ocean. French and English fight in the trackless forests of North America. Blood-thirsty savages aid the French, with the English red-coats stand rude Colonists who defend their homes against fire and scalping knife. The United States, as a nation, is still hidden in the future. If the great French general Montcalm can break through down the Hudson from Canada, America will be forever French."   (6:1)

This teleological picture of a nation seeking to be born in the face of "savages" permeates all that follows – but the nation must be fought for. The opening speeches at George II's court are used to set up the wrong ways of seeing America; it puts into the mouth of Lord Newcastle the "wrong" view that England has an automatic right to own America: "'tis the very nature of history that England should possess Massachusetts." Through the views of those who will lose runs a dismissive view of the "Americans."

Hawkeye now becomes a "super-ordinary American," one who can, with the wisdom of his position, apologize to his fellow colonials for the arrogance of the English, equating them with the equally barbarous "savages": "The red man's scalpin' knife is no more barbarous than the white man's arrogance" (6:20). And when Hawkeye is alone with Alice (the reversal of the names of Cora and Alice begins here, for no apparent reason), his debate with her, as she comes to appreciate his value, is all about that American future:

ALICE: (after a pause – muses): "You've known no other life – than here in the wilderness?"
HAWKEYE: (simply): "*This* is settled country (speaking with great emotion). Beyond those mountains beyond the Ohio, lies the *real* wilderness. In peace the Mohicans and I pioneer, blaze trails, open up new country, for civilization to follow – (pauses – turns to her) I wonder if you can understand the thrill of being *first!*"
ALICE: (enthralled): "As you tell it, I think I can."   (6:56)

This is a moment when Alice discovers herself, and apologizes to Hawkeye. He praises her courage. But notice the wording – "As you tell it, I think I can." Hawkeye embodies understanding, from whose words therefore can come a special realization. It is interesting that this phrasing *nearly* survives into the released film, but there Alice says only: "I think I can." On its own, this would be a minor indicator, but, in concert with all the other ways in which Dunne's version of Hawkeye as a *living proof* of "America" effectively vanished, it matters indeed.

Hear how it resonates again after the death and burial of Cora and Uncas. Now the mourning is conducted by Alice and Hawkeye:

HAWKEYE: "It was a right royal rite and for the last of the royal race of Mohicans (looks around the woods – and sighs). The time will come soon when the red man no longer hunts in these woods. The race is dyin' (looks off towards Chingachgook, nods). The Sagamore knows it."
ALICE: "And yet there's little death in the woods. They seem new and young – whispering that life is beginning – joyous and carefree."   (6:117)

Even the wilderness is turning against the "vanishing Americans," who know they are finished.

These two versions keep much from Balderston's, but make significant changes. The *overt* racism of the first scripts shifts now into the *irrelevance* of the Indians. When a new nation is waiting to be born, what hope for *anyone* who stands in its way?

Phase Three – Ralph Block's dreadful "western"

We know that at this point in the film's development, Dunne and Balderston left the project. Delays in the casting meant that they were not needed, so they moved on to other work. In August 1935, and still well before the preparation of the version that would go for vetting by the Production Code Administration (PCA), work moved to Ralph Block.

Block was a very different kind of writer, with a background first at Pathé, then at Fox writing westerns, then latterly at Warner Bros. He would soon largely abandon scriptwriting for a leading role in the emergent Screen Writers Guild, where he made his name as a campaigning liberal.[13] Three screenplay versions exist in the archive, all carrying his name (along with Dunne's, but that is surely a residual acknowledgment), through which it is possible to trace an evolution toward a whole different kind of film narrative. How far this narrative was motivated by a desire of the producers to generate an "audience pleaser" we shall see in a moment.

Across two versions – one labeled "Final" (August 26, 1935) and one bearing only handwritten dates ("8 October 1935, revised 14 October"), it is possible to trace several concurrent processes. First, a decline in all senses of the "mythic." Here Hawkeye is given a backstory, which presents him less as an all-powerful hero, more as a lucky survivor.[14] In this version speech passes out of the register of cultural representation to become caricatural. Upon our arrival in America, we meet General Braddock in debate with Hawkeye. Infuriated by Hawkeye's refusal to accept the wisdom of his commands, he replies: "Oddfish – infernal insolence" (7:15). Curiously, into this version comes the "real" figure of George Washington, to add a dash of authenticity. We are seeing a mix of real referents with generic fictionality.

But the big changes begin in earnest in the next version. By October, characters are becoming ever more stereotyped. The two women take on a melodramatic air (Alice becomes a huffy, arrogant missy, demanding that Hawkeye take her to her father). The reasons for actions are declining. Where, previously, we had seen the British motivated by the "raw materials of an Empire" to take America, now it becomes personal ambition. Pitt says to George II, simply, "Sire, I gave you India! Now I'll give you America" (8:4). Who needs a reason? But another influence is perhaps also showing: Small as producer is exerting a different, budgetary control. The massacre at Fort William Henry is reduced to a third-person report, eliminating all need for the big scene.

But the narrative is moving more generally in a new direction. Across Balderston and Dunne, characters were motivated by the *kind of people* they were, the *kinds of culture* they represented and embodied. Now, once past the increasingly dull, functional dialogue (HAWKEYE: "The fightin's stopped – what's happened?" SENTRY: "We've surrendered. But nonetheless you'll hang" [8:68]), characters relate primarily through accidents, coincidences, misunderstandings, mistakes, bluffs, and tricks. For example, at a crucial moment during the massacre, Hawkeye escapes from imprisonment in the English fort by tricking Heyward into coming too close and then "jumping" him to take his pistols.

Here the Indians are becoming trading post natives – stealing white folks' goods and drinking perfume for alcohol – or just plain nasty. In this version, strangely, Hawkeye knows Magua, but not as an old enemy – he approves Magua going as the women's guide. They only become enemies after Magua has tricked Uncas into a fight, for which he will be publicly flogged (Alice and Hawkeye have to rescue him). A great deal is made here of attempts, always failing, to get messages through. Tricks and countertricks prevail, with chases in between. Alice and Hawkeye quarrel like figures in a romantic comedy. (Peculiarly, although it might be argued that the original book is just vanishing, small parts that never appeared before now enter – a scene from Cooper's novel, for instance, with bears in a cave provides a "motive" for Alice to fall into Hawkeye's arms.) Now elements that will appear in the released film begin to enter – crucially, Hawkeye taking Alice's place at the stake. But in general Dunne's later claim that a bizarre, shapeless, directionless interference with the text had taken place seems borne out.

Phase Four – emergency action

At this point, Dunne was rehired – not, as he would later claim, so late that the film was effectively in production, but at the turn of 1935/6 (with actual filming five months off). Even so, it must have been clear to him that this was a time for desperate measures. On January 10, 1936, Dunne turned in a revised screenplay. The striking thing about this version is Dunne's attempts to reintroduce elements from his and Balderston's earliest versions. But only slimmed and diminished versions of Dunne's ability to make characters "speak their cultures" would survive into the final version. The question has to be: why?

This version, too, ends with Alice staying with Hawkeye. Quebec is gone – our best guess is that the accountant in Small had finally decided this, on cost grounds. Heyward, having (as in the to-be-released version) finally exonerated Hawkeye of treason at a postvictory trial, is ordered back to London, and leaves Alice in Hawkeye's "keeping":

ALICE: "Do you mind?"
CHINGACHGOOK: (gently but with strength): "Hawkeye is my brother, but his
                skin is pale. The white man will increase like grass in the
                spring – and Hawkeye will lead them. The day of the red men is
                past." FADE OUT. (10:117)

In this version Hawkeye has evolved – under Dunne's tutelage – into more than a scout, into a modern statesman, a leader, a man of the future not the past; and the Indians mourn but accept their own vanishing. If this is "liberalism," it is of a strange kind.

Indeed, this version is remarkable for Dunne having reinserted some of the crudest elements of racial ideology, which had gradually been expunged. At the scene of Magua's capture of the two women, Alice mocks him for his failures: "Aren't there enough women in your own tribe to be wives to such a great Chief?" Magua draws himself up proudly:

MAGUA: "Magua French – take white woman to squaw."
ALICE: "Oh, a half-breed. Is it possible that the pure-blooded women of your own people will have nothing to do with you?"   (10: 92)

It is evident that even these toned-down reintroductions were not acceptable. By the final versions, they are almost all gone. The April 10, 1936 version, we sense, is the version sent to the PCA – but not yet the version actually filmed. The ending would receive one more change. In the archives are four dated revisions to the April 10 script. The first two still have the residual figure of Gamut, a wandering preacher who travels with the two women and plays a small role in their rescue, but by the third he is excised. The first three keep George II as a caricatured German with a bad accent. By the fourth, surely at the behest of the PCA (which, as Ruth Vasey has shown well, concerned itself greatly with the "exportability" of films), this is changed.[15] The first three also return to the ending in which Alice returns to Europe with Heyward; only in the finally released (and approved) film does she get to stay – this has to have been a change on set. On April 13 the PCA received a script and wrote a long summary of it. With the exception of the ending, it is recognizable as the film that would be released. Joseph Breen, for the PCA, wrote to Small outlining its response. There were no overall problems, but there were many individual concerns about "too much gruesomeness throughout, with scalpings, violent death of all kinds, etc."[16] Script changes, or else great care in filming, were called for to cater for the criticisms. The completed and edited film was submitted to the PCA in July, and was passed with few problems. But we should note that the PCA recorded without comment that the ending had changed, to the "resolving" version.

How to explain this messy potpourri of changes? For the film as a whole: from epic, through world-historical individuals, to impoverished and discombobulated western, to a scrambled egg of a final film, not with some rhetorical challenge to isolationism, but with the relics of the original epic purpose. For the Native American characters: from a wider thematic in which they were irrelevant, to social Darwinian obsolescence, through western stooges, back to redundant fodder for the advance of "civilization."[17] For Hawkeye: from majestic figure, through incompetent, irascible chump, to a nice ordinary guy. Whatever the explanation, the one thing there is not is a purposeful politics. But that does not mean there is no politics at all.

The best clues to why this all happened in this way are contained in Small's (n.d) as-told-to autobiography. This three-volume compilation is a self-glorifying account, complete with a childhood tale of standing before a statue of an Indian chief, Tomo-Chi-Chi, in Savannah, Georgia, and dreaming of the past and his future: "When I thought of the Chief, I could picture the way our city was in days past, a beautiful panorama of forests and wild animals, of noble, brave warriors and tepees and tomahawks" (1:7). And thus, Small exclaims, his life-goals were set.[18]

But in among the self-aggrandizement there is some useful information. In 1932, when Small came together with Schenk and Goetz to form Reliance, Small took charge of actual productions – something he had long wanted to do. And he was, as Dunne later accused, a really interfering producer, for good or ill. Overall, Reliance did well. It had an early hit with *I Cover The Waterfront* (1933). Then Small conceived the idea of doing *The Count of Monte Cristo*. His account of the reasons bears consideration. He recalled arguments among the three of them. When he proposed that they do *Cristo*, Schenk and Goetz argued fiercely against him – they believed that apart from Cecil B. DeMille's, costume dramas were dead: "'People were worried about bread,' Goetz added, 'and you want to give them costumes.' I had learned my lesson as a kid. 'People want to escape,' I said stubbornly. 'The Depression's been around a long time. They're sick of worrying about bread'" (II:269). The precise conversations aside, this is a believable account – Small had come to pride himself on his ability to smell what the small folks will enjoy – or what he called "audience-pleasers."[19]

Cristo cost $435,000 to make, considerably over budget – but it made $5m. Small became angry because somehow Reliance seemed to see very little of the profit: "I became aware that something indeed was rotten – but not in Denmark and the rest of the foreign countries. It was in the United States. A look at the profits showed that only thirty per cent came from America, the other seventy per cent from the rest of the world. It made no sense – on a logical base" (II:276). The answer was corrupt practices at home – cinema owners misrepresenting the money they'd taken. "I concluded that the best way to fight their tactics was to make only films with subject matter slanted to do well in international theatres. Let the American exhibitors try to get their hot little hands on those box office receipts!" (II:277). Small would henceforth make films which best ensured overseas distribution.

If we follow this line of reasoning, the decisions that led to the *Mohicans* outcome was almost certainly an acute business judgment. This is the positive side. On the negative side, there is every reason to suppose that it was *not* ideological. Small recalls doing a biography of Rudolph Valentino. During its making, he had a battle with a "communist" writer, who tried to "insert propaganda" into one of his films – about a black man who could not afford false teeth. Sacking the writer, Small decided to get his own back, with a film called *Red Salute* (1935) vilifying communist propaganda. The film was attacked on its release and was boycotted, with stink bombs let off at its opening night in New York: "The attacks were successful. *Red Salute* failed. That was in 1935" (II:285). In the same year that he began to plan *Mohicans*, Small had his fingers burnt twice – by "communists." He half-regarded Roosevelt as a communist. No way would he have responded to a call for help from that source.

But as we have said, although there is not a scrap of evidence to sustain our original proposal of a direct political link to Roosevelt, that does not mean that there is no politics in this film. In fact, we would argue that its politics lie much more in the *kind of pleasure* it afforded audiences – a pleasure which is well captured in the repeated description of the film in many reviews we have read as an "old-fashioned blood." Frequent comparisons are made to silent-era westerns. Here is a film that decidedly refuses any of this "modern" nonsense about Indians. In the name of industrializing the countryside, it is possible to cheer and mourn simultaneously the "passing" of these lesser beings – even if we do admit, as they go, that "our side" may also have faults. Their irrelevance to the essential plot is nowhere better caught for us than in the fact we stumbled on, while doing our original research. The magazine *Picture Show* carried a pictorial synopsis of the 1936 *Mohicans* in its March 13, 1937 edition. Clearly prepared before the film's release, it declares that in saving Cora, "both Chingachgook and Uncas die." No such narrative importance survived the final edit. In the released version Chingachgook simply disappears after the death of his son – a true case of a "vanishing American."

The wider implication of this tale is, for us, the warning that it delivers about the dangers of textual interpretation unchecked against the routines and individual circumstances of a film's production regime. Political and ideological "readings" of films have become an academic

Table 1

	Hawkeye	Cora/Alice	Heyward	Chingachgook
Balderston: March 22, 1935	Returns to wilderness	Returns to London alone	Returns to London alone	Disappears after death of Uncas
Balderston: April 23, 1935	Returns to wilderness with Chingachgook	Returns to London alone	Returns to London alone	Returns to wilderness with Hawkeye
Dunne: June 14, 1935	Returns to wilderness with Chingachgook	Is reconciled with Heyward	Is reconciled with Cora	Returns to wilderness with Hawkeye
Block: August 26, 1935	Returns to wilderness with Alice and Chingachgook	Persuades Hawkeye to accept that she has changed	Dies, sacrificing himself to save Hawkeye	Returns to wilderness with Hawkeye and Alice
Block: October 8, 1935	Wounded; will be looked after by Alice	Commits herself to Hawkeye	Returns to London alone	Returns to wilderness alone
Dunne: January 10, 1936	Stays with Alice	Stays with Hawkeye	Disappears from narrative	Returns to wilderness alone
Dunne: April 10, 1936	Declines Alice	Returns to London with Heyward	Returns to London with Heyward	Disappears from narrative
Dunne: June 1, 1936	Accepts Alice; becomes scout	Will marry Hawkeye after the war	Returns to London alone	Disappears from narrative

game, which our error has forced us once again to recognize. Take the
very ending of the film. In our erroneous reading of this adaptation, the
end, and the ultimate fate of the characters, mattered greatly. The fact
that Hawkeye becomes a scout for the English, and will marry Alice,
signalled the film's anti-isolationist message. Now consider Table 1,
which summarizes the changing fates of key characters across the main
script versions that we have been able to examine in detail. This is
ending as afterthought, and the decisions look decidedly *ad hoc*.[20]

As a coda, we would like to point to one remaining puzzle. Namely,
the role of *Mohicans* director George B. Seitz. The Seitz who made a six-
chapter serial version of the *Leatherstocking Tales* in 1924, and made the
extant, Social Darwinian *The Vanishing American* in 1926. The Seitz who
then worked for many years at M-G-M, gained a long-term contract,
and carved a successful career making, among other things, the film
Andy Hardy's Dilemma (1938) about small-town American life. Why

Figure 1 This montage photograph was one of a number offered to
cinemas as posters for the 1936 adaptation of "the immortal classic"
The Last of the Mohicans. The central focus is evidently on the romance
between "the daring frontier scout hero Hawkeye and the lovely Alice
Munro."

was Seitz asked to direct this version of *Mohicans*? When was he taken on board and what input did he have, if any, to the writing of the script? Our sense, from hints and clues, is that he was marginal to the whole operation, as indeed was often the case in classical Hollywood production systems.[21] We have not managed to locate any substantial archive on Seitz. But if someone else can complete our story on this point, even if it challenges us on other points, we will be delighted.

NOTES

1. The film is rarely discussed in academic histories of the period. There is a short and interesting reference to it in an essay by Jeffrey Walker, who in less than a paragraph summarizes it as an adaptation blighted by fears of miscegenation (Walker, "Deconstructing an American Myth: *The Last of the Mohicans*," in Peter C. Rollins and John E. O'Connor, eds., *Hollywood's Indian: The Portrayal of the Native American in Film* [Lexington: University Press of Kentucky, 1998], p. 173), with a suggestion that this may have been the outcome of using George B. Seitz as director. This hurried conclusion, we will try to show, misses much that is important.
2. For any readers interested in the more general history of these adaptations, we would point to our book *The Lasting of the Mohicans: History of an American Myth* (Jackson: University of Mississippi Press, 1995).
3. This archival research was made possible by a grant from the British Academy, one of the UK's research funding bodies, to which we want to record our gratitude.
4. "Swelled by refugees from Nazi persecution and moved by the valor of loyalist Spain, Hollywood was ardently anti-fascist. Hollywood was also at this time informed by Washington that the President would welcome motion pictures that extolled democratic values and presented England in as positive a light as possible" (Dan Georgakas, "Robin Hood: From Roosevelt to Reagan," in Andrew Horton and Stuart Y. MacDougal, eds., *Play It Again, Sam: Retakes on Remakes* (Berkeley: University of California Press, 1998) p. 71).
5. David Culbert, "Our Awkward Ally: *Mission to Moscow* (1943)," in John E. O'Connor, ed., *American History/American Film: Interpreting the Hollywood Image* (New York: Continuum 1989), p. 128.
6. Edgar Eugene Robinson, *The Roosevelt Leadership, 1933–1945* (Philadelphia: J. B. Lippincott Company, 1955), p. 233.
7. See James McGregor Burns, *Roosevelt: The Lion and the Fox* (New York: Harcourt, Brace and Company, 1956), p. 255.
8. See, for example, Jack Warner, *My First Hundred Years in Hollywood* (New York: Random House, 1964).
9. See in particular Nick Roddick, *A New Deal in Entertainment: Warner Brothers in the 1930s* (London: BFI, 1983); David Culbert, ed., *Mission to Moscow* (Madison: University of Wisconsin Press/Warner Brothers Screenplays, 1980); and Michael E. Birdwell, *Celluloid Soldiers: Warner Bros.'s Campaign Against Nazism* (New York: New York University Press, 1999).

10. See Tino Balio, *United Artists: The Company Built by the Stars* (Madison: University of Wisconsin Press, 1986), pp. 117–118.

11. If space allowed, we would have much to say about these extraordinary archives. First, our thanks for the kindness, courtesy, and helpfulness of staff at each archive – you do a wonderful job. Second, great praise not only to those who run the archives, but to those who have taken care to hoard and safeguard such a wealth of materials. Without access to this depth of historical record, we would be left only with highly speculative accounts, and no ways to test even our own outlandish "textual" claims. Third, we record our own excitement at finding such amazing materials. In some ways, that they were incomplete made what was there even more exciting – the task of tracing patterns, finding connections, testing probabilities remains, simply, glorious.

12. All references and quotations in the following sections are, unless otherwise stated, taken from the production files for *The Last of the Mohicans* (1936), University of Southern California Cinema-Television Library.

13. Block would win an honorary Oscar in 1939 for "services to the industry through outstanding charitable endeavors."

14. The odd thing about this backstory is how closely it resonates with the opening given to the 1977 Schick Sunn version of *Mohicans*: (1936) Indians creep up on a lonely loghouse in an attack on a family, in which all die bar one boy – who grows up to be Hawkeye: (1977) Indians creep up on a lonely loghouse in an attack on a family, but this time Hawkeye appears at the last moment to drive off the Indians and rescue the family with the small boy – who then asks who is this person "La Longue Carabine" and thus launches the film.

15. Ruth Vasey, *The World According to Hollywood: 1919–37* (Exeter: University of Exeter Press, 1997).

16. Production summary and report, April 14, 1936. Letter from Joseph I. Breen to Reliance Pictures (April 16, 1936). Production Files, *The Last of the Mohicans* (1936), AMPAS Archive.

17. A wider set of issues is raised by the representation of Native Americans in this film. In a remarkable study, *The Vanishing American: White Attitudes and U. S. Policy* (Lawrence, KS: University of Kansas Press, 1982), Brian Dippie has traced the career of a persistent two-century-long ideology which preached, through every medium imaginable, that Native Americans were doomed, indeed were already dying out. However, by the early 1930s official policies were changing, not least as a result of the appointment of a new Head of the Bureau of Indian Administration, John Collier. Collier introduced substantial changes, many deriving from a principle of recognizing the authenticity and cultural worth of Native American cultures. Collier went on later in life to write a remarkable history of the American Indian peoples (Collier, *Indians of the Americas* [New York: New American Library, 1947]). None of this shows in the 1936 *Mohicans*. The publicity files in particular are replete with snide comments about Native Americans who appeared on set. There is casual talk of "braves," "squaws," and "bucks," and astonishment when they can ride bicycles. Mock references to films as "pictures that

talk like a man" present them as at best gauche, at worst rather stupid and backward. In the meantime, John Barrat, who played Chingachgook, is quoted in a press release declaring his interest in these cultures: "I was delighted to discover such interesting reading as are the old histories of the various of redskin tribes," Barrat declared. "I was amazed, too, to learn how speedily the North American Indian is vanishing, especially in the Eastern section of the country" (Publicity Files, *The Last of the Mohicans* [1936], USC Archive).

18. Edward Small, *You Don't Have To Be Crazy To Be In Show Business, But It Helps: An Autobiography* (as told to Robert E Kent), 3 vols. AMPAS Library, n.d., I:7. Further quotations will be cited parenthetically in the text.

19. Small's judgment on this was sustained by Joseph Breen, who wrote of *The Last of the Mohicans*, in the PCA's monthly report (July 31, 1936) as "an excellent audience picture based on the classic novel."

20. There remains a question. If the production of the film was not visibly influenced by the conflicts emerging in Europe, was its reception? By the time the film reached the cinemas, war was looking ever more inevitable. In November 1936 Mussolini announced the "Rome-Berlin Axis." The level of threat rose steadily thereafter. Could the film have been taken up in ways which turned its "history" into a contemporary moral lesson, about the need to unite against a common foe? We plan to explore this question in a separate essay. But from the surviving materials we have so far managed to examine, we can find no trace of such a "reading." In fact, there seems a determined wish to regard the film as a "return to an older style of film-making," or an "old-fashioned blood," as several reviews term it – denying it any contemporary reference points.

21. An example: in 1936 the magazine *Cinema Arts* ran an article on *The Last of the Mohicans*. We are not certain of the nature of the magazine, but it reads like something close to a publicity magazine, perhaps directed at exhibitors. The article is entirely positive. In recounting the story of the making of *Mohicans*, it devotes one sentence to Seitz, one paragraph to Dunne and his co-writers, and four long paragraphs to Edward Lambert, the film's researcher ("*The Last of the Mohicans*: James Fenimore Cooper's Undying Story of the Courage and Sacrifice of America's Pioneers," *Cinema Arts* 1 [1936], p. 24). The title alone warrants a pause for reflection if, as we suspect, this is effectively a piece of outreach publicity for the film. Not the Mohicans, not even Leatherstocking, but the "courage and sacrifice of the pioneers."

2 Romancing the letter: screening a Hawthorne classic

Michael Dunne

In *The Office of* The Scarlet Letter (1991), Sacvan Bercovitch calls Nathaniel Hawthorne's famous novel, written nearly a century and a half earlier (1850), "our most enduring classic."[1] This glowing compliment echoes dozens of others, including Henry James's judgment of 1887: "It is beautiful, admirable, extraordinary; it has in the highest degree that merit which I have spoken of as the mark of Hawthorne's best things – an indefinite purity and lightness of conception."[2] As these critical valentines attest, Hawthorne (1804–64) is one of America's indisputably canonical authors, and *The Scarlet Letter* is generally conceded to be his ultimate achievement. It is only to be expected, then, that there would be one or more attempts to present *The Scarlet Letter* on film. Mark Axelrod explains that "particular texts are preferable for standardization and exploitation within the Hollywood film industry because of the way they are written," so it comes as no surprise that Hawthorne's artful, stimulating, highly symbolic narrative should have been frequently chosen for cinematic adaptation.[3] For most of the twentieth century, from "artistic" silents, through studio entertainments obviously aimed at a mass audience, and high-minded European art films, all the way down to a starring vehicle for Demi Moore, *The Scarlet Letter* has been repeatedly adapted from the page to the screen. Curiously enough, these film versions simultaneously recognized the excellence of Hawthorne's classic text and sought to "improve" that text by adjusting it to the values of the contemporary cultures into which the films were released.

This development is both scandalous and perfectly understandable. It is something of a scandal that "our most enduring classic," Hawthorne's "beautiful, admirable, extraordinary" novel should be changed in any way by those who have chosen to adapt it for the screen, supposedly to make it more popular. On the other hand, critics have identified Hawthorne's own desire to hit the public's eye when writing *The Scarlet Letter* in the first place. As many scholars – including Edwin Haviland Miller in *Salem is My Dwelling Place: A Life of Nathaniel Hawthorne*

(1991) – have pointed out, Hawthorne and his family were in dire financial need at the time *The Scarlet Letter* was being written.[4] The need to strike a popular note with the reading public was thus acute. In keeping with this necessity, David S. Reynolds sees the book as the author's attempt to give the people of 1850 just what they wanted even while achieving a fine aesthetic finish: "Featuring a likable criminal, oxymoronic oppressors, a reverend rake, scaffold scenes, and sadistic women, the novel was a meeting ground for key stereotypes from the sensational press."[5] Brenda Wineapple seconds Reynolds's view, writing in her introduction to the Signet paperback edition of the novel: "A potboiler of love and crime and jealousy and revenge, the story is constructed with the sleek elegance of a Greek tragedy."[6] There is, then, a legitimate precedent for adapting the story of Hester Prynne to the demands of the market place. At the same time, one may be forgiven for feeling that some acts of adaptation are excessive and wrong-headed. As Bercovitch also observes, "Hawthorne's meanings may be endless, but they are not open-ended."[7]

When Jean Normand writes that "Hawthorne invented the visual techniques of the cinema on a literary level before the camera even existed," he helps to explain why so many cinematic adaptors have turned to Hawthorne's story about Hester, Arthur Dimmesdale, little Pearl, and Roger Chillingworth in preference to other great works of American literature.[8] The text of *The Scarlet Letter* forcefully supports Normand's argument. The narrative proper opens with a chapter entitled "The Prison Door," which provides a detailed picture of the people of seventeenth-century Boston, their clothing, their public institutions, their landscaping, and their physical relations to an exhaustively described prison door. The visual setting for the main characters' entrances is thus preestablished as in a film scenario. Twenty-four chapters later, the romance ends with a precisely drawn picture of a gravestone and its heraldic carving. No human characters are present as the novel fades to black with the words "ON A FIELD, SABLE, THE LETTER A, GULES." In between these pictures there are several arresting visual tableaux: Hester on a raised scaffold, holding the infant Pearl, with Dimmesdale looking down from a balcony and Chillingworth looking up from ground level; Hester, Pearl, and Dimmesdale, hand in hand on the scaffold at midnight, as Chillingworth looks up at them; Dimmesdale dying in Hester's arms in an ironic *pietà* framed by Pearl and Chillingworth. Obviously, these strikingly visual scenes are well suited to treatment on film. This list of cinematic opportunities could easily be expanded: Chillingworth's visit to Hester in prison in Chapter 4; Hester's and Pearl's visit to Governor Bellingham's mansion in Chapters 7–8; Hester's and Pearl's walk along the seashore in Chapter 14; Hester's meeting with Dimmesdale in the forest in Chapters 17–19; Chapter 21, called "The New England Holiday." It would appear that Normand is entirely correct about Hawthorne's cinematic potential. At least, a remarkable number of filmmakers dating back almost to the origins of the American film industry have agreed.

Beginning in early silent days, Gene Gauntier wrote and starred in a 1908 version. Three years later, Lucille Young starred as Hester, and she was succeeded in another version by Linda Arvidson in 1913. As the Internet Movie Database (www.imdb.com) attests, all these actresses – born within Hawthorne's own nineteenth century – can be considered serious film stars. Gauntier acted in films from 1906 through 1920, including appearances in such "artistic" films as *Evangeline* (1908), *The Taming of the Shrew* (1908), and *As You Like It* (1908), and she also contributed to the scripts for *Ben-Hur* (1907) and *Hiawatha* (1908). Young's career was in some ways similar to Gauntier's, beginning with her role as Hester in 1911 and concluding with the appropriate part of Mrs. Young in *Lightnin'* (1930). Arvidson was even more in demand, appearing in more than 150 silent films between 1907 and 1916, including her role as Bianca in the 1908 The *Taming of the Shrew*. The role of Hester came late in Arvidson's career. Whenever and however the role of Hester arose for each of these actresses, it is evident that it is a part that many female movie stars have coveted. Julian Smith recounts Lillian Gish's relentless struggle to get her own version filmed in 1926, and Judy Brennan reveals in *Entertainment Weekly* that "Meg Ryan reportedly lobbied hard for the part" that Demi Moore eventually landed in Roland Joffé's 1995 production of *The Scarlet Letter*.[9] Despite the unquestionable appeal of the role of Hester to actresses of different times and cultural situations, it is safe to say that none of the silent-screen actresses appearing in the 1908, 1911, or 1913 versions of the story lingers in the memories of most critics or film-goers today.

In fact, the first silent-screen version of *The Scarlet Letter* to attract much critical attention was the 1917 William Fox production, directed by Carl Harbaugh and starring Mary Martin. A February 16, 1917 reviewer in *Variety* apparently found this version rather subdued, which resulted in a judgment that the film was acceptable if unexceptional. However, this reviewer illustrated the widely held cinematic view that Hawthorne's classic tale was open to revision by suggesting that "[a] wide latitude could have been employed in the witchery or witchcraft scenes from the early Puritanical days that the tale speaks of to make this picture outstanding . . . It would seem 'The Scarlet Letter' could have been made 'big' if there had been less fidelity to the story and more attention to possibilities."[10] Although Hawthorne did not stress the possible witchcraft elements of the story, his original vision could apparently have been made even more "outstanding" if Harbaugh had exceeded the mandate that Hawthorne provided. It would be nearly eighty years before Joffé doggedly followed this advice to expand Hawthorne's original material wildly in his much-condemned 1995 version.

In the next version historically – the much-admired 1926 silent film featuring Gish as Hester – the director, Victor Seastrom, followed Hawthorne's lead in downplaying the resonances of the Salem witch trials. Perhaps as a result, a contemporaneous review in the *New York Times* by Mordaunt Hall surprisingly called this picture "as faithful a transcription of the narrative as one could well imagine."[11] *Variety* agreed that the film was "gripping," because "the story would make it that," even while conceding that *The Scarlet Letter* was "not a hot weather picture."[12] A half-century later, Mark W. Estrin still writes in *The Classic American Novel and the Movies* (1977) that this version "entertains by providing bright images to remember – particularly in Gish's luminous performance."[13] And, according to Pauline Kael, Gish's Hester "is one of the most beautifully sustained performances in screen history – mercurial, delicate, passionate."[14]

Despite most reviewers' praise of Gish and some reviewers' praise of Seastrom's textual fidelity, it must be conceded that the film's scriptwriter, Frances Marion, expanded Hawthorne's original narrative – though even she did not stress the witchcraft elements of the story. Chiefly, her additions concern a comic subplot involving the textually derived Mistress Hibbins and the purely invented Giles the barber. In this version Mistress Hibbins serves to articulate the most censorious female attitude toward Hester. Since, as Hall wrote in the *New York Times*, Gish's performance provides "an excellent conception of the courage of a young woman in the face of sneering, scorn and tittle-tattle," we can easily imagine that Hibbins would win few viewers' hearts.[15] Thus Giles seems cinematically justified when he contrives to get Hibbins into the sort of trouble with the authorities that results in her ducking in the village pond.

Even if we are fairly sure that this ducking episode does not appear in Hawthorne's book, we may begin to feel that there is some basis for the reviewers' overall statements about Seastrom's version. In the judgment of the *New York Times*, "The prudery of the ignoble bigots in Puritanical days is adroitly put forth in this picturization," while *Variety* affirms that the film makes "a strong plea against intolerance, for it makes the laws of the Colonies seem highly ridiculous and laughable, as judged by our present day standards."[16] Then, again, we may suspect that this is not exactly what Hawthorne's novel goes to show. Perhaps we may remember the judgment of Hawthorne's narrator that the Puritan elders "had fortitude and self-reliance, and, in time of difficulty or peril, stood up for the welfare of the state like a line of cliffs against a tempestuous tide."[17] Perhaps we will then conclude that reviewers of the 1926 film were responding to the values of their own antipuritanical times – the 1920s of H. L. Mencken and *The Sun Also Rises* (1926) – rather than to the times of the Puritans. Along these lines, Smith quotes the *New York Sun* reviewer who noted that Gish's character "is not Hawthorne's Hester Prynne, but she is yours and mine."[18] In the end, we may finally agree with Kael that Marion's script is less an "adaptation" of the book than a "diminution."[19]

This would seem to be the case also of the next filmed version of the romance, the 1934 talkie directed by Richard G. Vignola, with Colleen Moore as Hester and Henry B. Walthall reprising his 1926 role as Chillingworth. In this version Hawthorne's text is again expanded by a comic subplot, here the Miles Standish-John Alden-like courtship of Abigail Crakstone by Samson Goodfellow and Bartholomew Hockline. The widow Crakstone here fulfills the function assigned to Mistress Hibbins in the previous version, that of articulating female criticism of Hester. Admittedly, this function is textually derived. When Hester first appears before the people of Boston in Hawthorne's second narrative chapter, an "autumnal matron" articulates the feelings of the "wives and maidens" in the crowd that the magistrates have been too lenient in forcing Hester merely to wear a scarlet letter on her bosom. "At the very least," this woman says, "they should have put the brand of a hot iron on Hester Prynne's forehead. Madam Hester would have winced at that" (45). This lack of sympathy from most members of her own gender is an additional burden for Hester both in Hawthorne's romance and in these two filmed versions. In Vignola's film the lack of sympathy is exacerbated by the widow Crakstone's obnoxious children, Diggery and Humility, who persecute Pearl, knock her down, and throw mud at her and her mother.

Just as Mistress Hibbins's intolerance was opposed by the more forgiving male heart of Giles the barber, so Crakstone and her crone-like associates are balanced somewhat by Hockline, who even gets to articulate a line attributed to "a young wife" in Hawthorne's text: "[L]et her cover the mark as she will, the pang of it will be always in her heart" (45). This change typifies the war-between-the-sexes tone of the 1934 version. Although he offers to intercede for his friend Goodfellow with Abigail Crakstone, Hockline has no personal romantic designs on the widow's heart. He is happy in his bachelor life, as happy perhaps as Oliver Hardy, whom the actor Alan Hale physically resembles. In fact, the comic by-play between the looming Hale and the diminutive William Kent, who plays Goodfellow, closely resembles the routines with which Laurel and Hardy were accustomed to amuse audiences in the early 1930s. The comic relations between the two actors are especially illustrated in the film's adaptation of elements from the earlier film. Smith writes about the 1926 version: "Giles [the barber] is seen being rapped on the head for sneezing during religious service, seen courting the Beadle's daughter, Patience, through a speaking tube . . . and being denounced for stealing a kiss from Patience."[20] In 1934 Hockline, as churchwarden, raps Goodfellow on the head for sleeping during one of Dimmesdale's sermons, Hockline courts the widow Crakstone through a speaking tube, and Goodfellow is put in the stocks for laughing on the Sabbath. Experienced viewers would have little difficulty imagining Stan and Ollie engaged in similar antics while wearing period costume. As in the Laurel and Hardy shorts also, the "boys" are continually menaced and brow-beaten by the more mature women. After Hockline is dragooned into proposing to the widow Crakstone, he immediately becomes henpecked, followed to the tavern by his soon-to-be stepson Diggery, and threatened with the displeasure of his wife-to-be. The sailors who represent a wild alternative to the Puritan community in Hawthorne's text here commiserate with a fellow male caught in the trammels of domesticity. As a reviewer for *Variety* concluded, "Another venerated classic is wrecked on the rocks of comic relief."[21]

Colleen Moore's Hester fits into the gender patterns of the 1930s as well as the beleaguered males. Perhaps for this reason, the *Variety* review continues that "[i]t would be difficult to imagine a more happy choice for Hester than Colleen Moore." She is all melting eyes and nurturing instincts. Moore's successful silent-screen experience is evident in the long, full-screen close-ups with which she greets bad news – Chillingworth's promise to identify her lover, for example, or Bellingham's plan to remove Pearl from Hester's custody and turn her over to the widow Crakstone. When Dimmesdale says to Hester, "We must marry," Moore's Hester replies as any 1930s screen heroine might, "No, Arthur, it cannot be . . . Our lives must be a living penance." Later, when a dying woman named Allison apologizes to Hester for years of intolerance, the 1934 heroine dismisses her guilty confession with, "Oh, hush!"

Because of the mushy center at the heart of her character, this Hester does not command Dimmesdale to intercede with Bellingham to keep Pearl with her mother. Hawthorne's Hester says, "Look thou to it! I will not lose the child! Look to it!" (101). The Vignola/Moore Hester only looks beseechingly. This Hester also does not say to Dimmesdale in the forest, "Preach! Write! Act! Do any thing, save to lie down and die!" (180), because such aggressiveness might strike too Jean Arthurish a tone. Vignola's Hester does say – more or less textually – to Dimmesdale, "You shall not go alone!" (cf. 181), but she says it with fluttering eyelashes and with romantic string music in the background.

In other words, this is not exactly Hawthorne's story either, and not only because of the interpolated characters and subplot. This is a *Scarlet Letter* for the mid-1930s, as close to a romantic comedy as the material will allow. Even Pearl, played by Cora Sue Collins, comes across as a B-grade Shirley Temple, as when she and Hester march around the cabin playing soldiers because the Puritan children have refused to include Pearl in their grisly games. Imagine what Vignola and Moore could have done if only Dimmesdale did not have to die in the end! It will be another sixty years before Joffé and Demi Moore decide that he does not have to die after all.

As we might expect, changing social conditions and changing attitudes toward gender resulted in a changed *Scarlet Letter* when Hester's story next came to the screen in Wim Wenders's 1972 German version, *Der Scharlachrote Buchstabe*. As would be appropriate at that time, Hester's situation takes on gender-inflected countercultural resonances. Wenders's Hester is a young, sexy, independent woman opposed by older, repressed male authority figures. His principal additions to Hawthorne's narrative support this thematic emphasis. As James M. Welsh explains in his *Magill's Survey of Cinema* essay, Wenders originally intended to cast the gorgeous Yelena Samarina as Hester, but the money men demanded that the starring role of Hester go to the equally gorgeous, but better known, Senta Berger.[22] Wenders complied with their orders but cast Samarina as Mistress Hibbins. According to Welsh, whereas Hawthorne made the historical Mistress Hibbins older to suit his fictional design, Wenders made her younger. Wenders also made Hibbins much dishier and gave her a slave named Sarah, played by the equally attractive Laura Currie. Since Mistress Hibbins alone among the Puritans sympathizes with Hester, Wenders creates opportunities to show at least some form of female solidarity by filming Hester, Hibbins, and Sarah together in scenes cut contrastingly against shots of the joyless, sexless, Puritan male elders. The striking visuals support Wenders's 1970s vision thematically without introducing extratextual dialogue.

Wenders repeatedly gives Samarina visually appealing screen time, as when Hibbins – who seems in this version to be Bellingham's daughter rather than his sister – dons the governor's ceremonial robes and wig and parades in silence to the scaffold on which Hester has earlier stood. There she unsuccessfully attempts suicide by burning herself at the stake – without dialogue. In the following scene she does speak, relating to Chillingworth and Dimmesdale a disjointed tale about society, the prophet Jonah, and menstrual blood. Dimmesdale cannot bear to hear this speech and rushes from the room, reinforcing the viewer's early 1970s sense of his weakness as a character and as a male. Later, Hibbins gets to wear her own scarlet letter to church on the occasion of Dimmesdale's election sermon, and she gets to laugh maniacally when Dimmesdale reveals the *literal* letter "A" on his breast. Although largely without textual basis, these developments in Hibbins's character may be seen to fit smoothly into the thematic program of Wenders's film.

Thematic effectiveness is also the result of some other liberties that Wenders takes with Hawthorne's text. Because the studio officials also dictated that the film should be shot in Spain rather than in New England, the natural scenery available to Wenders called for some ingenious reinflections of Hawthorne's imagery. This is especially clear in the episode called by Hawthorne "A Forest Walk." The occasion is Hester's "resolve to make known to Mr. Dimmesdale, at whatever risk of present pain or ulterior consequences, the true character of the man who had crept into his intimacy" (165), that is, the fact that Chillingworth is her husband who is seeking revenge for his cuckoldry. The best place for this disclosure, Hester feels, is a secluded path in the forest. This location seems appropriate because the forest "hemmed [the path] in so narrowly, and stood so black and dense on either side, and disclosed such imperfect glimpses of the sky above, that, to Hester's mind, it imaged not amiss the moral wilderness in which she had long been wandering" (166). Without the forest primeval at his disposal, Wenders could not appropriate Hawthorne's symbolic location. Even so, he was able to represent Hester's conviction that "she would need the whole wide world to breathe in, while they talked together" (165) by means of location shots on the seashore showing the sea over Hester's shoulders and the rocky coast behind Dimmesdale. Since Hester will leave the community by sea and Dimmesdale will die ashore in the town, the shots are effective in foreshadowing the plot. The symbolism also effectively represents the wildness of Hester's character and the emotional rigidity of Dimmesdale's. All in all, Wenders makes a virtue of necessity in his use of scenery, all the while reinforcing the thematic emphasis of his adaptation.

Another change is more problematic since it concerns plot rather than setting. After Dimmesdale has confessed his guilt to the congregation and revealed the literal scarlet letter on his breast, he collapses. He is then carried back into the sacristy as Hester and Pearl make their way to the waiting ship. When Dimmesdale recovers from his faint, he tells the new governor, Fuller, that he can now rejoin Hester and Pearl with a clear conscience. Since Fuller has consistently articulated the most severe male judgment against Hester in this gender-inflected film, he cannot be pleased to hear that the Hester–Dimmesdale romance is about to have a happy ending. So he strangles Dimmesdale. The camera then cuts from the cruel and guilty Fuller to a saddened but departing Hester, and the political and gender conflicts animating the film are visually restated. Wenders thus achieves thematic closure, though the plot is decidedly twisted to make this possible.

The next development in the history of *The Scarlet Letter* on film is the 1995 version directed by Joffé and starring Demi Moore. About this version Bruce Daniels plausibly observes in *Journal of Popular Culture*, "Perhaps no movie was ever more widely and negatively reviewed."[23] David Denby can speak for many. Beginning with the premise that "life is not long enough to watch Demi Moore playing Hester Prynne," he writes that he watched only the first hour of the film. That was apparently enough: "What I saw in that dismaying and languid hour was a big swooning, 1955-style drama about repressed passion, nude bathing, and, finally, sex among the corn kernels (in the barn, you know)."[24] On a similar note, Owen Gleiberman writes that the sex-in-the-barn scene is "not the image I'll remember most. No, that would be Hester's teenage mulatto slave, who's hidden in the adjacent house, pleasuring herself in the tub as she enjoys a kinky communion with . . . a bird. A scarlet bird. You heard me."[25]

One might answer Gleiberman that the mulatto slave can most likely be traced back to the part of Sarah in Wenders's film and that the bird probably derives in some strange way from Hawthorne's text. When Governor Bellingham first sees Pearl, he says, "What little bird of scarlet plumage may this be?" (97). Later, while Dimmesdale is inside delivering the election sermon, Pearl dances through the market place, making "the sombre crowd cheerful by her erratic and glistening ray, even as a bird of bright plumage illuminates a whole tree of dusky foliage, by darting to and fro, half seen and half concealed, amid the twilight of the clustering leaves" (222). To Denby's criticism one might answer that there was probably as much sexual repression among the Puritans as among any other group of human beings. By the same token, some sort of sex surely took place between Hester and Dimmesdale, or Pearl would not be dancing in the market place or anywhere else. At the same time, we must conclude that – any remote similarities to Hawthorne's text notwithstanding – the Moore/Joffé version is the clearest evidence to date that filmmakers continually revision *The Scarlet Letter* in the terms provided by their own cultures.

One patent form of revisioning involves the film's 1990s version of Christian theology. Hawthorne's Dimmesdale says to Hester in the forest, "Were I an atheist – a man devoid of conscience – a wretch with coarse and brutal instincts – I might have found peace, long ere now. Nay, I never should have lost it! But, as matters stand with my soul, whatever of good capacity there originally was in me, all of God's gifts that were the choicest have become the ministers of spiritual torment" (173–174). The Dimmesdale played by Gary Oldman in 1995 is less bothered by spiritual issues because he is less capable of distinguishing theologically between good and evil. When Hester asks him, "Do you believe we've sinned? Dimmesdale can answer only, "I know not." Hawthorne might find Oldman/Dimmesdale's theological confusion suitable punishment for his flirtatious quip to Hester earlier in the film: "And here I thought comprehending God was going to be my greatest challenge." Clearly, the filmmakers feel that the quip demands no punishment, since they end their film with a voiceover in which the now-grown Pearl asks, "Who is to say what is a sin in God's eyes?" One suspects that the citizens of seventeenth-century Boston would happily volunteer an answer.

Then, again, this film is not really about sin or any other complicated issues, as a glossy advertising insert from *Entertainment Weekly* demonstrates:

As relevant today as when Nathaniel Hawthorne wrote it almost 150 years ago, 'The Scarlet Letter' stars Demi Moore as Hester Prynne, a spirited and sensual young woman who is branded an adulteress and cast out by a harsh Puritanical society that seeks to punish her for being human . . . 'The Scarlet Letter' is a story about the corrosiveness of fear and how it breeds racial and cultural hatred. But it is ultimately a tale of the redemptive power of love.[26]

In other words, the 1995 *Scarlet Letter* was conceived and executed as an overlong dramatization of sex, multicultural tolerance, and sexual politics – an ideal mix for mid-1990s American culture.

The patently sexual aura of Joffé's updated film understandably disturbed many viewers. Mituba's autoerotic scene in the tub that proved so bothersome to Gleiberman, for example, is intercut with the scene showing Hester and Dimmesdale in the barn. The sequence is clearly intended to show that everyone in the Puritan community is doing something sexual most of the time, as American popular culture today assumes. Thus in Joffé's film Brewster Stonehall tries to rape Hester, Chillingworth wants to sleep with Hester as soon as he returns from

Indian captivity, the women of the community are interested primarily in whether a character named Mary was sexually abused during her Indian captivity, and the community elders reveal obvious sadomasochistic tendencies as they brutally question Mituba about Hester's possible involvement in witchcraft. A comparable list of sexual activities might be gleaned from the television listings during sweeps week.

Joffé's film is also up to date in terms of multiculturalism in a way that Hawthorne could not be. Dimmesdale's first sermon segues easily from the need for the Puritans to establish a city on a hill to the need to love their neighbors irrespective of race or religion. Hester is unconvinced that the Algonquins really need Dimmesdale's translation of the Christian Bible or that Christian morality is superior to what the tribes already practice. On the other hand, the Puritan elders in this film see Native Americans, Quakers, dissenters, and independent women as variations of the same problem – nonconformity. In a totally fabricated incident, Chillingworth tells these elders that his former community in Virginia came to ruin through these agents of "Otherness," and the terrified white males accept Chillingworth's analysis without question. False charges, suborned testimony, a jack-booted posse – all the modes of phallocentric totalitarianism familiar to watchers of television documentaries today – soon follow. Since none of this political subtext seriously threatens the love plot involving Hester and Dimmesdale, viewers are encouraged to condemn oppression and bask in their own unchallenged tolerance without intellectual distraction. Easy answers are Joffé's speciality.

This is true also of the film's central feminist message. The community of women embracing Hester and Mistress Hibbins is clearly preferable to the male power structure that includes Chillingworth and Governor Bellingham – as Wim Wenders already told us. Hibbins – usually called Harriet in this version – naturally assists Hester during Pearl's birth, Demi Moore's most demanding, least coiffed, scene. Appropriately, Hibbins encourages Hester to sit up during the delivery, following the recent female recovery of birth techniques repudiated by the male medical profession. Even among the Native Americans, women's greater wisdom is evident. After the captive Chillingworth goes more native than the natives, it is the elder women of the tribe who decide – in subtitles – that he should be sent back to the white community. When Dimmesdale naively assumes that some sort of accommodation can be worked out between the male elders and the women accused of witchcraft, Hester asks, "What has happened to the man I love?"

Hester is right, of course, as we might expect on the basis of Demi Moore's name above the film's title. And yet, Hester's triumph is mixed. Despite her professed self-reliance, she is well on her way to being hanged when the dashingly attired Dimmesdale finally arrives to declare his love and save the day. Significantly, Hester and the other accused women are gagged as well as bound in this scene. Significantly also, final victory arrives not through Dimmesdale's confession but through the *deus-ex-machina* device of a Native American attack just at the crucial moment. Joffé thus both strikes a note of feminism and sings the lyrics of a violent finale, proving to his 1990s audience that – despite puritanical hang-ups suggesting the contrary – you really can have it all.

In her opening-day story on this film in *USA Today*, Susan Wloszczyna writes, "As the film's star Demi Moore has bluntly declared, 'Not very many people have read the book.'"[27] Clearly, both she and Moore were mistaken, and not only about readers in 1995. Nearly a century of cinematic representations of *The Scarlet Letter* demonstrate that generations of directors and screenwriters have read Hawthorne's original

Figure 2. The 1995 Entertainment/Hollywood production of *The Scarlet Letter* emphasizes the doomed romance between Hester (Demi Moore) and the erstwhile Reverend Dimmesdale (Gary Oldman).

text and also that each has done so under the ruling assumptions of a different social context.

NOTES

1. Sacvan Bercovitch, *The Office of* The Scarlet Letter (Baltimore: Johns Hopkins University Press, 1991), p. xxii.
2. Henry James, *Hawthorne* (1887), (New York: AMS, 1968), p.109.
3. Mark Axelrod, "Once Upon a Time in Hollywood; or, The Commodification of Form in the Adaptation of Fictional Texts to the Hollywood Cinema," *Literature/Film Quarterly* 24:2 (1996), p. 204.
4. Edwin Haviland Miller, *Salem is My Dwelling Place: A Life of Nathaniel Hawthorne* (Iowa City: University of Iowa Press, 1991), pp. 274ff.
5. David S. Reynolds, *Beneath the American Renaissance: The Subversive Imagination in the Age of Emerson and Melville* (New York: Knopf, 1988), p. 263.
6. Brenda Wineapple, "Introduction," Nathaniel Hawthorne, *The Scarlet Letter* (New York: Signet, 1999), p. xii.
7. Bercovitch, *The office*, p. xi.
8. Jean Normand, *Nathaniel Hawthorne: An Approach to an Analysis of Artistic Creation*, trans. Derek Cotman (Cleveland, OH: Case Western Reserve University Press, 1970), p. 311.
9. Julian Smith, "Hester, Sweet Hester Prynne – *The Scarlet Letter* in the Movie Market Place," *Literature/Film Quarterly* 2 (1974), pp. 101–102; Judy Brennan, and Jess Cagle, "News & Notes," *Entertainment Weekly*, February 4, 1994, pp. 8ff.
10. "Review of *The Scarlet Letter*, directed by Carl Harbaugh," *Variety*, February 16, 1917.
11. Mordaunt Hall, "Review of *The Scarlet Letter*, directed by Victor Seastrom," *New York Times* August 10, 1926, 19, p. ?
12. "Review of *The Scarlet Letter*, directed by Victor Seastrom," *Variety*, August 11, 1926.
13. Mark W. Estrin, "'Triumphant Ignominy' on the Screen," in Gerald Peary and Roger Shatzkin, eds., *The Classic American Novel and the Movies* (New York: Ungar, 1977), p. 29.
14. Pauline Kael, *Kiss Kiss Bang Bang* (Boston: Little, Brown, 1968), p. 345.
15. Hall, "Review ," *New York Times*, p. ?
16. Ibid.; "Review," *Variety*, 1926.
17. Nathaniel Hawthorne, *The Scarlet Letter* (1850), (New York: Signet, 1999), pp. 216–217. Further quotations will be cited parenthetically in the text.
18. Smith, "Hester," p. 102.
19. Kael, *Kiss Kiss*, p. 345.
20. Smith, "Hester," p. 104.
21. "Review of *The Scarlet Letter*, directed by Richard G. Vignola," *Variety*, September 25, 1934.
22. James M. Welsh, "*The Scarlet Letter (Der Scharlachrote Buchstabe)*," in Frank N. Magill, ed., *Magill's Survey of Cinema: Foreign Language Films* (Englewood Cliffs, NJ: Salem Press, 1985), VI, pp. 2658–2661.

23. Bruce Daniels, "Bad Movie/Worse History: The 1995 Unmaking of *The Scarlet Letter*," *Journal of Popular Culture* 32:4 (Spring 1999), p. 3.
24. David Denby, "Review of *The Scarlet Letter*, directed by Roland Joffé," *New York Times* October 23, 1995, pp. 43–44.
25. Owen Gleiberman, "Red Letter Daze," *Entertainment Weekly*, October 20, 1995, pp. 43–44.
26. See Judy Brennan, and Jess Cagle, "News & Notes," *Entertainment Weekly*, February 4, 1994.
27. Susan Wloszczyna, "Is the 'A' for Adaptation or Abomination?," *USA Today*, October 13, 1995, p. 1D.

3   The movies in the Rue Morgue: adapting Edgar Allan Poe for the screen

Paul Woolf

Poe's paradoxical popularity

Type the name Edgar Allan Poe (1809–49) into the search facility of the Internet Movie Database (www.imdb.com) and you will discover that there have been 141 cinema and television films based, to varying degrees, on Poe's works.[1] This is more than Herman Melville (25 entries in the database), Henry James (67) and even Mark Twain (83). While not an entirely scientific exercise, this does suggest that Poe is the most-filmed American author of the nineteenth century.[2]

Bare statistics, however, only tell us so much. Poe is a uniquely popular figure for the screen industry. But, in comparison with other major authors, it is to a greater than usual extent and with greater than usual frequency that feature-film and television versions of Poe's works depart radically from the texts from which they claim to originate. This is clear from my own viewing, and from books such as Ronald L. Smith's *Poe In The Media* (1990) and Don G. Smith's comprehensive critical filmography *The Poe Cinema* (1999).[3]

Usually when one watches a screen adaptation of a familiar literary text, one looks for changes to the storyline, details that have been modified, and characters that have been conflated or dropped completely. With Poe adaptations, it is sometimes more a question of spotting the few details, characters, and elements of plot that have been retained at all. Rather than adaptations, many are best described simply as new stories featuring a scattering of Poe's ideas. The *New York Times* said of *The Black Cat* (Edgar G. Ulmer, 1934) that the film, supposedly based on Poe's tale of the same name, "is not remotely to be identified with Poe's short story."[4] Such comments are almost a commonplace of reviews of Poe-derived films.

Some "Poe" films happily throw in together incidents from more than one Poe story or poem. It is as if Poe's works were one vast repository of characters, events, and themes, from which filmmakers are happy to select the items they want and disregard all others. This has been so

43

since 1908 when the very first Poe adaptation, *Sherlock Holmes and the Great Murder Mystery*, took the crime from Poe's short story "The Murders in the Rue Morgue" (1841) and gave the case to Arthur Conan Doyle's famous English detective.

This is, by the way, not a complaint; there have been some terrific films, as well as more than a few turkeys, made using bits and pieces from the Poe repository. I am, though, interested in this paradoxical popularity of Poe with screenwriters, directors, and producers. It would be possible to write an entire essay on why filmmakers love to use Poe's name but so consistently ignore his texts. This essay would touch upon issues ranging from Poe's widespread popularity outside America (many of the 141 films have been produced in Europe), to the brevity of the majority of his surviving works (do filmmakers treat short stories and poems with a different attitude than they bring to novels?). It would discuss the way in which many "Poe" films, while dispensing with the original narrative, create what reviewers often refer to as "the feeling of Poe" or "the Poe atmosphere."[5] What exactly is this "atmosphere," and why do filmmakers find it more useful than Poe's texts? The essay would also explore the longstanding debate over Poe's "literary merit."[6] Has Poe's dismissal by numerous significant figures, from Henry James to T. S. Eliot to the influential critic Harold Bloom, enabled filmmakers to feel less reverential toward Poe's works than they might toward texts by less disputed members of the literary canon such as, say, James?

This chapter, though, addresses the question of how we study films as audiovisual adaptations of texts when they bear very little resemblance to their literary progenitors. I pay particular attention to "The Murders in the Rue Morgue."

"As much as anyone ever invents a genre, Poe invented the detective story," wrote the critic F. O. Matthiessen about "The Murders in the Rue Morgue," the short story generally acknowledged as "the founding text" of detective fiction.[7] It is the first of three tales set in 1840s Paris and featuring as their central character Auguste Dupin. "The Mystery of Marie Rogêt" (1842/3) and "The Purloined Letter" (1845) are the others. Dupin is an idiosyncratic, reclusive "young gentleman" (414) who in "The Murders in the Rue Morgue" "take[s] an eager delight" (415) in exercising his exceptional intellect on solving the "horrible" (420) murders of a mother and daughter.[8] The women have been killed and "fearfully mutilated" (420) in their own bedroom but the police have "not . . . the shadow of a clue" (425), baffled by the apparent motivelessness of the murders and the seeming impossibility of the killer escaping from the locked and secure room. Dupin, with his formidable powers of "observation" (417) and "analysis" (411), discovers material evidence that the police have missed and deduces how the murderer was able to exit the room. He ultimately reveals the killer to be an escaped, razor-wielding orangutan.

Tales of crimes and criminals were a feature of newspapers and novels long before Poe, but it was his concentration on describing the detective and narrating the process of detection that gave the Dupin tales what one contemporary called their "original character."[9] The name that Poe gave to his Dupin stories – "tales of ratiocination"[10] – offers some idea of what he considered to be their key focus: the rigorous logical thinking through which Dupin solves crimes. They are stories above all else about the workings of an extraordinary man's powerful intellect.

In the hundred years since the now-lost *Sherlock Holmes and the Great Murder Mystery*, "The Murders in the Rue Morgue" has been adapted for film or television on at least eight more occasions.[11] Of these, a further three are unavailable to view, leaving five extant versions. I will focus first on the earliest and most famous of these films – *Murders in the Rue Morgue* (Robert Florey, 1932).

The Universal Poe

In 1929 Carl Laemmle, Jr. succeeded his father as head of production at Universal Pictures.[12] He instituted a new policy of making high-budget movies based on prestige works of literature. As part of this policy, Universal purchased the film rights to a popular stage adaptation of Bram Stoker's *Dracula* (1897) and turned Mary Shelley's *Frankenstein* (1818) into a screenplay. Both were released as movies in 1931 and both, in the depths of the American Depression, became enormous box-office successes.[13] As the film historians Bruce Dettman and Michael Bedford note, it was "more than enough to convince Laemmle Jr. that he had hit upon a virtually unexplored (at least in America) and financially potent field of filmmaking – the Monster movie."[14] The studio quickly went into production with a series of films now referred to as "the Universal horror cycle," a group that also soon included *The Invisible Man* (James Whale, 1933) and *The Bride of Frankenstein* (James Whale, 1935).

"The Murders in the Rue Morgue" was one of the first texts to which Universal turned for material for its new "horror cycle." Shooting on *Murders in the Rue Morgue* began in October 1931 with Bela Lugosi, the Eastern European actor who had starred as the title character in *Dracula*, as the lead.[15] But Lugosi, as I explain below, was not playing Auguste Dupin.

When *Murders in the Rue Morgue* was released in 1932, posters advertising the film clearly situated it as a successor to the earlier horrors:

We warned you about 'Dracula.' We warned you about 'Frankenstein.' Now we warn you that the blood will run cold in your veins at the amazing, almost unbelievable things you'll see in this picture . . . the terrible things that only Poe could imagine and only Universal dared picturize. With . . . Bela Lugosi ('Dracula' himself).

Large text at the bottom of the same posters informed potential cinemagoers that the film is "Based on the story by EDGAR ALLAN POE."[16]

Poe's fame and his reputation as primarily a writer of horror tales, developed during his lifetime and consolidated in the decades after his death by press articles that focused on the "diablerie," "horrible monstrosities" and "wild and perverse" nature of his stories, gave him an obvious appeal to Universal as the studio sought to market its movies as spine-chillers.[17] Universal returned to Poe twice more as the "horror cycle" continued, producing Ulmer's *The Black Cat* in 1934 and *The Raven* (Louis Friedlander) in 1935. Both films starred Lugosi and Boris Karloff ("Frankenstein" himself) and both "ow[ed] little to Poe sources."[18]

It was not just Poe's literary status that endeared him to Laemmle, Jr., however, but also the prevalent public image of the author as an isolated, morally destitute, and very possibly insane genius. This image had been popularized by the infamous obituary written by Rufus Griswold in 1849, which, though always contested by those more favorable to Poe, had persisted.[19] The Universal pressbook for *The Raven* suggested that journalists consider in their articles the question "Was Edgar Allan Poe a mental derelict?" and drew parallels between Poe himself and Dr. Vollin (Lugosi), the Poe-obsessed, isolated, morally destitute, and very definitely insane genius whom the screenwriters created as the film's central character. According to Don G. Smith, the "pressbook also refers to 'Frankenstein' Karloff, 'Dracula' Lugosi, and 'Goose-Pimple' Edgar Allan Poe as 'the big three'" of horror movies.[20] Poe was, it seems, almost as much a part of the Universal horror family as the studio's two biggest stars.

Famously, another film company, American International Pictures (AIP), would similarly appropriate Poe for a series of horror movies, directed by Roger Corman, in the 1960s. Both sets of films – Corman's so-called "Poe cycle" and Universal's three Poe adaptations – are still much loved and watched today, all available to buy on VHS and/or DVD. The intimate association of Poe with the horror-film genre has undoubtedly helped to shape the popular conception of him today. Many of the websites about Poe maintained by fans, for instance, use the gothic and "blood-dripping" typefaces associated with horror-film posters and title sequences.[21] Poe's popular legacy is, literally, written by the genre.

What is evident, however, is that Poe's name was of more value to Universal and to AIP as a marketing tool than his works were as direct sources for screenplays. The advertising for *Murders in the Rue Morgue*, for example, might claim that "only Poe could [have] imagine[d]" the film's "almost unbelievable" events, but the fact is that it was Universal's screenwriters, and not Poe, who supplied its basic premise, its storyline, and the majority of its scenes.

Murders in the Rue Morgue (1932)

Murders in the Rue Morgue, set in Paris in 1845, opens at a carnival where we meet the dashing young medical student Pierre Dupin (Leon Waycoff) and his beautiful fiancée Camille L'Espanaye (Sidney Fox). As various theorists, most famously Mikhail Bakhtin, have argued, carnival can be seen as a time in which the usual social order is temporarily overturned, moral boundaries disrupted and otherwise repressed urges released.[22] The film thus immediately indicates that what follows is likely to be a period in which accepted social and moral norms are challenged and unsettled.

Among the carnival's semi-naked Arab dancing girls and Wild West displays is a sideshow marquee, standing over the entrance to which is an enormous cut-out of an ape. A ringmaster urges spectators to come inside to see Erik the Ape (played by Charles Gemora in an unconvincing monkey costume), "the ape man . . . the monster who walks upright . . . the beast with a human soul." Entering the tent, Pierre and Camille are greeted by Dr. Mirakle (Lugosi). Mirakle's strange hair, boggling eyes, and unidentifiably foreign accent ("I never heard an accent like it," Pierre says) – not to mention the fact that this is "'Dracula' himself" – immediately denote him as sinister.

Mirakle takes to the stage, the backdrop of which is a pictorial narration of stages in human evolution from amoeba to man. Mirakle addresses the audience, assuring them that he is "not a sideshow charlatan" and promising that in Erik he is "not exhibiting a freak, a monstrosity of nature, but a milestone in the development of life." Mirakle orders his servant, Janos "The Black One," to unveil Erik's cage. Noble Johnson, who plays Janos, was one of the best-known black actors of the 1930s, and for the role he wears light face make-up. Depending on a scene's lighting, this at times gives him an appearance almost as pale as Mirakle's, despite being called "The Black One." At other times, Janos is noticeably darker-skinned than his master. This willful confusion of blackness and whiteness suggests that not only social and moral boundaries, but also any stable notions of racial identities, are under threat during this carnival period.

"Behold," Mirakle exclaims as Janos takes the covering from Erik's cage, "the first man!" Mirakle converses with Erik, translating into English the noises made by the ape. "My home is in the African jungle . . . but I was captured by a band of hairless white apes . . . I am lonely," Erik laments. The crowd noisily decry Mirakle's invocation of evolutionary theory and his claims of man's genetic likeness to apes. Someone shouts "Heresy!" from the floor. As much of the audience walks out in disgust, Mirakle responds angrily. "My life is consecrated to a great experiment," he shouts. "I tell you I will prove your kinship with the ape. Erik's blood will be mixed with the blood of man!" Pierre, clearly intrigued by the doctor, and Camille are among the few remaining spectators. Mirakle invites them to take a closer look at Erik. The "lonely" ape seems attracted to Camille and, through the bars of his cage, grabs her bonnet. Mirakle starts to look at Camille with menacing interest.

It soon becomes clear that, as part of his "great experiment," Mirakle is responsible for the deaths of a number of young women, all of whose bodies have washed up from the Seine. We see Mirakle abduct a "woman of the streets" (Arlene Francis), as the credits name her. We cut to Mirakle's mad-scientist laboratory where the prostitute, stripped to her underwear, is strapped to an X-shaped cross and is screaming, the film displaying the classic horror movie's penchant for scenes of sadism that are simultaneously terrifying and titillating. Mirakle is extracting blood from the woman to test its suitability for mixing with Erik's. The experiment fails when Mirakle discovers that she has "rotten blood" – presumably syphilitic, certainly not virginal. "Your blood is rotten! Your beauty was a lie!" he shouts irately at her, at which exact moment she dies.

Mirakle stays in Paris once the carnival has left town and turns his attention to tracking down Camille. Importantly, we always see Camille in virginal white, she always wears a crucifix, and Pierre has already described her as "pure." Her blood is definitely not "rotten." Mirakle's first attempt to lure Camille to his tent fails when Pierre, intuitively suspicious of the doctor, intervenes, but it is obvious that, if Mirakle has his way, Camille will be "the pride of science," the woman whose "pure" blood will prove his theory. It is never explained why only a virgin's blood will mix with Erik's.

By this stage, we have already learned of Pierre's own macabre fixation – obsessively investigating the deaths of the young women by examining with his microscope samples of their blood, which he has procured illegally by bribing the morgue-keeper. Pierre has discovered that the women did not die of drowning, as supposed, but because "some foreign substance" has been "introduced into the bloodstream."

Meanwhile, Mirakle makes another attempt to see Camille, visiting her late at night. When she refuses to let him enter the home she shares with her mother, Mirakle sends Erik to kidnap her. Just after we have seen Camille pray in front of a crucifix, the ape breaks into the house, murders Madame L'Espanaye, and takes away Camille, who has fainted. Madame L'Espanaye's murder is the first time that the screenwriters use a detail taken directly from Poe's narrative: in Poe's original story the daughter's mutilated corpse is discovered stuffed up the chimney; here Madame L'Espanaye's body suffers the same fate. Across Paris, Pierre finally deduces that "the foreign substance" in the murdered women's blood is gorilla's blood and, realizing that Mirakle must be involved and Camille is in danger, sets off to rescue his fiancée. Pierre gets to Camille's home too late to help Madame L'Espanaye and is briefly himself suspected of her murder before persuading the police to accompany him to Mirakle's house-cum-laboratory. As they arrive, Mirakle has just discovered that Camille's blood is suitably "pure" for his nefarious purposes. But Erik now attacks him, apparently to prevent the doctor experimenting further on his beloved Camille. He kills him, grabs the unconscious Camille, and runs off with her again, this time taking to the rooftops. Pierre pursues Erik and the film climaxes with the medical student shooting the ape dead and, finally, saving Camille.

Poe's "Murders" and Universal's Murders

Although the film's opening credits announce it to be "Based on the immortal classic by Edgar Allan Poe," Poe's "The Murders in the Rue Morgue" makes only fleeting appearances in Universal's *Murders in the Rue Morgue* – some characters' names, the nature of Madame L'Espanaye's murder, and a dispute among her neighbors over the killer's native language (crucial to Poe's story but played for in-consequential laughs here) are the only conspicuous traces of it. Whether Universal ever intended to produce a more faithful version of Poe's story, the success of *Frankenstein,* which outperformed even *Dracula* at the box office,[23] makes it unsurprising that the studio decided instead to transform "The Murders in the Rue Morgue" into another "mad-scientist and monster" movie. In doing so, they not only dispensed with Poe's plot but also shifted the focus away from the process of detection, the key interest of the original narrative.

However, while the two plots may be profoundly dissimilar, the film nonetheless addresses many of the same issues explored by Poe in his version of the "ape terrorizes city" story. I want to suggest now that this may be a fruitful point of entry into studying Universal's *Murders in the Rue Morgue* as an adaptation of Poe's "The Murders in the Rue Morgue" – seeing the film as a continuation of, or even commentary on, themes that lurk just below the surface of Poe's text.

There are many topics that one could discuss here. It would, for example, be interesting to compare the way in which the two works depict the city, specifically the European city, as a site of violence and of sexual immorality. I want, however, to concentrate on an issue that appears in comparatively oblique form in Poe's story, but is pushed to the foreground of the 1932 movie – that is, an intersecting interest in race, sex, and science.

Throughout "The Murders in the Rue Morgue," Dupin's detective work has an air of scientific method about it. A conversation between Dupin and the narrator at the start of the story touches on, among other things, "nebular cosmogony" (a form of studying the beginnings of the universe) and the contemporaneous astronomer John Pringle Nichol (419–420). It is during this conversation that Dupin's remarkable use of logic to understand other people's thoughts and behavior is revealed, thereby affiliating his techniques to wider modern scientific discourse. This sense of Dupin's scientific ability is reenforced as he solves the case. In looking at material evidence and deducing from it the only possible series of events that could lead to its appearance at a certain place and time, Dupin reasons, he says, "*'a posteriori'*" (431) (backward from finish to start), much as a cosmogonist would in attempting to recon-struct events leading up to the creation of matter from the material evidence of the universe as it exists today.

As Dupin reaches his revelation of the murderer's identity, however, his work does more than simply *resemble* scientific procedure; he actually turns to a scientific text, the nineteenth-century French natural historian Georges Cuvier's *Animal Kingdom* (1817), to clinch his proof.[24] It is when Dupin shows to the narrator Cuvier's "minute anatomical and generally descriptive account of the large fulvous Ourang-Outang of the East Indian Islands . . . [its] prodigious strength . . . [and] wild ferocity" that the narrator says he finally "understood the full horrors of the murder" (437). Only an orangutan as described by Cuvier, Dupin then illustrates, could have left the marks found on the murdered women's bodies. Cuvier's book both informs and lends authority to Dupin's theories. It seems appropriate, then, that at the very end of "The Murders in the Rue Morgue" we learn that the recaptured orangutan has been sold to the Jardin des Plantes (444), Paris's public zoo and botanical gardens, and the place where Cuvier carried out his research. This is, the story implies, the appropriate home for a ferocious African animal in Paris, where it becomes both public spectacle and scientific specimen. Dupin draws on Cuvier to demonstrate that even the most "'perplexing'" (425) mystery of the modern city can be interpreted through the application of modern science. Cuvier's work contains both figuratively (in *Animal Kingdom*) and literally (in the Jardin des Plantes) the "wild" (433) threat of the orangutan.

As "The Murders in the Rue Morgue" gathers pace and moves towards its denouement, in which Dupin and the narrator confront the sailor from whom the orangutan has escaped, it is easy to overlook the significance of the reference to Cuvier. If anthropological science seems incidental or submerged in Poe's story, however, it is from the very beginning visible and central in Universal's rendering of the tale. Dr. Mirakle's controversial diatribe about man's descent from apes establishes the subject of evolution as a focal point of the narrative.

The 1932 film was topical: the argument in America between evolutionists and antievolutionist Christians was still raging in the wake of the infamous Scopes trial of 1925 (and, with revived intensity, persists today). One historian has described Scopes as "the best-known legal contest in American history" until "the trial of O. J. Simpson."[25] Ostensibly a dispute over whether schools in Tennessee should teach their students about mankind's evolution from apes or about biblical creation, in essence the Scopes trial publicly pitted against each other two very different explanations of the origin of the universe, one based on science, the other on Scripture. This debate is played out in microcosm in Dr. Mirakle's marquee.

Murders in the Rue Morgue seems to negotiate a path between the two sides of the Scopes controversy. It carefully avoids either fully endorsing or rejecting evolutionary theory. Pierre tells his skeptical roommate Paul (Bert Roach) that Mirakle "might be right" about evolution, and nothing in the film ever disproves the doctor. The question of whether or not Mirakle is right, however, is forgotten in the excitement of the action sequences toward the end – Erik's and Mirakle's fight, the rooftop chase. The film leaves Mirakle's theories still possible, but unproved. Indeed, it seems to suggest that this might be best. Like Universal's *Frankenstein*, *Murders in the Rue Morgue* argues that the quest for scientific knowledge is not justifiable if certain moral boundaries must be breached. Some things, simply, are best left unknown and Mirakle, the classic "mad scientist," is punished by nature, killed by Erik, for trying to know too much.

If Mirakle represents evolutionary science gone bad, however, Pierre represents its more positive capabilities. It is Pierre's investigation into the murdered women's blood samples that establishes Mirakle's guilt and takes him to Mirakle's house (just) in time to save Camille. "Good science'" can tame nature at its most dangerous (Pierre in turn kills Erik), and, in this way, Pierre's science performs in the film the same role that Cuvier's text does in Poe's story. Crucially, Pierre's science is compatible with Christianity, as evidenced by his impending wedding to the chaste, praying, crucifix-wearing Camille. The film, released at a time when America was still divided by Scopes, at first glance manages tactfully to balance evolutionary science with Christianity.

But, looking harder, *Murders in the Rue Morgue* is more unsettling than that. It offers plenty of hints that distinguishing between good science and bad science is not straightforward. Throughout the film Mirakle and Pierre are doubled.[26] Both obsessive scientists, they dress almost identically (black cape, white shirt, black necktie, black hat, sturdy cane). Mirakle follows Camille and Pierre through the Paris streets to find out where she lives and Pierre later does the same to Mirakle. At one point, Paul, infuriated by his roommate's relentless research and morbid infatuation with morgues and blood samples, says that Pierre's "eyes are getting glassy, just like that old charlatan" (meaning Mirakle) and accuses Pierre of being a "vampire," one who steals blood, just like Mirakle. Paul also points out that Pierre's research is not part of his official studies. Mirakle, working in a carnival rather than a university and not, as he says, producing any research "to be shown," may be a rogue scientist, but so to an extent is Pierre. Like Mirakle, his work is not sanctioned nor, carried out at home, supervised by any official authority. And, of course, Pierre's scientific brilliance is only made possible by Mirakle's murders – the doctor indirectly supplies the female bodies on which Pierre works. The dividing line between good science and bad science is, at best, blurred here.

The climactic rooftop chase scene, in which the emphasis is on Pierre as a brave and chivalrous hero, again diverts our attention away from more troubling aspects of Pierre's character. Nonetheless, by insisting upon the similarity between Pierre and Mirakle, the film plants a seed of anxiety about the dangers of even well-intentioned science. Pierre could easily become Mirakle. Indeed, *Phantom of the Rue Morgue* (Roy Del Ruth, 1954) develops this idea. It features as its villain Dr. Marais (Karl Malden), a mix of Cuvier and Freud, who turns from good scientist into murderously bad scientist as he tries to prove his theories about animal and human psychology. Both movies imply that it is an inherent risk of scientific pursuit that the scientist might lose sight of accepted norms of ethical behavior. In this sense, both might be seen to be questioning Poe's apparently more unequivocal enthusiasm for science as a means of supplying order to the modern, urbanized world, turning a story that celebrates the power of science into a cautionary tale about its negative implications.

In both Poe's story and Universal's film, the issue of science is intimately related to questions about race. Georges Cuvier was most famous for producing in *Animal Kingdom* a hierarchical system of classifying all human and animal life. In Cuvier's league table, African people constituted the lowest subsection of humans, and orangutans came just below humans. Throughout his work, Cuvier emphasized the supposed physical and behavioral similarities between orangutans and Africans, revealing, according to Elise Lemire's account of "The Murders in the Rue Morgue," "sensibilities and intentions plainly in line with enduring but specious speculations proposing the subhumanity, or inferior developmental or evolutionary state, of Africans and their descendants."[27] In nineteenth-century America the idea that black people shared both physical characteristics and bestial tendencies with apes was a matter of scientific "knowledge" among white people. Lemire demonstrates how Poe's story, with its deeply sexualized account of an orangutan brutally killing two white women in their own bedroom, would have been understood by the author's contemporaries as a tale about unrestrained black men raping vulnerable white women, the reference to Cuvier pointing the way to such a reading.

The fantasy of "interracial rape," as has been well documented, permeated American culture throughout slavery, deployed by white racists to justify governance of and violence against black people.[28] Theories such as Cuvier's offered scientific "proof" that black men, like apes, could not control their sexual urges. The rape of a white woman by a black man became arguably the most feared of all crimes, suggesting as it did the inability of white men to protect their families and wider communities from imagined black bestiality. Poe's story was just one of innumerable texts to invoke such fears.

Miscegenation paranoia persisted beyond slavery, through Reconstruction and into the twentieth century (and has not yet disappeared). As Rhona Berenstein has described, it underpins the "jungle-horror" movies of the 1920s and 1930s, of which *King Kong* (Merian C. Cooper and Ernest B. Schoedsack, 1933) is the most famous example, and to which *Murders in the Rue Morgue* might be considered a cinematic cousin.[29] Anxiety about miscegenation was certainly in evidence in 1931, the year when *Murders in the Rue Morgue* went into production, in the notorious Scottsboro rape trial. The case, which generated nationwide interest, saw nine young black men accused of raping two white women in Alabama and, despite the suspect nature of the evidence against them, convicted. The men were likened in the southern press to "savages" and described as "beasts unfit to be called human"; their alleged crime "savored of the jungle . . . the meanest African corruption."[30] It was clear from such reports both that black-on-white rape was still considered, in the words of one newspaper, the most "heinous" of crimes and constituted "a wholesale debauching of society," and that Cuvieresque notions of black "subhumanity" were still widespread.[31]

It does not require a long leap of imagination to view *Murders in the Rue Morgue,* released while the Scottsboro case was still national front-page news, as a film that plays quite consciously on themes of miscegenation and its connection to evolutionary theory. The supposed similarity between black men and apes, which had been underlined for some sections of white society by Scottsboro, might well have been enough for contemporary audiences to see Erik as a figure for a black man. From the very start, the movie certainly establishes an evolutionary scale based on race. As we move with the characters through the carnival at which the film opens, we are presented with Arab dancing girls described as having "skin so brown" and "snake hips," and in the Wild West show with "bloodthirsty savages . . . redskins from the wilds of America." Anything "brown" or "red," anything other than whiteness, in this carnival, is associated with animalism and savagery. As its one racially mixed character, Janos, whose presence is actually not entirely necessary to the plot, is key to the film, directing our understanding of its evolutionary scale. As Erik's keeper, he may be above the "beast with a human soul" on the evolutionary ladder, but his ape-like movements and monosyllabic dialogue suggest him as some kind of "missing link" between Erik and the film's other human characters, all of whom are clearly white and none of whom displays any of Janos's primate traces. By implication, then, it is the black part of Janos "The Black One" that keeps him in a state of semi-evolution. Here whiteness equates to articulate, fully evolved, and fully civilized, and nonwhiteness to inarticulate, unevolved, and uncivilized. The film gives Janos some whiteness (quite literally, "gives" it to him by putting light make-up on Noble Johnson's face), enabling him to talk, hold down a job, and drive a carriage, like the white characters, but it also makes sure we know that Janos is still "The Black One," still ape-like.

Having made this connection between apeness and blackness, the film then invites us to see Mirakle's experiments on women as a series of symbolic rapes, with not only Mirakle but also Erik the Ape figured as the rapist. The fact that the first woman we see Mirakle experiment on is a semi-naked prostitute instantly sexualizes the doctor's work. That he then goes in search of a virgin as his next victim also relates his experiment to sexuality. This is further underlined in Erik's murder of Madame L'Espanaye, who is wearing only a nightdress, in a frenzy that looks as much sexual as it is violent, and in his kidnapping of the similarly semi-dressed Camille. Most potently, however, it is Mirakle's insemination of Erik's bodily fluids into the bloodstream of the women he experiments on that raises the idea of rape and, specifically, inter-racial rape. Even with Mirakle dead, and the threat of his elusive and sinister foreignness dispelled, Erik's instinctive attraction to Camille prolongs the threat of his raping her and only Pierre's heroics prevent its realization.

By killing Erik, Pierre restores stable racial boundaries, guaranteeing that there will be no interspecial/interracial mixing. In case we missed the point, Janos, the film's emblem of racial confusion, is also killed during the final minutes. The carnival is well and truly over.

Like Poe's Dupin, Pierre asserts the supremacy of the white, rational male over the bestial racial "Other" (Poe's orangutan; Mirakle, Erik, and Janos in the film). The detective–scientist preserves whiteness, both Camille's racial whiteness and her virginity. In this sense, *Murders in the Rue Morgue* simultaneously reenforces a racial as well as a sexual hierarchy in which the powerless (fainting, unconscious) white woman must be protected from the ape/black man by a white male empowered both by scientific expertise (for Pierre, his microscope; for Poe, Cuvier) and by firearms (the gun with which Pierre shoots Erik).

Later adaptations of "The Murders in the Rue Morgue"

As indicated above, the 1954 *Phantom of the Rue Morgue* continues the debate over science and race. It is perhaps most interesting for its interest in the psychopathology of serial killers and its portrayal of ineffectual police attempts at criminal profiling. The film ridicules nineteenth-century criminological theories that facial appearances, especially racial characteristics, indicate a person's tendency to criminality. It argues that events in a person's life turn them into killers, not their biological inherit-ance. In this way, the film speaks back to its 1932 cinema predecessor and to Poe's story, questioning the treatment of race in both.

Phantom of the Rue Morgue contains slightly more of Poe's story than Universal's version. The next screen adaptation, *Murders in the Rue Morgue* (1971), though, has even less. The film, a slightly psychedelic horror movie, features a theater company performing a stage version of

"The Murders in the Rue Morgue." Otherwise, though, it is a classic non-Poe Poe movie, containing almost none of the original narrative whose title it shares, but making a number of gestures toward the author's work, including a maniacal dwarf and two premature burials.

In an interview included on the DVD release of the film, director Gordon Hessler argues that it would be impossible to make a film faithful to Poe's original text: "You can't make that film because it's a detective story when, once you know the denouement – it was the monkey who did it, the whole thing is over. So you've got to invent within that."[32] Hessler reveals the difficulty of turning "The Murders in the Rue Morgue" into a screen detective story. I teach an undergraduate course on detective fiction, and Poe's story is the first text we read. Students, many of whom have read impressive amounts of twentieth-century detective fiction, often respond to "The Murders in the Rue Morgue" by saying that they feel "cheated" that the culprit turns out to be, in Hessler's words, "the monkey." The students feel that the tale does not play by the rules of later detective stories. Their expectation is that a detective story will put forward a number of suspects and keep readers trying to work out until the end which one is the guilty party. With "The Murders in the Rue Morgue," one simply could not, on the first reading, predict that the murderer will turn out to be an orangutan. Poe has Dupin withhold too many clues from us (for instance, that he found nonhuman hair at the murder scene) until immediately before he reveals the murderer's identity for an accurate advance guess to be possible. For my students, then, the issue is not so much that the killer is a monkey, but that the story denies them the key attraction of detective fiction: figuring out whodunit.

Of course, this is unfair to Poe, who did not have these rules to play by and whose focus in the tale seems to be celebrating Dupin's prodigious use of scientific rationalism rather than having his readers guess the killer's identity. It does present a problem, though, for any filmmaker wishing to reproduce Poe's narrative for an audience who, like my students, expect from a detective story a mystery in which they can participate. The most faithful adaptation of "The Murders in the Rue Morgue" I have seen is an American made-for-television movie of that title (Jeannot Szwarc, 1986). The film, a much more typical screen adaptation of a well-known work of literature, retains Poe's essential narrative but changes some features of the original (Dupin, played by George C. Scott, is a retired police detective) and introduces some new elements. The most important of these is a romantic subplot involving Dupin's daughter (Rebecca De Mornay) and his young sidekick (Val Kilmer). The film, in my opinion, fails to achieve any degree of suspense.

Of course, this might just be because it is badly acted, poorly directed, and terribly written (which it is). But, I believe, it is also because it tries to stay fundamentally close to Poe's plot and so cannot offer any other plausible suspects for viewers to evaluate before it reveals an orangutan to be the killer. It is worth noting that *Phantom of the Rue Morgue*, which is much more successful as a thriller, creates dramatic tension through its use of new characters, scenes, and storylines and not through its use of Poe's tale.

This is not to say, however, that there is nothing of interest in the 1986 film. It would, for example, not be too far-fetched to read it as a story shaped by mid-1980s fears over AIDS, specifically the (then)speculative identification by some scientists and journalists of African monkeys as the source of HIV.[33] This *Murders in the Rue Morgue* was produced at a time when public concern over AIDS was reaching levels of hysteria, with supposedly promiscuous African men (again, that fear of unrestrained black sexuality) as well as homosexual men demonized as purportedly irresponsible carriers of the disease. Whether intended as such, the movie's depiction of Paris as a place of homosexuality and of heterosexual promiscuity that is terrorized by a murderous African monkey does provoke such a contextualization.

The most recent version of "The Murders in the Rue Morgue" is *Killed By Lightning* (Yevgeni Yufit, 2002), a Russian art film whose central character is a contemporary evolutionary scientist. Described by its director as "a free improvisation of" "The Murders in the Rue Morgue," its narrative has even less to do with Poe's than any of the other films discussed here.[34] But *Killed By Lightning* could be said to hold a conversation with Poe's story about evolution; it certainly invites us so to see the film by claiming kinship with the original tale.

Conclusion

"The Murders in the Rue Morgue" poses, as we have seen, a very specific challenge for any filmmaker who has textual fidelity in mind. One would have to write a different essay for each Poe story or poem – "The Black Cat," "The Pit and the Pendulum," "The Tell-Tale Heart," and "The Raven" are other frequently adapted works – to determine how and why each one has been treated on screen exactly in the way it has. What I hope to have demonstrated by using "The Murders in the Rue Morgue" as an example, however, is that it seems to me most fruitful to watch film adaptations of Poe stories not in order to measure the "amount of Poe" they have in them, given that so many have very little, but for the ways in which they enter into debates over

Figure 3. Universal Pictures' 1932 production of Edgar Allan Poe's *Murders in the Rue Morgue* shows strong influence from German Expressionism in its art design and themes.

issues raised in the original texts. This provides an opportunity to see how those debates have developed over the past century and a half or so, and how they have been recapitulated and reframed in very different sociohistorical contexts.

NOTES

1. Internet Movie Database, http://www.imdb.com. Site accessed August 11, 2004. Figures correct at time of writing.
2. As far as I have found, only Arthur Conan Doyle, with 159 entries, Charles Dickens (181 entries), and Shakespeare (555) have been more adapted for the screen than Poe.
3. Ronald L. Smith, *Poe in the Media: Screen, Songs and Spoken Word Recordings* (New York: Garland Publishing, 1990), and Don G. Smith, *The Poe Cinema: A Critical Filmography of Theatrical Releases Based on the Works of Edgar Allan Poe* (Jefferson, NC: McFarland and Company, 1999).
4. *New York Times* (May 19, 1934), quoted in Smith, *Poe Cinema*, pp. 45–46.
5. William K. Everson, *Classics of the Horror Genre* (Secaucus, NJ: Citadel, 1974), reviewing *The Black Cat*, quoted in Smith, *Poe Cinema*, pp. 44, 43. The phrases appear recurrently in reviews of Poe-derived films.

6. Harold Bloom, "Introduction," in Bloom, ed., *Modern Critical Views: Edgar Allan Poe* (New York: Chelsea House, 1985), p. 3, quoted in Jonathan Elmer, *Reading at the Social Limit: Affect, Mass Culture, and Edgar Allan Poe* (Stanford: Stanford University Press, 1995). For further discussion of this issue, see Elmer, *Reading at the Social Limit*, and J. Gerald Kennedy, "Introduction: Poe in Our Time," in Kennedy, ed., *A Historical Guide to Edgar Allan Poe* (Oxford: Oxford University Press, 2001), pp. 3–17.

7. F. O. Matthiessen, "Poe's Influence" (1948), reprinted in Graham Clarke, ed., *Edgar Allan Poe: Critical Assessments*, 4 vols., *Volume IV: Poe in the Twentieth Century* (Mountfield, East Sussex: Helm Information, 1991), p. 181; Catherine Ross Nickerson, *The Web of Iniquity: Early Detective Fiction by American Women* (Durham, NC: Duke University Press, 1998), p. 6.

8. Edgar Allan Poe, "The Murders in the Rue Morgue" (1841), in Poe, *Tales of Mystery and Imagination* ed. Graham Clarke (London: Everyman, 1993), pp. 411–444. Further quotations will be cited parenthetically in the text.

9. Unsigned review in *Tait's Edinburgh Magazine* (Edinburgh: September 1845), reprinted in Graham Clarke, ed., *Edgar Allan Poe: Critical Assessments*, 4 vols., *Volume II: Poe in the Nineteenth Century* (Mountfield, East Sussex: Helm Information, 1991), p. 159.

10. Poe used the term in a letter written to a friend in 1846. Quoted in Dana Brand, *The Spectator and the City in Nineteenth-Century American Literature* (Cambridge: Cambridge University Press, 1991), p. 104.

11. These do not include the lost 1912 film *The Raven* (director unknown) in which "Edgar Allan Poe" dreams scenes from various of his stories, including "The Murders in the Rue Morgue," nor 1934's *Maniac* (Dwain Esper), which features a character "having hallucinations in which he imagines himself to be the murdering orangutan from Poe's 'The Murders in the Rue Morgue'" (Smith, *Poe Cinema*, p. 48) but which is otherwise derived from another Poe tale, "The Black Cat" (1843), (see Smith, *Poe Cinema*, pp. 9, 48). A 1914 silent film called *The Murders in the Rue Morgue* (Sol A. Rosenberg) is lost (Smith, *Poe in the Media*, 85), and two television versions of the story, one British (James Cellan Jones, 1968), and one French (Jacques Nahum, 1973) are, to the best of my knowledge, also no longer available to view.

12. Information in this paragraph is taken from Bruce Dettman and Michael Bedford, *The Horror Factory: The Horror Films of Universal, 1931–1955* (New York: Gordon Press, 1976), pp. 7–8.

13. *Dracula* (Tod Browning, 1931); *Frankenstein* (James Whale, 1931).

14. Dettman and Bedford, *Horror Factory*, p. 7.

15. Smith, *Poe Cinema*, p. 38.

16. The poster is reproduced ibid., p. 37.

17. Quotations taken from unsigned review in *The Spectator* (London: August 1845); George Ripley, review in *New York Daily Tribune* (New York: January 1850), both reprinted in Clarke, ed., *Poe in the Nineteenth Century*, pp. 155, 248; and Constance Rourke, "Extract from *American Humour*," reprinted in Clarke, ed., *Poe in the Twentieth Century*, p. 61.

18. Smith, *Poe Cinema*, p. 57.

60 _Paul Woolf_

19. For further discussion of this, see Kennedy, "Introduction: Poe in Our Time," pp. I14–15, and Joan Dayan, _Fables of Mind: An Inquiry Into Poe's Fiction_ (Oxford: Oxford University Press, 1987), p. 3. Griswold's article, "Death of Edgar Allan Poe" was originally printed in the _New York Daily Tribune_ (October 9, 1849) and can be found in I. M. Walker, ed., _Edgar Allan Poe: The Critical Heritage_ (London: Routledge and Kegan Paul, 1986), pp, 294–302.
20. Don G. Smith, _Poe Cinema_, p. 58.
21. See, for example: M. Cullum, _The Poe Page_, http://www.geocities.com/Area51/Corridor/4220/poe.html; P. Forrest, _Edgar Allan Poe's House of Usher_, http://www.comnet.ca/~forrest; Christoffer Nilsson, _Qrisse's Edgar Allan Poe Pages_, http://www.poedecoder.com/Qrisse. All three sites were among the first twenty returns from Google (http://www.google.com) when I entered the name "Edgar Allan Poe" into the search engine on August 30, 2004.
22. Mikhail Bakhtin, _Rabelais and His World_, trans. Helene Iswolsky (Bloomington: Indiana University Press, 1984). For a discussion of carnival and the horror film, see Jack Morgan, _The Biology of Horror: Gothic Literature and Film_ (Carbondale and Edwardsville: Southern Illinois University Press, 2002).
23. Dettman and Bedford, _Horror Factory_, p. 7.
24. Baron Georges Cuvier, _Animal Kingdom: Arranged According to its Organization_ (1817), trans. H. McMurtrie (London: Orr and Smith, 1834). Information on Cuvier is drawn from Lindon Barrett, "Presence of Mind: Detection and Racialization in 'The Murders in the Rue Morgue,'" in J. Gerald Kennedy and Lillian Westberg, eds., _Romancing the Shadow: Poe and Race_ (Oxford: Oxford University Press, 2001), pp. 167–169; Lawrence Frank, "'The Murders in the Rue Morgue': Edgar Allan Poe's Evolutionary Reverie," _Nineteenth-Century Literature_ 50:2 (September 1995), pp. 168–188; Shawn James Rosenheim, _The Cryptographic Imagination: Secret Writing from Poe to the Internet_ (Baltimore: Johns Hopkins University Press, 1997), pp. 68–85; and Ronald R. Thomas, _Detective Fiction and the Rise of Forensic Science_ (Cambridge: Cambridge University Press, 1999), pp. 46–56.
25. Ronald L. Numbers, _Darwinism Comes to America_ (Cambridge, MA: Harvard University Press, 1998), p. 76. For further information on Scopes, see pp. 76–91.
26. For a fuller discussion of the similarities between Dr. Mirakle and Pierre, see Ken Hanke, "_Murders in the Rue Morgue_: Robert Florey's Consolation Prize." Originally published as "Robert Florey's _Murders in the Rue Morgue_: Almost a Classic," _Phantasma_ 1:3 (1981).
27. Elise Lemire, "'The Murders in the Rue Morgue': Amalgamation Discourses and Race Riots of 1838 in Poe's Philadelphia," in Kennedy and Westberg, eds., _Romancing the Shadow_, p. 168. See Lemire's chapter for a fuller discussion of race and science in the story and in nineteenth-century American culture in general.
28. For more on this subject, see David Aaron, "The 'Inky Curse': Miscegenation in the White American Literary Imagination," _Social Science Information_

22:2 (1983), pp. 169–190; George M. Fredrickson, *The Black Image in the White Mind: The Debate on Afro-American Character and Destiny* (1971), (Hanover, NH: Wesleyan University Press, 1987); and bell hooks, *Yearning: Race, Gender and Cultural Politics* (London: Turnaround, 1991), pp. 57–64.

29. Rhona Berenstein, *Attack of the Leading Ladies: Gender, Sexuality and Spectatorship in Classic Horror* (New York: Columbia University Press, 1996), pp. 160–197.

30. For information on Scottsboro, see Dan T. Carter, *Scottsboro: A Tragedy of the American South* (Baton Rouge: Louisiana State University Press, 1969), and James Goodman, *Stories of Scottsboro* (New York: Vintage Books, 1994). The quotations are taken from Carter's survey of southern newspaper reports of the trial (Carter, *Scottsboro*, p. 20). Carter also notes that one of the defendants, Willie Roberson, was commonly referred to as "that nigger ape" (ibid., p. 45).

31. Quoted in Goodman, *Stories of Scottsboro*, p. 15.

32. Hessler interviewed in "Stage Tricks and Screen Frights" (Greg Carson) on *Cry of the Banshee and Murders in the Rue Morgue* double DVD, MGM, 2003.

33. See Gabrielle Griffin, *Representations of HIV and AIDS: Visibility Blue/s* (Manchester: Manchester University Press, 2000).

34. The film's entry at www.imdb.com lists Poe as one of its writers. The phrase "free improvisation" was used in an email to me from the director, May 12, 2004.

4   Readapting *Uncle Tom's Cabin*

Stephen Railton

During film's silent era between 1903 and 1927, Harriet Beecher Stowe's *Uncle Tom's Cabin* (1852) was adapted for the screen nine times. Some of the nine made film history. The 1903 Edison–Porter version, which preceded even the same year's *The Great Train Robbery* (usually cited as the first American narrative film), was the first American movie adapted from a novel, and also the first to use titles.[1] Vitagraph's 1910 version was the first dramatic movie longer than two reels: its three reels were shown one at a time on three different days. The 1914 World adaptation was probably the first feature film to feature an African-American (instead of a white actor in blackface) in a central role. Nine adaptations in twenty-five years is almost certainly a record, too. More significant, however, is what together these films have to say about cultural history as itself a process of continuous selective adaptation.

All nine were called *Uncle Tom's Cabin*:

  1.   Edison–Porter (1903, 1 reel)
*2.   Sigmund Lubin (1903, 1 reel)
  3.   Vitagraph (1910, 3 reels)
*4.   Thanhouser (1910, 1 reel)
*5.   Imp (1913, 3 reels)
*6.   Kalem (1913, 2 reels)
  7.   World (1914, 5 reels)
*8.   Famous Players-Lasky-Paramount (1918, 5 reels)
  9.   Universal (1927, 13 reels)

The five marked by asterisks have been lost. You can view versions of the remaining four at *Uncle Tom's Cabin* & American Culture: A Multi-Media Archive, an online resource that I have been building since 1998 to enable users to explore the story of Stowe's story as a cultural phenomenon.[2] Only in the case of the Edison–Porter film, however, is the version available in the archive the same film that its original audience saw. The Vitagraph and World films are available only as they were rereleased in the late 1920s, when they were edited for home viewing to take advantage of the stir aroused by Universal's 1927 big-budget *Uncle Tom's Cabin*.[3] Kino International has recently made Universal's adaptation available on VHS and DVD, but Kino's source is the 114-minute version that Universal prepared in 1928 for nationwide distribution; the originally released 141-minute version is not available either. Altogether about fifty minutes are missing even from the four movies we have.

Then there is the question about what "text" the moviemakers were adapting. The answer starts, of course, with the novel that Harriet Beecher Stowe (1811–96) published in 1852. Often cited as the bestselling nineteenth-century American novel, Stowe's book was still widely read at the time movies were born. When her copyright expired in 1892, dozens of publishers rushed to produce new editions in every kind of format. A survey of the branches of the New York City public library system in 1899 found that *Uncle Tom's Cabin* was the single most frequently checked-out title.[4] But Stowe's story was always more than a text. It was adapted into a range of other media wide enough to surprise anyone who thinks that merchandising a popular success is a modern idea: *Uncle Tom's Cabin* was spun off into children's books, songs, lithographs, porcelain figurines, even card games and jigsaw puzzles.

The adaptation that matters most to an account of *Uncle Tom's Cabin* on film is its transformation into the play that Harry Birdoff, with only a hint of hyperbole, has labeled *The World's Greatest Hit*.[5] On stage *Uncle Tom's Cabin* set yet more records. By 1853 four different dramatizations were playing simultaneously in New York City, and for the next seventy-five years multiple touring companies kept the play continuously in performance. Stowe refused to authorize any dramatic representation of her novel, but in the nineteenth century the laws of copyright did not apply to adaptations into new media. The most successful antebellum script, by George Aiken, was relatively faithful to Stowe's text, but in the decades after the Civil War the "Tom Shows," as the plays came to be called, acquired a performative life of their own. The dramatic adaptations themselves were constantly adapted to enable companies to compete with other forms of mass entertainment. For example, when the Fisk Jubilee Singers began drawing huge audiences to their fundraising tours in the early 1870s, African-American singers soon became part of every larger Tom company's troupe, and right after P. T. Barnum's circus merged in 1881 with J. A. Bailey's, the "Tommers" unveiled the "Double Tom Show," advertising "Two Topsys" and "Two Markses." Playing in "opera houses" during the cold months and in tents during the summer, "Tommers" took *Uncle Tom's Cabin* into every

American city and almost every American town every year. No reliable numbers are available, but in all probability for every one of the many readers the book had, dozens (perhaps hundreds) of people saw Eliza cross the ice or Simon Legree beat Tom to death in a live performance. Early twentieth-century audiences were at least as familiar with "Tomming" as viewers in our time are with a top-rated television show.

The film adaptations of *Uncle Tom's Cabin* were deeply influenced by the conventions of these preexisting dramatic adaptations. In fact, the first two film versions, both 1903, draw their actors, costumes, sets and theatrical "business" from two different Tom companies. Subsequent films often boasted of their fidelity to Mrs. Stowe's book, but in every case the representation of the story is mediated by elements that derive from its long stage history. In her review of Universal's *Uncle Tom's Cabin* (1927), for instance, Harriette Underhill supports her claim that "Harry Pollard, the director, was filming the story exactly as it was written," with three examples: that Tom is a comparatively young man, that Eva and Topsy are played by girls, and that moviegoers will get to see "real bloodhounds and not mastiffs" chase Eliza across the ice.[6] To Pollard's credit, his conception of Tom is closer to the novel's (in which Tom is a vigorous man with a new baby) than the typical theatrical "Uncle Tom" (who could always be identified by his bald head fringed with white hair and his feeble posture). And stage Topsys were usually grown women (occasionally, grown men). But as careful readers of the novel know, there are no dogs of any kind in the scene where Eliza crosses the ice. After decades of seeing posters and performances featuring "8 Man-Hunting Siberian Bloodhounds" or "10 Genuine Cuban Blood Hounds" as stars of the Tom Shows, however, film audiences in 1927 would have felt about as cheated watching Eliza cross the river without dogs in pursuit as they would have were she not holding a child in her arms.

The popularity of *Uncle Tom's Cabin* with playgoers helps to account for its appeal to the early movie industry. Not only had it proven itself as a box-office attraction, it was also a story that audiences were already very conversant with. The people who made the early movies and the people who paid to see them all had to learn the new language of cinematic representation, and while the new technology of film opened up all kinds of possibilities for enlightening and entertaining and astonishing audiences, it also imposed severe limits on filmmakers. A "full-length" movie in 1903 was one reel (at most fifteen minutes) long, and before 1927 the only ways to provide dialogue or exposition were through interpolated title cards or an external showman-narrator who talked directly to the audience while the movie played. The best compensatory solution to these technical constraints was an audience's prior knowledge of whatever story a movie was "telling," which explains why so many early narrative films adapt books, plays, and fairy tales. No story was more familiar to early twentieth-century American audiences than *Uncle Tom's Cabin*. As soon as the actress playing Eliza puts her hand to her ear, they could "hear" the dogs in pursuit. If Eva coughs, they know she is dying. A Quaker hat means Phineas Fletcher; an umbrella identifies Marks. But that audience's knowledge does complicate our twenty-first-century relationship to the silent movies that survive. We can read Stowe's text and we can view the film adaptations, but we cannot fully recover the experience of going to the turn-of-the-century Tom Show, which played so constitutive a role in defining the expectations and interpretations of the films' original audiences.

An example might help to suggest how much we can lose. Scene 11 of the 1903 Edison version, directed by David A. Porter and featuring an uncredited troupe of Tommers, is "The Auction of St. Clare's Slaves." From a narrative point of view, its most important event is Tom's sale to his third and final owner, Simon Legree. The minute-long scene is shot in one take, from a camera set up in exactly the position of a playgoer with a center seat ten rows back in the orchestra section. Watching any movie more than a hundred years old requires adjustments on our part, but the representational conventions by which Legree's villainy and Tom's dismay are established still communicate to us. On the other hand, the scene's first half is probably incomprehensible to a modern viewer. It begins with two groups of blacks in front of the auction block; the ones on our left are kneeling and the ones on our right are dancing and clapping. They move aside hastily as the auction begins. A young, well-dressed African-American who has not been seen before is sold, while a white character with a top hat and an umbrella whom we saw earlier in the film jumps in and out of the bidding, only to be scolded and driven away by the auctioneer as the climax to this sale.

If you refer to Stowe's account of the auction, you discover that the first slave to be sold is St. Clare's valet, Adolph, but Stowe's text will shed no light at all on the rest of this episode, which is drawn instead from the story's theatrical incarnation. There are no scenes of slaves dancing in groups anywhere in Stowe's novel, but one stage adaptation (by a Boston writer named Conway) enlivened the auction scene with a dance as early as 1853, and by the 1870s the auction almost always provided the occasion for a major musical number featuring the company's black performers. Porter's production uses the right side of the screen to serve up a twelve-second gesture toward that tradition. The group of slaves on the left are shooting craps; gambling, playing on the stereotypical association of blacks with dice (called "Ethiopian dominoes" in the late nineteenth-century "Coon Shows"), was introduced into Tom Shows much later than dancing, perhaps as late as 1890, but in any case in plenty of time for the people watching the movie in 1903 to know exactly what those kneeling slaves were up to. And from the umbrella the audience would immediately recognize that frantic white bidder. Marks is a minor figure in Stowe's novel, appearing only in the North-moving storyline, but on stage he became a central character, appearing throughout the play mainly to make audiences laugh. His behavior at the auction was a well-worn shtick: he buys Adolph with a final bid of "seventy-five," then offers the outraged auctioneer one dollar instead of seventy-five and asks for his twenty-five cents change.

None of this explanation would have been necessary to Americans in 1903 (who would have seen *and heard* Marks's auction routine on stage). Nor would the film's use of the slave auction as an occasion for minstrel show entertainment and comic relief as well as pathos struck them as a violation of the story. It is true that in Stowe's novel the scene of Tom's sale is drenched in his suffering and her narrator's moral indignation, and most of that is vitiated by the film's depiction of the event. But by 1903 "the story of Uncle Tom" was no longer just Stowe's. It was a cultural text that had already been adapted and revised many times before movies could take hold of it.

This earliest film adaptation does contain two conspicuously cinematic moments, where we can see Porter self-consciously experimenting with the new medium's potentialities: the use of miniatures and electric lighting to create the "Steamboat Race between the *Robert E. Lee* and *Natchez*," with an explosion, fire, and thunderstorm, and the use of double exposure in the "Death of Eva" to show an angel descending to carry her spirit aloft while her body remains on earth. The authority for these events is not Stowe's novel, which never even mentions steamboat racing and only describes Eva *descending* to comfort Tom in two posthumous visions, but again the Tom Show, which had been using wires to pull Eva *up* into heaven for fifty years, and using scrolling dioramas to simulate boat races for half as long as that. By our standards, the effects in these scenes are comically primitive, but Porter seems quite proud of the ability the camera gives him to control scale, lighting, and exposure to impart a more realistic look to them; at least, the steamboat scene is drawn out to almost a minute, and the sequence of Eva both lying in the bed and simultaneously climbing into the angel's arms is shown twice (in case audiences missed it the first time?).

This kind of display is the first sign of what becomes a pattern in the film adaptations: a determination to outperform the stage adaptations in the representation of the episodes that provided the Tom Shows with their dramatic climaxes, such as Eliza crossing the ice or Eva's death. One hundred years ago, the competition for customers between acting companies and film exhibitors was often very direct; in many towns up until the 1920s movies were shown in the same "opera houses" as plays, with local managers deciding which entertainment form was likely to attract more customers. It is in the context of this competition that we have to understand the promotional claim the films often made of "follow[ing] the book rather than the stage version."[7] Their concern was not fidelity to Stowe's original intentions and emphases, but giving patrons an experience that the Tom Shows could not, which meant using "the almost unlimited possibilities of the screen"[8] visually to top what the Tom Shows did. Just how far all this remained from Stowe's novel can be heard in the following typical comment, by a reviewer in 1914: "Eliza trod real ice in a regular river, without racing all the way on property cakes, the length of a bloodhound's nose ahead of the howling pack."[9] Thanks to the camera and location shooting, the ice is real, but the inevitable presence of the dogs reminds us that what we see is not Stowe's fiction.

While interesting as a very early example of the art of moviemaking, the chief value of the 1903 Edison–Porter *Uncle Tom's Cabin* is as a shorthand record of the Tom Show as it had evolved over the second half of the nineteenth century to adapt Stowe's novel to changing cultural circumstances. The film's subtitle is *Slavery Days*, which reminds us of the most relevant and fundamental change: at the end of the Civil War slavery was abolished, removing both it and Stowe's impassioned protest against it from the arena of social cause to the archive of historical memory. Stowe's antebellum readers could identify slavery as a specifically southern evil, but after abolition slavery as a 250-year-long fact of the nation's past presented Americans with different problems. What had it been like? How should slavery be re-presented? And what would such representations say about Americans as a nation? Like the Tom Shows after Reconstruction, the 1903 film almost entirely transforms Stowe's act of protest into a minstrel show. Not counting the titles, the film runs just over eleven and a half minutes. Almost two minutes of that consist of four different scenes of slaves dancing (in addition to the auction scene, a group dances briefly at a levee, Topsy cavorts before a shocked Ophelia, and a very well-dressed ensemble stages an elaborately choreographed cakewalk in St. Clare's garden). Eliza has to flee to save her child, and Tom and Emmeline still suffer from Legree's villainy, but almost all the other blacks fit perfectly into the stereotype of the "happy darky" that blackface minstrelsy created before the Civil War to amuse and reassure white audiences. There were bad masters like Simon Legree, the film implies, but otherwise "Slavery Days" are nothing that America needs to feel guilty about.

The 1903 film offers the most eulogistic account of slavery. Except for Topsy, no one dances in the 1910 Vitagraph film; instead, groups of slaves are shown sadly trudging onto a steamboat to be carried down-river or working in Legree's cotton field under the lash of his drivers. Between 1903 and 1910, the camera has become more mobile, as film-makers experimented with shooting a scene from a number of angles. This innovation enabled them to offer filmgoers a way of seeing *Uncle Tom's Cabin* that the stage plays never adopt: the point of view of the enslaved. Like Stowe's narrative, but unlike the Tom Shows, the film takes us *inside* Tom's cabin. More striking is the moment at which the camera moves around behind the table at which two white men – Shelby and Haley – are discussing "whom to buy and sell and for how much" to film them through the crack in the door through which Eliza spies in horror as she hears her son being sold. Stowe's narrative can give us Eliza's feelings at this moment, but in the novel those feelings are mediated by the narrator's unmistakably white voice. The film, by showing us how the moment looks through Eliza's eyes, brings us closer, I think, to sharing the slave mother's violated helplessness.

On the whole, all four surviving films "tell" the story from perspectives that remain outside the slaves' point of view, but the 1914 and 1927 films also contain moments at which the audience sees the system of slavery from the vantage of its victims. The most surprising instance occurs at the end of the 1914 World picture. In her novel Stowe does not depict the death of Legree. This is one of the first things that changed when the book was dramatized: the dynamic of live entertainment demanded that spectators be shown the villain's ultimate punishment, and in the Aiken script that became the basis for the Tom Shows, Marks kills him. We also get to see Legree die in all but the 1910 film. In the World film, however, he is killed by a young male slave avenging Tom's death. The scene is shot from behind a clump of bushes as Legree rides past along a trail. When a black hand holding a pistol comes into the frame from the right and shoots, viewers find themselves in the position of an armed, violent black killing a white person. The next scene is a close-up of the man, as a satisfied smile appears on his face and he moves off toward freedom with the gun still in his hand. Stowe's book, of course, includes the heroic episode in which George Harris shoots Loker; while Tom's Christian forgiveness of his oppressors remains her ultimate standard, through Harris's character she legitimizes black anger and even black violence in self-defense. In its representation of what amounts to a slave rebellion, however, the film takes the white viewer much further toward a new angle of vision on the world.

This is also the first film to employ an African-American to play Tom, though the actor, Sam Lucas, had already enacted Tom thousands of times on stage. The movie begins with a shot that includes a large group of dancing slaves, but here, too, the perspective challenges white complacency. The dancers appear in the distant background, while diagonally across the middle of the shot Tom limps down a path away from the camera, and in the foreground opposite the tiny dancing figures Chloe stands absolutely motionless, watching Tom toil his way. There is no caption, and the scene is followed by a shot of happy black children fishing and mugging for the camera in stereotypical "pickaninny" fashion, but as a way of establishing the conditions of slave life, the opening scene, especially the eloquently dignified body language of Tom's and Chloe's nearer figures, seems implicitly to subvert, or at least to estrange the viewer from the comfortable image of a circle of dancing black bodies.

Silent films, of course, were hardly ever truly silent. The nickelodeons and theaters that showed them employed musicians to accompany the images. It would be wonderful to know what the pianists played as this first scene was projected. If they chose a lively piece to accompany the dancers in the distance, Tom's apparently painful walk would look absurd by contrast, but if they chose a slow and serious selection in keeping with his image, the jumping dancers would be made to seem as grotesque as Ralph Ellison, writing to expose cultural archetypes as racist stereotypes, made the "dancing Sambo" doll in his 1952 novel *Invisible Man*.

On the other hand, no adaptation of *Uncle Tom's Cabin* in this period could afford to mount too direct an attack on slavery without taking too big a risk at the box office. Universal's 1927 version, for example, originally budgeted at $500,000, wound up costing $1,763,008 – almost another record for *Uncle Tom's Cabin*, but two silent movies did cost more. As production dragged on, one of the main concerns of Carl Laemmle, head of the studio, was not to offend the white South. When southern papers protested that any remake of Stowe's novel was "a direct insult to the old true South,"[10] Universal created focus groups of white southerners, which led to another kind of remaking. As shot, the film opened "at the Slave market in New Orleans,"[11] where Cassy is bought by Legree while her infant daughter Eliza is pulled from her arms and sold to the Shelbys, a Kentucky couple in the city on their honeymoon. Although it does not narrate it directly, Stowe's novel provides textual justification for most of this auction scene, but when the focus groups objected, Universal deleted it entirely (though it is still described in the movie's twenty-page, twenty-five cents souvenir program).

The version that premiered in New York begins at the Shelby plantation on the wedding day of Eliza and George Harris, another event referred to though not directly narrated in Stowe's text. Instead of initiating audiences into slavery through the scene of a mother and her baby being torn apart, the film now introduces its story through scenes of white ladies and gentlemen playing croquet before the ceremony and waltzing that evening, black children stealing and devouring watermelons, slaves getting a holiday to attend the wedding and afterwards staging their own minstrel equivalent to the waltzing in the big house, while the "almost" white Harrises are treated as members of the family by Mr. and Mrs. Shelby, "whose gentle rule of the slaves," as an early caption puts it, "was typical of the South." In a remarkable effort to have it both ways, the filmmakers chose for the very first image that the audience sees a full-screen close-up shot of Robert E. Lee in his Confederate uniform, who gazes at us with benign dignity for several seconds before the following words appear over his face: "There are few, I believe, in this enlightened age who will not acknowledge that slavery as an institution is a moral and political evil – Robert E. Lee, 1856." Trust Hollywood to find a way to suggest that Mrs. Stowe and General Lee were on the same side all along.

This use of Lee reminds us that in one strange way Stowe did share a concern with her film adaptors from which the Tom Shows were exempt. Stage companies could plan their itineraries to stay out of regions that might be hostile to their production, and even the most active of them could only get to so many cities or towns in a season on the road. Stowe and the motion picture companies thought instead in terms of a national market. She knew that a book protesting against a social evil could be effective only if it was read, and she took care to make her novel as palatable as possible to the white southerners whose hearts and minds she hoped to reach and change. For the film industry, the secret of profitability was getting its product distributed as widely as possible: a 300-seat theater in Alabama had the same hold on film companies' attention as a 300-seat theater in Maine or Iowa. Yet if moviemakers indulged white southern audiences, and that part of the larger national audience that remained under the spell of the Magnolia Myth, with scenes of elegant wealth and contented slaves at the Shelby and St. Clare estates, it was Stowe who, in the first two-thirds of her story, imaginatively designed and constructed those sets in the first place. The silent-screen versions of her novel make it possible to draw a fairly straight line from her bestselling nineteenth-century novel to

Margaret Mitchell's bestselling twentieth-century one. The Shelby mansion that Pollard built on the back lot at Universal could have served as the blueprint for Tara in *Gone With the Wind*.

At the end of the souvenir program, Laemmle promises moviegoers in 1927 that "through the limitless possibilities of the motion picture camera" they will see "picturized" both "the sunshine and the shadows of the plantation life of the glorious Old South."[12] Calling the slavery era "glorious" flatters white southern audiences, but ultimately the film spends most of its time in the shadows. When Haley drives Tom away from his Kentucky home and family, the caption locates us in a darker story: "Uncle Tom – caught in the black and hopeless stream of human souls – destined down the river." Even Eliza gets caught in that stream, as this adaptation has her recaptured and carried downriver by Marks, and eventually sold with Tom to Legree. Her suffering is the movie's focal point: just before the intermission, for example, she loses Harry in a long and heart-wrenching scene. Despite the cuts that Universal had already made, several reviewers at the New York premier complained that "the hardships and cruelty are never depicted with the slightest idea of restraint," and one predicted that the film's inclusion of "Sherman's men" marching to Eliza's rescue "likely queers its chances below the [Mason-Dixon] line."[13] The amount of anguish registered on Eliza's white face troubled critics less than Pollard's depiction of Legree and his two overseers whipping Tom to death: "so realistic, in fact, that this sequence took on an aspect of pathos and horror never before equaled" in film.[14] Within days, in response to these criticisms and disappointing ticket sales at the Central Theater, Universal edited out much of the whipping scene (including its "employment of a picture of Christ," which, though authorized by Stowe's text, struck reviewers in 1927 as "distasteful"[15]).

Neither in New York nor in Los Angeles, where it opened next, did the box-office numbers meet Universal's expectations, so much more drastic cuts were made (from thirteen reels to ten) for the film's general release in September 1928. In April 1928, Universal had tested the southern market with a version that "eliminated . . . the scenes of Sherman's march";[16] in this form it seems to have done about as well in the South as in every other edited form it did throughout the rest of the country, which is to say, well enough almost to earn back its cost, but not nearly as well as it was supposed to do. According to one account, it was the sixth most popular movie of the year.[17] Among the films it had to compete with was *The Jazz Singer*, which brought the silent era to a noisy end as Al Jolson, in blackface and with tears in his eyes but looking nothing like the many unhappy black faces we see in the second half of the Universal film, sang "Mammy." It is hard to know whether it was mainly the sound of Jolson's voice, or his more ingratiating representation of race, or Universal's often noted problems with the distribution of its feature films, or yet other factors, that best explains this adaptation's relative lack of success.

Stowe died in 1896, before *Uncle Tom's Cabin* went to the movies. One of her descendants did protest on her behalf against the concessions Universal made to southern audiences,[18] but Stowe herself, who expressed no public reaction of any kind to the Tom Shows, might have felt that it was similarly beneath her to notice any of the film adaptations. Less probably, she might even have recognized how completely her story had become a cultural text that every new generation and each new media would adapt to suit its own ends. In an introduction for a new edition that Jewett published in 1878, she suggested that since *Uncle Tom's Cabin*'s original purpose, the abolition of slavery, had been achieved, it would continue to live most meaningfully as an "illustration of Christianity," that Tom's Christ-like witness would inspire others besides Eva, St. Clair, and Cassy to "follow [him]."[19] All the movie versions, however, minimize the novel's theological motifs, and what religiosity they retain is associated mainly with Eva, not Tom (there is not one shot of his black figure being taken to heaven). The most didactic moral element in the movies concerns temperance: both the 1903 and 1927 versions show the villainous men drinking almost continuously, and in the 1910 and 1914 versions Legree staggers drunkenly through most of his scenes. This emphasis is consistent with Stowe's text, but since the silent era was also the age of prohibition, the anti-saloon imagery of these films probably owes more to contemporary cultural politics than to Stowe's vision. We have lost the 1918 adaptation, but its advertising campaign allows us to see how much more committed the filmmakers were to their twentieth-century audiences than to their nineteenth-century source: when the film was released, America was at war against the Germans in Europe, so Stowe's apocalyptic attack on the sins of American society could be billed as "the greatest piece of democratic propaganda ever conceived."[20]

The freedom with which moviemakers manipulated Stowe's narrative to serve their immediate ambitions is entirely in the tradition of the book's life on stage. And just as Tom Shows were shaped by developments in other theatrical forms such as minstrelsy or the circus, so film adaptations reflected what was being shown on other movie screens. The most popular silent-film genre, for example, was the western – if you did not already know that, it could be inferred from the way the 1914 adaptation elongates and orchestrates the scene in which Harris declares his freedom (Chapter 17 in the novel) as a shoot-out at the pass between the fugitives and a posse of slavecatchers. With its extraordinary repertoire of dramatic and melodramatic characters and scenes, *Uncle Tom's Cabin* gave filmmakers hooks on which they could hang a broad range of interpretations. Nellie Revell, writing in *Variety*, observed that the 1927 Universal version "looked to me as though it should have been called 'The Perils of Eliza.'"[21] Since Eliza was played by Margarita Fischer, director Pollard's wife, the decision to structure the film around close-ups of her anguished face struck some contemporary viewers as an uxorious act. It is also, in a sense, faithful to the spirit of Stowe's text, which sees reality and the evil of slavery essentially from a woman's point of view. But Revell's observation links the Universal film to *The Perils of Pauline*, the Pathé serial that starred Pearl White, one of about a dozen movie serials featuring imperiled women (*The Hazards of Helen*, *The Exploits of Elaine*, and so on) that like westerns were a major staple of the diet that early movies fed their audiences.

This essay only begins to explore all that the silent *Uncle Tom's Cabins* can tell us – about the power of Stowe's story, about the nature of film as a new media, about America's cultural history – but I cannot end it without acknowledging that these nine films are in fact only a part of the picture. During the silent era, *Uncle Tom's Cabin* appeared in almost a dozen other movies, including films about traveling Tom Shows, parodic and burlesque treatments, even an *Our Gang* comedy. Universal's 1927 version turned out to be Hollywood's last full-scale treatment of the property. In 1946, M-G-M considered a remake, but an NAACP campaign led it to cancel the plan.[22] The only feature-film version in the past seventy-five years was produced in Germany, in 1965. On the other hand, *Uncle Tom's Cabin* continued to make appearances in the movies, most famously as "The Small House of Uncle Thomas" in the 1956 film of Rogers and Hammerstein's 1949 Broadway musical *The King and I*. It was adapted twice for television, for Omnibus in 1955 and for Showtime in 1987. The relative insignificance of these productions, especially when compared with the phenomenal popularity of the television mini-series *Roots* (1977), might seem to suggest that Stowe's representation of slavery can no longer be adapted to fit the cultural needs of a post-Civil Rights era America. The opprobrium that now attaches to the term "Uncle Tom" might also seem to suggest that as a cultural text Stowe's story is now out of fashion. I think, however, that Stowe's Uncle Tom lives on at the movies under a lot of other names. When he is *Driving Miss Daisy* (1989's Best Picture), he is called Hoke. When he cures the ills of white folks while locked up on *The Green Mile* (a 1999 nominee for Best Picture), he is called John Coffey.[23] When as an inner city black teenager he teaches a suburban white girl to dance while healing her soul (in MTV's 2001 box-office smash *Save The Last Dance*), he is called Derek. This list, the list of movies which use the formula that Stowe established in *Uncle Tom's Cabin* for defining the role of the African-American, no matter how harshly constrained his own life is, as serving the emotional or spiritual needs of white folks, could go on and on. Our movies show few signs of freeing themselves and us from this sort of Tomming. It survives because it fits so well the repressions and fantasies that white audiences continue to bring to any American relation of race.

Figure 4. Cassy being sold at auction in New Orleans, and separated from her child Eliza. This is the original opening scene of Universal's 1927 Super-Jewel production of *Uncle Tom's Cabin*. (Harry Pollard Papers, Wichita State University Libraries, Department of Special Collections.)

Figure 5. Guests at the Shelbys' plantation for the wedding of Eliza and George. This is the opening scene of the movie as released. The photo is from the Grosset & Dunlap movie edition of the novel (New York: 1927).

NOTES

1. Charles Musser, *History of the American Cinema*, 10 Vols., Volume I: *The Emergence of Cinema* (New York: Charles Scribner's Sons, 1990), p. 349.
2. The URL of the archive is www.jefferson.village.virginia.edu/utc. It also contains all the primary texts quoted in this essay, as well as hundreds of other items relating to "UTC AT THE MOVIES."
3. Cf. Ben Brewster et al., *Theatre to Cinema* (Oxford: Oxford University Press, 1997), pp. 60–76.
4. Thomas F. Gossett, *Uncle Tom's Cabin and American Culture* (Dallas: Southern Methodist University Press, 1985), p. 339.
5. Harry Birdoff, *The World's Greatest Hit* (New York: Vanni, 1947).
6. Harriette Underhill, "Uncle Tom's Cabin Wins Praise as Film," *New York Herald Tribune*, November 5, 1927.
7. George Blaisdell, "Review of *Uncle Tom's Cabin*," *Moving Picture World*, August 22, 1914.
8. Vanderheyden Fyles, "Review of *Uncle Tom's Cabin*," *Movie Pictorial*, September 19, 1914.
9. "Review of *Uncle Tom's Cabin*," *New York Herald*, August 25, 1914.
10. Mrs. Mary Forrest Bradley, president of the Memphis chapter of the United Daughters of the Confederacy, quoted in "'Uncle Tom' Gets Walloped:

Insult to Film Slavery Story Here, Forrest Chapter Says of Movie Plan," *Memphis News Scimitar*, November 5, 1926.

11. Anonymous, "The Story of the Picture," souvenir program (New York: Universal Pictures, 1927), p. 7.
12. "Another Universal Achievement," souvenir program, p. 20.
13. Mordaunt Hall, "Simon Legree and His Slaves," *New York Times*, November 5, 1927; "Sid," "Review of Universal Pictures' *Uncle Tom's Cabin*," *Variety*, November 9, 1927.
14. "Review of Universal Pictures' *Uncle Tom's Cabin*," *Billboard*, November 12, 1927.
15. Cf. Mordaunt Hall, "'Uncle Tom's Cabin' More Desperate in Its Villainy Than Any Other Portrayal," *New York Times*, November 27, 1927. Hall had called the use of Christ "distasteful" in his 5 November review, where he also gives us the best available description of what the excluded footage showed: "Mr. Pollard depicts Uncle Tom as if he had been crucified and then brings forth a picture of Christ." Stowe's original illustrator, Hammat Billings, included Christ in his drawing of the whipping scene in Jewett's 1853 illustrated edition of the novel.
16. Anna Aiken Patterson, "'Uncle Tom's Cabin' Takes the Test," *Weekly Film Review*, April 28, 1928.
17. This ranking was established by James Mark Purcell and appears in Richard Koszarski, *History of the American Cinema*, 10 Vols., *Volume III: An Evening's Entertainment: The Age of the Silent Feature Picture, 1915–1928*, (New York: Charles Scribner's Sons, 1990), p. 33.
18. "Great Grand-Niece Has Grouch Over U's Tom," *Variety*, August 29, 1928.
19. Harriet Beecher Stowe, "Introduction," *Uncle Tom's Cabin* (Boston: Jewett & Co., 1878), p. 38.
20. "Review of *Uncle Tom's Cabin*," *Photoplay Magazine* (August 1918).
21. "Nellie Revell in New York," *Variety*, November 16, 1927.
22. See Peter Noble, *The Negro in Films* (Port Washington: Kennikat Press, 1969), p. 218.
23. See Linda Williams, *Playing the Race Card: Melodramas of Black and White from Uncle Tom to O. J. Simpson* (Princeton: Princeton University Press, 2001), pp. 301–310.

5   Screening authorship: *Little Women* on screen 1933–1994

Deborah Cartmell and Judy Simons

"We haven't got father, and shall not have him for a long time," says Jo sadly as the four March sisters cluster around the family hearth at the start of *Little Women* (1868).[1] From its very first page, Louisa May Alcott's *Little Women* is demonstrably a book about women existing in a world without men. Framed by the action of the American Civil War, the story creates a nineteenth-century space in which women can legitimately take on male roles while the able-bodied breadwinners – husbands, fathers, sons, and lovers – are away from home at the battle-fields. As the sisters gather at the fireside in an act of communal reading to hear the letter from father who is "far away, where the fighting was" (11), the text dramatically illustrates the importance of the written word that gives presence to what is absent.

This chapter examines the cinematic representation of this dysfunctional world and the accompanying exploration of female autonomy in *Little Women*. In this context, it considers, too, the specific role of writing and reading in the novel as offering a route to female independence, both mental and material, and the ambivalent treatment this receives on screen. For whereas the novel is packed with literary allusions and forcefully conveys the potency of literature as a survival mechanism, film has tended to present *Little Women* in a much milder light as a sentimental story for girls, its subject that of the American family and the socialization and triumph of its unruly heroine.

Significantly, the American Civil War, which provides the backcloth to the domestic story, was a war fought on moral principle. It was not a battle for literal but for metaphorical territory, its impetus that of human rights and social justice. So Alcott's little women fight a similarly figurative war, as they battle against the personal demons that beset each of them in different ways. And the novel exposes both their internal tensions and the class and other conflicts of the new, modern America. For the world in which the four sisters and their mother, the saintly Marmee, find themselves is one for which they are singularly unprepared. Brought up to expect male protection as a prerequisite for middle-class respectability, they have seen their fortunes decline and their income fail to match their aspirations. In a society where the traditional parameters have suddenly shifted, the March women are forced to redefine their social and personal roles – as providers, stalwarts, and upholders of moral justice – in a reconfigured community where women must acquire strength if they are to find financial stability or personal independence. That negotiation is at the heart of the novel.

For Alcott (1832–88) herself, the key to such independence lay in her writing. Her own struggles as an author are reflected in the struggles experienced by Jo March in *Little Women*, which in its narrative progression expresses the difficulties that beset the female artist in the mid-nineteenth century. As has been noted elsewhere, Jo is a projection of her creator's aspirations who "serves to emphasize the frustrations that women's imaginative creativity encounters."[2] Jo, like Alcott, has to establish herself in a professional milieu that requires observing certain conventions regarding gender roles. The tension between public pressures and artistic integrity poses a familiar dilemma for nineteenth-century women writers, but it has particular resonance for Alcott's work and for the films it has engendered. For while the act of writing has a crucial part to play in *Little Women*, the significance of authorship is depicted more diffidently on screen. Similarly, the different films of *Little Women* vary considerably in acknowledging the presence of the war; yet that war had an undeniable impact on the growth of a new America, which in turn produced the emancipated woman of whom Jo March is a prototype.

Little Women has always been an extraordinarily popular work. Its first edition of two thousand copies sold out within the first month of publication and the book has featured on the bestseller lists on both sides of the Atlantic ever since. The novel quickly became known as an American classic, if not the seminal classic novel of American girlhood. It has been described as "*the* American female myth, its subject the primordial one of the passage from childhood, from girl to woman,"[3] and a number of eminent modern writers and critics have commented on its inspirational impact on their own thinking.[4] The archetypal qualities that endeared it to children and adults alike at the time of its first appearance – a winning struggle against the odds, a feisty heroine, and the awkward growth from childhood to adulthood – have also been the qualities that have endeared it to filmmakers. In addition to the film versions, there have been cartoon and comic strip stories, television serials, abridged editions, stage plays, and radio and audiotape dramatizations and readings, and even an opera. In concentrating on the narrative epicentre of the novel – the March women, and in particular,

Jo's personal development – the adaptations have invariably excised what might seem to be the less immediately appealing features of the text. Yet it is precisely those features that are the most intriguing for a modern reader. The Christian framework, the presence of the Civil War, the incipient feminism, and the unrealized tensions of the book do not fit easily into the Hollywood ethos of heroism, romance, and harmonious resolution. Whereas recent textual critics of *Little Women* have tended to focus attention on the contradictions of the novel and the problematic contexts of its production,[5] the films accentuate family values, sisterly love, and a fantasy of female authorship – their emphases echoing the cultural values of their time.

Playing to their audiences' expectations, few of the adaptations thus allow themselves the luxury of hinting at the darker edges around the novel's soft centre of family togetherness. Nonetheless, as Catherine Stimpson has pointed out, the tensions that underlie the representation of family are one of the work's most seductive features for they reflect the ordeals experienced by every girl reader and by extrapolation every girl viewer as well. As she suggests, "Both female and male readers love any text that gives an experience of division and self-division"[6] and Jo's growing up is characterized by the pull between family conformism and her adolescent rebellion. The screen versions of *Little Women* vary significantly in the ways in which they expose or conceal these tensions, and in particular the ways in which they explore the role of writing (and reading) in Jo's life. For while authorship provides a route to financial independence for Jo, as indeed it did for Alcott, market forces compromise her urge for self-expression. Both Mr. March and Professor Bhaer deplore Jo's proclivity for gothic thrillers and fantasy writing. When Bhaer tells Jo, in the sequel, *Good Wives* (1869), "I would more rather give my boys gunpowder to play with than this bad trash," she burns her manuscripts rather than risk his further disapproval:

They *are* trash and will soon be worse than trash if I go on; for each is more sensational than the last. I've gone blindly on, hurting myself and other people, for the sake of money; – I know it's so – for I can't read this stuff in sober earnest without being horribly ashamed of it; and *what should* I do if they were seen at home, or Mr. Bhaer got hold of them? (280)

One of the most fascinating aspects of *Little Women* is its interrogation of authorial status for women and its double-edged nature. Bitterly disappointed at the condemnation of her work, Jo is nevertheless prepared to accept Bhaer's judgment as authoritative. Professor Bhaer, the older man and surrogate father, represents a view of a hierarchy of culture that dogged Alcott all her life. Writing under the name of A. M. Barnard in the early part of her career, Alcott produced the sorts of thrillers so disparaged by Bhaer; she was persuaded to renounce them by her father and publisher in favor of the domestic realism that was ultimately to bring her fame and fortune.

Interestingly, the three films of *Little Women* examined here become increasingly explicit in their acknowledgment of the place of authorship in determining the significance of *Little Women*, as they respond to and reflect their own cultural condition. Their readiness to interrogate the subversive undercurrents of the novel can of course be attributed to the period in which they were produced and the political and cultural forces that shape them. The three most famous screen adaptations of *Little Women* are George Cukor's film (1933), starring Katherine Hepburn in the role of Jo, Mervyn LeRoy's film (1949) with June Allyson, and Gillian Armstrong's postfeminist adaptation (1994) with Winona Ryder as Jo and Susan Sarandon as Marmee. Variously, they represent a history that has become embedded in the American female psyche. According to the librettist-composer Mark Adamo (who has turned the novel into an opera), "Hollywood has had to film the piece once every 20 years or so to slake the recurring appetite [for it] and indeed, each film creates its own very different 'little women.'"[7] This chapter explores the tensions between the literary and visual media in the cinematic versions of *Little Women*. It also explores the ways in which these tensions are used to mirror the more profound thematic dissonances that lie beneath the harmonious surface of a book that has traditionally been categorized as an anodyne work, suitable only for the uncritical child reader.

With its opening narrative tableau of the four sisters and their mother reading the father's letter, an image reproduced in the illustrations to countless editions of the novel as well as on screen, *Little Women* foregrounds the moral and imaginative power of text as well as that of family. The letter is, however, only the first of the indications that literature serves as a moral signpost for readers. Mr. March's letter, which conjures up such poignant emotions in the girls, is followed swiftly by the Christmas gift that Marmee gives her daughters: John Bunyan's allegory of spiritual development, *The Pilgrim's Progress*. In a period when books were something of a luxury in even a middle-class household, it is telling that Bunyan's novel is thought to be so potent that each girl is provided with her own personal copy. By providing a stable reference point in a morally fragile society, the book acquires a symbolic status, becoming a substitute for the guiding hand of their absent father.

But the power of literature is by no means presented simplistically. Texts can be inspirational forces for good, but they also hold risks. If Christmas morning shows the March sisters quietly absorbing Bunyan's

Christian messages, Christmas night shows them exuberantly playing out an exotic melodrama, written by Jo, for the entertainment of their friends and neighbors (and based on an adolescent piece of Alcott's own).[8] *Norna; or the Witch's Curse, an Operatic Tragedy* allows all sorts of unruly fantasies to run riot, as Jo puts on male costume in order to perform the roles of both villainous seducer and dashing hero: "I always wanted to do the killing part," (15) she declares boldly, visualizing herself somewhat ambitiously in the role of Macbeth. On the one hand, then, *The Pilgrim's Progress* is offered as a positive influence that shapes the narrative; on the other hand, *Little Women* shows the equally power-ful attractions of alternative fictions, not only the thrillers that feed Jo's transgressive desires, but also the staples of Victorian adolescent reading, such as *The Wide Wide World*, *The Heir of Redclyffe*, and *The Pickwick Papers*.[9] All are presented as formative influences on the budding writer.

Little Women itself, of course, contains a similar duality with its oppor-tunities for differing textual positions. Does Jo blaze a trail for female autonomy or does the ending of the novel show her meekly conforming to the orthodoxy of becoming a "little woman"? Is Marmee a model of American motherhood or a secretly mutinous advocate for women's rights? And is Jo's writing an act of liberation or merely another example of her ultimate compliance with the demands of a traditional society? Given her own dedication to writing and the complicated role that it played in her life, it is perhaps not surprising that Alcott should draw attention to the act of authorship as an outlet for passion and invest it with a host of symbolic meanings. Neither should we be surprised that filmmakers have found it easier to gloss that complexity with a conservative spin. A close look at the opening frames of the films in-dicates the level of their unease with the radical undercurrents of the novel. Indeed, the way in which the titles are presented says it all. The picture-postcard images of the Cukor and LeRoy films as the opening credits roll recall a nostalgic longing for a Christmas past with its echoes of family harmony, peace, and goodwill. This is reinforced by the mu-sical accompaniment, "There's No Place Like Home," which underlines the sense of wistfulness in recalling a time long past. Even Armstrong, who makes authorship a central thematic strand of her adaptation, succumbs to the temptation of the Victorian fantasy by utilizing traditional bookplate designs as borders for the film's titles.

Yet the awareness of dissident nuances in the story is not just a late twentieth-century development. Cukor's *Little Women* opens in what might seem to be a sweeping departure from the text but which is in fact close to it in spirit. The novel begins on Christmas Eve with the four sisters clustered together in front of the fire, awaiting their mother's return home. Both Cukor and LeRoy start their films with exterior shots of a snowy New England landscape before drawing the viewer in to the warmth of the domestic interior. In both films these exterior scenes are prolonged, but with quite different impact. Cukor, somewhat unexpectedly, sets the opening in the center of his New England town. Snow is thick on the roofs of buildings and piled on the sidewalks, and the title music segues into the sound of a military band. The camera moves to the mission with its conspicuous banner announcing "United States Christian Commission: Concord Division," patently indicating the correspondence between the film and Alcott's own home town. The military march gains in volume and a line of soldiers emerges to fill the center screen cheered on by the bystanders, who stop their business to watch the young men go off to war, while children chase the regiment as they disappear from view. The scene switches to the inside of the mission, where Mrs. March is at work, providing clothes and provisions for the unfortunate. She listens to the sad tale of an old man whose four sons have all signed on; two have already been killed, one is a prisoner, and he is off to seek the fourth, lying sick in a military hospital. Deeply touched by the story of parental self-sacrifice, Mrs. March gives the father money from her own purse in addition to the overcoat she has found for him from the stores. As she ponders her own inadequacy, the supervisor reassures her of her vital role in both the war effort and as a mother of daughters.

These opening scenes perform multiple functions. They establish the military context for the unfolding domestic action, and locate the women in a community that sees its young, virile men disappear. However fleetingly, that community is made real for the viewer in all its parochialism and hardship with visible references to the impact of war on a civilian population. The scene inside the mission, for instance, shows an entirely female workforce, incessantly busy throughout Mrs. March's conversation with the old man, and a female manager. The opening thus depicts Marmee, unusually, in her life outside the home as a working woman, and situates her not as an exceptional case but as one among many parents who must make sacrifices for the war. The theme of women's capability and employability is developed as Cukor's direction moves to show both Meg and Jo earning their own living as, respectively, a nursery governess and a paid companion. Before we ever reach the famous sigh, "Christmas won't be Christmas without any presents," with which the novel opens, a spirit of free thinking in relation to women's lives has been firmly established.

While Cukor's film was produced at a time when concern over the influence of Hollywood on American morality was mounting, LeRoy's *Little Women* was made under the restrictive and firmly established Production Code that dictated the content of Hollywood films from 1934 to the mid-1950s. LeRoy's film epitomizes the values of M-G-M at the time, characterized as "typically American middle class ones of optimism, materialism and romantic escapism."[10] His postwar version adopts a strikingly different note, despite the fact that it consciously draws on Cukor's adaptation, even to the extent of using the same sets and retaining the plot changes from the earlier film; both films used the same screenwriters: Sara Y. Mason and Victor Heerman. In keeping with the post-World War II move to domesticate women and return them to their prewar roles of homemakers, the liberal attitudes to female emancipation of the early 1930s have by 1949 been almost totally eradicated. Produced in a period in which there was a forceful backlash against independent women,[11] this version, significantly, makes little reference to the war, we do not see Beth die, and the March home and the girls' dresses reveal an opulence that blatantly contradicts Alcott's representation of genteel poverty. In direct contrast to the actual first sentence of the book, the first words of LeRoy's film, "Merry Christmas," emit a positive rather than negative message; this is endorsed by the opening frames which accentuate the welcoming comforts of home, as the warmth of the March family parlor forms a dramatic opposition to the bare, wintry landscape. The repeated images of windows in the first scenes strengthen this division: Meg, Beth, and Amy press their faces against the window to watch Jo as she leaps over the fence; Laurie appears at the window of his cold, grand house watching the cosy March home opposite; Jo goes to the window to spy on Laurie; and the four girls gaze longingly through the window of the general store as they go out on Christmas Eve to spend their dollar Christmas gift from Aunt March. There is nothing to disturb the unruffled surface. The Victorian parlor is snug and inviting, the sisters are a devoted group, and Marmee herself appears to be completely unaffected by the chilly conditions outside as she steps across the doorstep into the warmth of home. The frictions that are a natural part of family life – and that make Alcott's depiction of it so authentic – are nowhere in sight.

To twenty-first-century viewers of Cukor's 1933 adaptation, the portrayal of Jo is an arresting one; boyish and physically awkward, Katherine Hepburn's gawkiness is remarkably close to the coltishness that is attributed to Alcott's Jo in the first part of the book, even though Hepburn is clearly considerably older than fifteen. Hepburn's performance has been attacked as mannered, brassy, and loud,[12] but it stresses

Jo's eccentricity and her deviation from conventional female behavior. By 1949, this adolescent awkwardness has gone, to be replaced by a softer June Allyson, whose costume emphasizes her mature female figure and who cannot even whistle convincingly. This Jo does not dominate in the way that Hepburn's does – she is, if anything, overshadowed by the sentimental and surprisingly young Beth (played by Margaret O'Brien), the strikingly attractive and fashionably dressed Meg (Janet Leigh), and the pouty and startlingly voluptuous Amy (Elizabeth Taylor). Even Jo's longing to go to the battlefields is transmuted by LeRoy into a desire to be a nurse rather than the character's original aspiration "to go and fight with papa" (13).[13] Her literary ambitions, too, are modified, as she announces her wish to be a writer for purely monetary motives with no mention of the powerful artistic impulses that feature so centrally in the novel.

Yet Alcott's women have no alternative but to be strong in a society that has stripped them of their men. With the father away, the only men around in the thinly disguised New England town of Concord are those who are wounded or are either too old or too young to go to war. While on the one hand celebrating female spiritual wealth and the accompanying strength and independence, Alcott's work also shows how the women's material poverty is alleviated by men, notably by the affluence of their grand neighbors, the wealthy Laurences. Significantly Mr. Laurence and Laurie are disqualified from the sexual or marriage stakes, at least as far as the original text of *Little Women* is concerned. The grandfather and the adolescent boy are desexualized, and their lack of machismo is reinforced by the backcloth of war. For they are men who are either too old or too young to go to war and by implication too old or too young to be sexually active. Indeed, Alcott was determined that romance should have no defining part in her narrative. "Girls write to ask who the little women marry, as if that was the only aim of a woman's life," she complained bitterly when faced with her copious fan mail. "I *won't* marry Jo to Laurie to please anyone!"[14]

Alcott's rejection of the romantic format could not, however, be sustained by Hollywood, and the different screen versions of *Little Women* incorporate the sequel to the novel, first published as *Good Wives*, which takes the girls through to their ultimate destinies, glamorized by the cinematic conventions of their respective periods. But the novel poses other challenges to orthodoxy. The portrait of Jo March, striking her bid for freedom, uncomfortable with the constraints of femininity, and embarking on her independent career as an author, is at odds with some of the overt messages of the text that advocate propriety and restraint as well as promoting the subservience of women to men. Marmee becomes an explicit conduit for this ambivalence, as she confides in Jo that even she has only managed to achieve self-control over her unruly and unfeminine temper as a result of her husband's guidance. Despite the fact that she is portrayed in the novel as an exemplar of female self-sufficiency, she gives out contradictory messages when she advises her daughters, "To be loved and chosen by a good man is the best and sweetest thing which can happen to a woman" (84). Her statement can easily be perceived as undermining the overriding narrative thrust toward female independence, the ideal for which Jo strives – and to which Alcott was personally so committed. Significantly the films of *Little Women*, determined to convey an uncomplicated message, elide this ambiguity by presenting Marmee either as domestic goddess (Cukor and LeRoy) or as prototype feminist (Armstrong). Neither portrait accurately reflects the uncertainties of the text.

Looking at all three films, we can see how the exceptionally "unfilmic" novel is increasingly adapted according to Hollywood conventions. In particular, all three films restructure the text so that it has a definite beginning, middle, and end.[15] There is no suggestion of a two-part structure (comprising the dramatically different texts of *Little Women* and *Good Wives*), and all three conclude with Bhaer's proposal, unlike the novel where we see a married Jo and family settled at Plumfield. Against Alcott's declared feelings, the films increasingly romanticize the marriage of Jo to the Professor from 1933 to 1994, with Bhaer becoming incrementally youthful and attractive. The 46-year-old Paul Lukas is awkward and fatherly in appearance, while Rossano Brazzi in the 1949 adaptation, at thirty-three, once he has lost his glasses, looks quite glamorous. Indeed, the romantic direction of that film is announced at the beginning when Brazzi is given star billing in the credits, despite the fact that Bhaer is a minor and relatively shadowy figure in the novel. Surprisingly perhaps for such an openly feminist director, Armstrong casts Gabriel Bryne, a very young-looking 44-year-old, smoldering with undeclared passion, as by far the sexiest of the three. The Bildungsroman genre of the novel is transformed into romantic comedy, and visuals increasingly replace dialogue. In keeping with the globalization of Hollywood films, the Christian context is virtually obliterated in the latest version.

Consistent with postmodern Hollywood, Armstrong's film is highly self-reflexive. In part, this introversion is conducted through the figure of Marmee; in her repeated musings on female independence, she becomes Alcott's spokeswoman in the film. The shift of emphasis is exaggerated by the casting of Susan Sarandon, an actor well known for her feminist sympathies, in the role. Additionally, however, the film explicitly foregrounds the literary act and makes overt connections between the dramatic events and the life of their author. Armstrong draws heavily on her reading of Alcott's biography, and extracts from Alcott's journals occur intermittently in the screenplay, blurring fiction and fact. The autobiographical voiceover that introduces the opening scenes of the film positions Jo as the author/narrator and structures the film's events as retrospective. However, Armstrong sidesteps the frustrations that beset the real author as she found herself under pressure to compromise, and that bubble through the pages of the novel. Indeed, as Elaine Showalter has observed, *Little Women* "stands as one of the best studies we have of the literary daughter's dilemma: the tension between feminine identity and artistic freedom, and even more important, between patriarchal models of the literary career and those more relevant to women's lives."[16]

In the novel Marmee's role is the antithesis of that portrayed by Sarandon. In fact, rather than offer liberation, Mrs. March transforms her three independent daughters into "little women," stamping out their envy (Meg), pride (Amy), and aggression (Jo) so that they can become as perfect as their sister Beth, Alcott's "Angel in the House." *Good Wives* concludes with a celebration of Mrs. March's triumph – she is last seen enthroned as "the queen of the day," surrounded by her dutiful and thankful daughters, who are unrecognizable at the end of the book in their translation into wives and mothers.[17] Indeed, it could be argued that by the conclusion of the sequel, Mrs. March has achieved her aim of converting all her daughters into versions of Beth, inert women who lack a life and identity of their own. On the verge of death, Beth asks Jo to take her place – "you must take my place, Jo, and be everything to father and mother when I'm gone" (327) – and, after Beth dies, Jo does become "another" Beth in her resignation to family duties, sacrificing her artistic principles in the process.[18]

Certainly, it is indisputable that Jo undergoes an alarming character reversal in part two of the novel as she changes from aspiring writer who renounces marriage to a wife and mother with no time for writing. What Marmee begins, Professor Bhaer completes, forcing her to accept the mutilation and ultimate destruction of her early writing. When Amy burns Jo's manuscript in the first novel (a premonition of her ultimate destruction of Jo's story when she marries Laurie), Marmee tells Jo that she must grin and bear it: "As Jo received her good-night kiss, Mrs. March whispered, gently – 'My dear, don't let the sun go down upon your anger; forgive each other, help each other, and begin again tomorrow'" (65). And when Professor Bhaer convinces her that she should not write sensational stories, to prove her devotion and compliance, this time in an ultimate act of self-sacrifice, she burns them herself. Jo's change in attitude toward her writing as dramatized in *Little Women* mirrors the change in tone between the original novel, published in 1868, and its 1869 sequel. It reflects Alcott's reluctant recognition of the value of the milch cow that would provide for her family's prosperity and her obliteration of the disturbing undercurrents that give such life to the first volume. It is also probably the reason why many readers prefer to think of *Little Women* as solely the 1868 version.

Alcott's anxieties about succumbing to expectations and betraying her principles as an artist are reflected in Jo, who, in the sequel, gradually abandons her ambitions to remain single and become a great author. In reality, Alcott wrote *Little Women* as a guide to young girls against her inclinations, at the behest of her publisher. Her distaste for the task is recorded in her journal:

May 1868. – Mr. N wants a girls' story, and I begin 'Little Women.' Marmee, Anna and May all approve my plan. So I plod away, though I don't enjoy this sort of thing. Never liked girls, or knew many, except my sisters; but our queer plays and experiences may prove interesting, though I doubt it.[19]

She later complained in 1869 that her publishers are "very *perverse* & wont let authors have their way so my little women must grow up & be married off in a very stupid style."[20]

While the pressures on the female writer to either sell out or abandon ambition altogether are at the heart of the sequel, Alcott's concerns about self-betrayal are entirely omitted from the screen adaptations. All three films reject the clearly delineated two-part narrative structure and choose to end the film at the penultimate chapter, with Jo agreeing to marry Professor Bhaer, under his umbrella. But even this is radically altered. Alcott's account of the proposal is unsettling as she refuses to romanticize the meeting or make Bhaer seem anything but awkward and fatherly:

It was certainly proposing under difficulties, for, even if he had desired to do so, Mr. Bhaer could not go down upon his knees, on account of the mud, neither could he offer Jo his hand, except figuratively, for both were full; much less could he indulge in tender demonstrations in the open street, though he was near it; so the only way in which he could express his rapture was to look at her, with an expression which glorified his face to such a degree that there actually seemed to be little rainbows in the drops that sparkled on his beard (372).

Bhaer's god-like status is enhanced by the little rainbows on his beard and both Bhaer and Mr. March are invested with divine gravitas. It is their judgment on Jo's writing that is accepted as final, and writing itself that gives the emotional game away. Bhaer comes to visit Jo because he has come across her poem, "In the Garret," in a newspaper and surmises from it that she is in love with him. Significantly, the poem is only of value in bringing the two together and after it has been read, Jo self-deprecatingly dismisses it as "bad poetry" while Bhaer agrees: "Let it go, – it has done its duty, – and I will have a fresh one when I read all the brown book in which she keeps her little secrets,' said Mr. Bhaer, with a smile, as he watched the fragments fly away on the wind" (299).

His remark is chillingly indicative of the future of their relationship. It also echoes the approach of the Alcott children's journals; each night they were invited to pen their innermost secrets ready for their parents' inspection while they were asleep. How the reader is to judge the poem is a different matter. "In the Garret" abbreviates the novel's narrative, describing the contents of each sister's little coffin-like chest, with Jo symbolically closing the lid on each sister's aspirations. The poem is, in fact, an elegy, not just to Beth, but to all the March girls, and especially Jo. In the penultimate chapter Alcott has Jo kiss goodbye to her career as a writer by agreeing to marry Bhaer.

This, above all, is a challenge for film adaptation and all three films choose to delete the ordeal that Jo faces and by doing so radically change Alcott's ending. The choice, between husband and career, patriarchy and independence, obedience and rebellion, is erased in all three versions. While renowned as a "women's director," Cukor initiates this rewriting in 1933, possibly resulting in Hepburn's accusation that the director never managed to finish reading the book.[21] It is inviting to speculate that Hepburn felt let down by the ending of the film in its refusal to give expression to a dilemma at the very heart of the novel and one which she, undoubtedly, experienced herself. In the 1933 film Bhaer apologetically informs Jo that he does not like her stories and wishes her to write from the heart – advice that she seems to accept, though Cukor does not show Jo burning her precious manuscripts. While he is physically paternalistic (she pats him on the back rather than giving him a kiss), Hepburn's Jo takes command of the relationship and yanks him into her house to meet the family in a reversal of the groom carrying the bride across the threshold. The film reshapes the novel in daringly allowing Jo to survive the moral lashings of her mother and Professor Bhaer, emerging at the end as the independent author she promised to be in the first book. The final frame offers a painting of the house (in fact Alcott's own home, Orchard House), a nostalgic recreation of nineteenth-century domesticity, as if frozen in time.

The 1949 film, directed by LeRoy, presents an even more pronounced romanticized ending. Jo is shown writing her novel, now entitled *My Beth*, and sending it to Bhaer who, as in the earlier film, brings the published version to her in the closing moments. Happiness is overflowing in this version, with Beth being resurrected through the book,[22] literary success being guaranteed for Jo, and Jo and Bhaer walking arm in arm against a painted background into the house – again, a replica of Orchard House; the crude sentimentality of the ending is crowned by a technicolor rainbow, an intertextual reference to LeRoy's earlier film, *The Wizard of Oz* (1939), while also replicating the rainbows that Alcott describes in Bhaer's beard. By implication, Bhaer has saved Jo from a life of artistic solitude, symbolized by his bringing her the rainbow with its underlying message of stasis as articulated in Dorothy's famous line, "There's no place like home."

Although ostensibly closer to the novel,[23] the 1994 adaptation parts company with the text in the closing moments and chooses to end the film like its predecessors, this time with Bhaer leaving the proofs of a novel behind for Jo to approve. This builds on the previous films, which had Bhaer clearly "correcting" Jo's writing without consulting her. In this version there is a marked emphasis on Jo's writing; her rage at Amy's burning of her manuscript and her disappointment with Bhaer's criticisms are prominently featured in the film. Indeed, once she meets Bhaer, she begins to write the "real thing" her creative output, as in the previous films, is implicitly linked to her awakening sexuality. Working against the book, the *Little Women* films increasingly endorse a romantic theory of literary authorship, one that interestingly becomes explicitly articulated in other films of the 1990s, including John Madden's highly successful *Shakespeare in Love* (1996), where creativity merges sexuality, writing, and romance.[24]

In Armstrong's film it is Amy who draws artistic inspiration from the home, presenting her parents with the gift of her painting, of Orchard House, visually echoing the closing frames of the Cukor and LeRoy films. (The painting of the home, like the film itself, pays homage to its source in what Amy – and Armstrong – self-deprecatingly admit to be an imperfect copy.) Bhaer and Jo are left outside in the closing moments. Armstrong's Jo does not quite fit under Bhaer's umbrella and the rain is used in this later version to call attention to her body and the steamy sexuality of the pair. Adopting Stella Bruzzi's categorization of clothes on film, in the early films of *Little Women* clothes are used to "look at," especially the extravagant costumes of the 1949 version. Here the clothes, unmistakably, are used to "look through."[25] Paradoxically, Alcott's thematic concerns with an author selling out are fully enacted in Armstrong's film as the director herself succumbs to the demands of Hollywood, romanticizing and sexualizing Alcott's ending. This is the only version in which they actually kiss, compatible with

Byrne's portrayal of Bhaer as less stiff and more sensual than that of his predecessors.

In 1933 Bhaer produces an unnamed book; in 1949 the book becomes *My Beth*, and in 1994 it is embodied as proofs of *Little Women*, reflecting the growing tendency to draw out the correspondences between author and character. All three films do precisely what Alcott's text resists, perpetuating a view of the author who writes, successfully, from the heart. Yet as Alcott's journals depressingly demonstrate, professional authorship was a soul-destroying and grinding task:

January, 1879. – When I had the youth I had no money; now I have the money I have no time; and when I get the time, if I ever do, I shall have no health to enjoy life . . . duty chains me to my galley.[26]

Alcott and Jo depart company at the end of *Good Wives* (Alcott the unmarried writer, Jo the mother with no time for books); the films increasingly insist on having it all. Indeed, in all three films Jo becomes a serious writer only once she has met the love of her life. For a woman to achieve her ultimate creative potential, according to Hollywood rules, she must have a man. The films end by filling the void of the husband or father, a "void" articulated and celebrated so clearly in Alcott's opening chapter, a void which is vital to the novel's success.

Little Women, seemingly against all the odds (that is, in spite of its "unfilmic" narrative structure and its "un-Hollywood" values), is, if not *the* most adapted, one of the most filmed of all American novels.[27] Hollywood continues to be fascinated by literary authorship, but it is clear that there is a growing divide between literary scholarship and cinematic adaptation. Hollywood's increasing tendency to romanticize the writer is in direct opposition to the repeated insistence of Alcott (and her recent critics) on the converse. Armstrong's film uses Alcott scholarship both as a means to claim cultural authority for the production and as a shield to conceal its equivocation. For in reality the film remains reliant on a popular cultural conception, an old-fashioned and inaccurate construction of "the author" as romantically inspired. Ironically, the films progressively intersect with the novel in unwittingly raising the issue of the commodification of literature.[28] And it is this very relationship, between literature and the market place, so pervasive in the novel and in its cinematic reconstructions, that is at the very heart of the study of literary adaptation.

Figure 6. The George Cukor version of Louisa May Alcott's *Little Women* is dominated by a star-studded female cast, including Spring Byington, Joan Bennett, Frances Dee, Katharine Hepburn, and Jean Parker.

NOTES

1. Louisa May Alcott, *Little Women* (1868), ed. Anne K. Phillips and Gregory Eiselein (New York and London: W. W. Norton & Co. 2004), p. 11. Further quotations will be cited parenthetically in the text.

2. Shirley Foster and Judy Simons, "Louisa May Alcott: *Little Women*", in Foster and Simons, *What Katy Read: Feminist Re-readings of "Classic" Stories for Girls* (London: Macmillan, 1995), p. 87.

3. Catherine Stimpson, "Reading for Love: Canons, Paracanons and Whistling Jo March," *New Literary History* 21 (1990), p. 958.

4. These include most famously Simone de Beauvoir. See Elaine Showalter, *Sister's Choice: Tradition and Change in American Women's Writing* (Oxford: Clarendon Press, 1991), and Stimpson, "Reading for Love," for further discussions of this phenomenon.

5. See in particular Foster and Simons, *What Katy Read*, for a summary of these debates.

6. Stimpson, "Reading for Love," p. 970.

7. www.pbs.org/wnet/gperf/littlewomen/look.html, accessed April 19, 2004. The opera was first aired on August 29, 2001.

8. Louisa May Alcott, *Norna; or the Witch's Curse, an Operatic Tragedy* (1847–49), published in *Comic Tragedies* (1893).

9. Susan Warner, *The Wide, Wide World* (p. 18), *The Heir of Redclyffe* (p. 18); Charles Dickens, *The Pickwick Papers* (p. 183).

10. David A. Cook, *A History of Narrative Film* (1980; rpt. New York: Norton, 1990), p. 304.

11. See Carol Gay, "*Little Women* at the Movies," in Douglas Street, ed., *Children's Novels and the Movies* (New York: Ungar, 1983), pp. 28–38.

12. User comment September 3, 2002. www.imdb.com/title/tt0024264/users' comments 15.04.04.

13. In the text Jo expresses a wish to fight and only subsequently to be a vivandiere, drummer, or nurse. LeRoy significantly omits the more active, male aspiration and prioritizes the ambition to be a nurse over that of drummer.

14. Louisa May Alcott, *Louisa May Alcott, Life, Letters and Journals* ed. Edna D. Cheney (London: Sampson, Low, Marston, Searle & Rivington, 1889), p. 201.

15. As has been observed, Hollywood has remained surprisingly fixed in its adherence to a rigid set of conventions. See Pam Cook and Mieke Bernink, *The Cinema Book*, 2nd edn (London: BFI, 1999).

16. Showalter, *Sister's Choice*, p. 44.

17. Alcott's portrayal of saintly motherhood is not without reservation; ironically, at the beginning of the novel, Marmee benefits materially from her teaching her daughters that virtue is its own reward with the girls turning their dollars into presents for her.

18. This argument is propounded by a number of recent critics of *Little Women*, including Angela M. Estes and Kathleen Margaret Lant, in a provocative essay, "Dismembering the Text: The Horror of Louisa May Alcott's *Little Women*," *Children's Literature* 17 (1989), pp. 98–123. "The experimental

transformation of Jo March into a proper 'little woman' – performed and delineated in a textual laboratory which masquerades as an informative and supportive guidebook for children – turns out to be a 'gothic' study in horror, the very kind of story Alcott so longed to write but which she renounced, or tried to, for the sake of her young, impressionable reader" (p. 103). Other more measured critical interpretations of this life change are expounded by, among others, Martha Saxton, Judith Fetterley, and Elaine Showalter.

19. Alcott, *Life, Letters and Journals*, p. 198.
20. Quoted by Estes and Lant, "Dismembering," p. 569.
21. Quoted in Gay, "*Little Women* at the Movies," p. 32.
22. Holly Blackford writes about the connections the films draw between Beth's death and Jo's writing in "*Little Women* on the Big Screen: Heterosexual Womanhood as Social Performance," in Deborah Cartmell, I. Q. Hunter, Heidi Kaye, and Imelda Whelehan, eds., *Sisterhoods Across the Literature/Film Divide* (London: Pluto, 1998), pp. 32–47.
23. A number of episodes omitted from the earlier versions are included in Armstrong's adaptation, making the experience of the film seem more like the book. However, as Armstrong has herself implied, this may be due to technological advances – her description of the filming of the skating episode, for instance, would be far too technically challenging for the earlier films. See *Little Women*, DVD, Columbia Pictures Industries, 1994; Layout and Design, Columbia Tristar Home Entertainment, 2001.
24. For an analysis of the representation of the author in *Shakespeare in Love*, see Richard Burt, "Shakespeare in Love and the End of Shakespeare," in Mark Thornton Burnett and Ramona Wray, eds., *Shakespeare, Film, Fin de Siècle* (London and New York: Palgrave, 2000), pp. 203–231.
25. Stella Bruzzi, *Undressing Cinema: Clothing and Identity in the Movies* (London: Routledge, 1997). For a discussion of the clothes in *Little Women* films, see Pat Kirkham and Sarah Warren, "Four *Little Women*: Three Films and a Novel," in Deborah Cartmell and Imelda Whelehan, eds., *Adaptations: From Text to Screen, Screen to Text* (London and New York: Routledge, 1999), pp. 81–97. Gillian Armstrong discusses the pains taken to make the dresses look worn in her comments on the DVD of the film.
26. Alcott, *Life, Letters and Journals*, pp. 272–273.
27. See the unnamed review at www.katherinehepburn.net/reviews/littlewomen.html.
28. While the issue was profoundly troubling to Alcott at the time of *Little Women*'s composition, it became less so when she produced the later sequels, *Little Men* and *Jo's Boys*, which openly cashed in on her early success.

David Lavery

Investigating the "erotics of reading" in *The Pleasure of the Text* (1975), Roland Barthes once pondered why "we do not read everything with the same intensity of reading," why "our very avidity for knowledge impels us to skim or to skip certain passages (anticipated as 'boring') . . . (no one is watching) descriptions, explanations, analyses, conversations." Of course, no author, Barthes concedes, can predict in advance what will be skipped:

> he cannot choose to write *what will not be read*. And yet, it is the very rhythm of what is read and what is not read that creates the pleasure of the great narratives: has anyone ever read Proust, Balzac, *War and Peace*, word for word? (Proust's good fortune: from one reading to the next, we never skip the same passages.)[1]

Certainly, no two readers of *Moby-Dick* (1851), nor the same reader reading subsequently, nor two screenwriters preparing, forty years apart, to adapt the classic novel by Herman Melville (1819–91) for the film medium, skip the same passages or discover the same text. *Moby-Dick*, after all, is full-to-overflowing with "descriptions, explanations, analyses, conversations" inviting anything but the avid, easily bored student, the supposedly disinterested but often with an ax-to-grind scholar, and the medium-determined and cost-driven screenwriter to pass on by. But it is by no means certain, as with *Remembrance of Things Past*, that Melville's text has been the beneficiary of these lapses. There are few great books more often misread or maladapted.

Adapting *Moby-Dick*

Soon after the release of *The Scarlet Letter* (Roland Joffé, 1995), a film featuring Demi Moore as Hester Prynne that perverted Nathaniel Hawthorne's original novel by supplying a happy ending, a cartoon appeared in the *New Yorker* that speculated on what might happen if she were to star in a new version of another classic novel of the American Renaissance. Over a caption which reads "Demi Moore's *Moby Dick*," we see the actress standing, like a competitor at a fishing contest, beside her prize catch: a giant, dead, white whale, hanging from a hook. So far, the Moore version of Melville's classic novel *Moby-Dick* (1851) has not yet been made, but we need not wait for a movie *Moby-Dick* with a happy ending.

Two early twentieth-century incarnations of Melville's book, both from Warner Brothers, the silent *Sea Beast* (Millard Webb, 1926) and the talkie *Moby Dick* (Lloyd Bacon, 1930) – both starring John Barrymore as "Captain Ahab Ceely" – had Ahab vanquishing the whale and living to tell about it. Both even added a love story, with Ahab battling his half-brother Derek (George O'Hara, Lloyd Hughes) for his fiancée, Esther Harper (Dolores Costello) in the first, Faith Mapple (Joan Bennett) in the second. In both films Ahab loses his leg to the whale after being pushed overboard by the scheming Derek and seeks revenge against the beast who, he fears, has ruined his marriage prospects. In both Ahab not only slaughters his watery nemesis but returns from his mission to murder Derek *and* get the girl.[2]

In two later, more authentic adaptations of *Moby-Dick*, a 1956 version (again from Warner Brothers) directed by John Huston from a screenplay by the science fiction writer Ray Bradbury, and a 1998 Hallmark Hall of Fame/USA Network made-for-television production directed by Franc Roddam, Ahab's battle with the whale is finally fatal, and neither includes a love story. But neither do these more superficially faithful and ambitious films make the slightest attempt to render Ishmael as the novel's central intelligence, nor capture even a trace of the book's wicked, often blasphemous humor, nor fully engage Melville's complex metaphors. The literary critic Charles Feidelson was perhaps thinking of decades of often uncomprehending literary readings of *Moby-Dick* when he insisted that "Certainly no interpretation is adequate which fails to take into account the multiplicity of possible meanings in the white whale and in *Moby-Dick* as a whole."[3] If the same standard is applied to film "interpretations," both of the latter twentieth-century film adaptations of *Moby-Dick*, the focus of my attention here, must be judged failures. One of the greatest of all novels still awaits a film version that captures Melville's novel in all its intricacy.

Moby Dick (1956)

Speaking of his then recently completed *Moby Dick* to the film critic Arthur Knight, John Huston would recall that "Ray [Bradbury] and I tried to be as faithful to the meaning of the book as our own understanding and the special demands of the movie medium would allow."[4]

Taking the director at his word, we might well conclude, given the film they produced, that both their comprehension of the novel and their vision of the possibilities of cinema were imperfect and limited.

Huston, then an internationally known director of such films as *The Maltese Falcon* (1941), *Key Largo* (1948), *The Treasure of the Sierra Madre* (1948), *The Asphalt Jungle* (1950), *The African Queen* (1951), and *The Red Badge of Courage* (1951), with a penchant for adapting literary works and a larger-than-life personality, had been contemplating filming *Moby-Dick* since the early 1940s. He initially hoped to cast his father Walter Huston as Ahab. When he finally secured the funding to make the film in the mid-1950s and cast the usually mild-mannered Gregory Peck as the monomaniacal Ahab,[5] he invited Bradbury, then in his thirties, whose work, especially *The Martian Chronicles* (1950), he admired, to try his hand at writing the script. Huston, Bradbury would recall in self-congratulatory fashion, saw "the poet in my writing" (Atkins "An Interview," 44).[6]

Bradbury claimed never to have read *Moby-Dick* before accepting Huston's assignment, but under contract he would read and reread the book and turn out (by his own estimation) more than 1,200 pages of outlines and text in the process of generating 140 pages of screenplay (Atkins "An Interview," 51). During a sojourn in London during the run-up to filming – at nearby Elstree Studios, in Wales, Ireland, and off the coast of Portugal – Bradbury even convinced himself that he was channeling *Moby-Dick*'s author: "I am Herman Melville," he began to feel. "The ghost of Melville was in me" (46). Bradbury persuaded himself as well that the changes he made in Melville's narrative would have been enthusiastically approved by the author (47).

With Huston's wholehearted approval (44), Bradbury decided to leave out the mysterious Fedallah and his infernal crew entirely. "He's a bore," Bradbury concluded. "He's horrible. He's the thing that ruins the whole book. I don't care what the Melville scholars say, he's the extra mystical symbol which breaks the whale's back, and he would be unbearable on the screen" (44) He inserted early glimpses of Stubb and Flask and even Ahab, melodramatically lit by a lightning flash, during the arrival of Ishmael (a bland and unengaging Richard Basehart) at the Spouter Inn. He combined Chapters 28 and 36 ("Ahab," "The Quarter-Deck: Ahab and All") in his version of Ahab's first appearance on *The Pequod*, fusing Ishmael's and the crew's first glimpse of their captain as "a man cut away from the stake, when the fire has overrunningly wasted all the limbs without consuming them, or taking away one particle from their compacted aged robustness"[7] with his initial stratagems (nailing the gold ounce to the mast; asking the crew to splice hands; crossing the lances) for entangling them in his quest, but delaying for a later scene below decks in Ahab's cabin his very public explanation to the skeptical Starbuck of "the little lower layer" (Chapter 36), the deeper, epistemological reasons for his vengeance.

Bradbury changed, too, the order of several key events, the better to enhance the drama, or so he thought. He moved the encounter with the British ship the *Samuel Enderbey* and its Captain Boomer, who remains jovial despite losing his arm to Moby Dick, from the final third of the novel ("Leg and Arm," Chapter 100) to the first hour of the movie and making Boomer sillier than in the book. He delayed Ahab's confrontation with the "clear spirit" of a storm at sea and his "I blow out the last fear" taming of the St. Elmo's Fire ("The Candles," Chapter 119) until after his refusal to aid the captain of *The Rachel*'s hunt for his lost son ("*The Pequod* Meets *The Rachel*," Chapter 128).

Queequeg's realization of his coming death likewise departs substantially from the novel. Melville has the harpooner fall ill from a mysterious fever, which leads him to order the carpenter to prepare a coffin. When his fever breaks, his resignation ends as well. In the Bradbury version he reads the signs of his death while casting his bones, orders a coffin made, gives all his worldly possessions to Ishmael, and becomes a living statue, roused from his deathwatch only when his bosom friend's life is threatened.

Bradbury inexplicably recasts the ending as well, having First Mate Starbuck decide to pursue Moby Dick even after the Captain's death. According to French, Bradbury's original screenplay even had Starbuck taking up Ahab's pursuit and killing the whale: "the most disturbing adaptative change," French argues, "is that Starbuck in the movie actually succeeds in killing Moby Dick. (The black blood in the film and a reference in the script to 'the dying whale' confirm the murder.) One can't kill the phantom of life in the novel, but evidently in Bradbury's estimation, Moby Dick was, after all, just a whale" (French, "Lost at Sea," 61).[8]

Bradbury also had Ahab, entangled in harpoon lines, go down with the whale – an idea which, more than any other, convinced him that Melville was his co-pilot.[9] (This change, in turn, required a reformulation of Elijah's prophecy to Ishmael and Queequeg earlier in the story so that it would be properly self-fulfilling.) But Bradbury's "inspiration" was clearly, as Linda Costanzo Cahir and John C. Tibbetts hint (154), a case of what is now sometimes called "cryptonesia," a clandestine creative theft, conveniently forgotten.[10] We need not look far to discover the source of Bradbury's scripted end for Ahab. In "The Chase – Third Day" (Chapter 135), the missing Fedallah – the character that Bradbury conveniently threw overboard – is found in a similar prophecy-fulfilling pose:

at that moment a quick cry went up. Lashed round and round to the fish's back; pinioned in the turns upon turns in which, during the past night, the whale had reeled the involutions of the lines around him, the half torn body of the Parsee was seen; his sable raiment frayed to shreds; his distended eyes turned full upon old Ahab. (433)

Inspiration indeed.

"It's a pretty good blend," Bradbury would conclude after viewing the film that Huston made from his first screenplay: "It almost worked. The film is almost magnificent" (Atkins, "An Interview," 50). An exaggeration, no doubt, but the film does get many things right. Orson Welles's performance as Father Mapple, minister to the whaling industry, who sermonizes on Jonah from a pulpit in the shape of a ship's prow accessible only by a rope ladder, could not be improved upon. The whaling scenes, combining studio work with actual whaling footage, are often quite gripping. Harry Andrews is completely convincing as "I know not all that may be coming, but be it what it will, I'll go to it laughing" Second Mate Stubb. The opening credit sequence, utilizing contemporary paintings of whaling scenes; the film's emphatic score, composed by Philip Sainton; its innovative cinematography (by Oswald Morris) that fused Technicolor and black-and-white prints of the same shot – all these factors succeed splendidly in establishing tone and mood and atmosphere.

"Our biggest problem," Huston would recall, "was to turn Melville's expositional passages into characteristic dialogue."[11] Bradbury would, in turn, characterize the challenge the filmmakers faced as a fusion of "the Shakespearean approach which is sheer language and the cinematic approach which is pure image" (50). Much was lost in the process. As French argues, the film eliminated "most of the documentary (whaling as a commercial occupation) and the philosophical dimensions,"[12] and "these deletions cut the story loose from its moorings as 'the real living experience of living men' in Ishmael's words" (French, "Lost at Sea," 53; Ishmael's words are from "Moby Dick", Chapter 41).

Moby Dick (1998)

Directed by Franc Roddam (*Quadrophenia* [1979], *The Lords of Discipline* [1983], *K2* [1992], *Cleopatra* [1999]) from a screenplay he co-authored with Anton Diether (*Night Games* [1980], *Cleopatra* [1999]), the television version of *Moby Dick* was filmed in Australia at an air force base near Melbourne and off the coast. Although graced, thanks to its broadcast format, with an extra hour of narrative time in which to render Melville's 200,000-plus word novel (the film was aired as a three-part mini-series) and the beneficiary of more than forty years of advances in cinematic art and science since the Huston/Bradbury version, the 1998 *Moby Dick* remains an uninspired disappointment.

As "'Thar She Blows!' The Making of *Moby Dick*," a behind-the-scenes video included on the DVD of the 1998 version, makes abundantly clear, the filmmakers behind the most recent attempt to get the story of Ahab and the white whale right were driven by high ambitions. Patrick Stewart, best known at the time for his role as another captain (Jean-Luc Picard on *Star Trek: The Next Generation*) and, later, as Professor Charles Xavier in *The X-Men* franchise, spent eight months immersed in the world of Herman Melville preparing for the "role of a lifetime" as Ahab. Piripi Waretini, the Maori who plays Queequeg as part of the film's more international, more multiethnic cast, wrote his M. A. thesis on Melville. Those responsible for what the narration calls the film's "state of the art" special effects and "totally believable whales" reveal the secrets of their trade. Peck, who narrates the documentary and turns in a unmemorable performance as Father Mapple in the film, insists that this new version, unlike the one in which he himself starred, is more faithful to both Melville's philosophy and his "great Victorian rolling prose." Despite such pretensions, it would be difficult to argue that the film that resulted is a pronounced improvement in any respect.

Closer in age than Peck to Ahab and suitably scarred and wizened,[13] Stewart is certainly adequate as *The Pequod*'s captain, yet he never succeeds in convincing us of the character's high purpose, his proximity to madness, or his power to exercise his will over the crew. In response to contemporary criticism of Peck's performance in his film, Huston had insisted that the "next generation will appreciate it more than the last."[14] Stewart's understated but hardly exemplary turn helps to confirm Huston's prediction: his Ahab only enhances our estimate of Peck's work.

Once again, Ishmael, played this time by Henry Thomas, sixteen years after starring in Spielberg's *ET* (1982), is barely developed as a character. On "'Thar She Blows!'" director Roddam insists that the film is really all about his journey, his great adventure, his learning, but in fact he is, from beginning to end, a humorless, dull, pessimistic cipher.[15] As in the 1956 film, we learn almost nothing about him; we are seldom invited to see the wonders of whaling through his eyes. The filmmakers choose instead to devote a sizable portion of their additional time to Ishmael and Queequeg's relationship, now reduced to buddy film clichés, and to Ishmael's initiation as a "new pup" sailor. We must endure several scenes of the novice's hazing by his shipmates (pouring grog over his blistered hands, for example). As both the novel and the Huston/Bradbury version make clear, Ishmael is a veteran sailor, though not an experienced whaler; Roddam and Diether make him a neophyte, completely "at sea," all the better to abuse him.

Roddam and Diether take other liberties. Elijah (Bruce Spence) is made at once more prominent – we see him stalking Ishmael upon his first arrival in New Bedford – and less ominous: more a crazy street person than a mad prophet. The Spouter Inn is populated with prostitutes; Stubb (Hugh Keays-Byrne) is seen exiting with two in tow. (In a continuity error, Ishmael will soon run into Stubb and his women again in an upstairs hall.) Precious time is frittered away transforming *Moby-Dick* into *Mutiny on the Bounty*: both Starbuck (Ted Levine) and the crew contemplate a hostile takeover of the ship, and at one point Ahab puts an end to such plotting with a rifle. While being more politically correct in casting Queequeg (Huston, after all, had used his Austrian friend Frederick Ledebur), Roddam and Diether rob him of nearly every ounce of dignity, having him behave more like a Polynesian party animal than a prince and giving him a full head of hair (he is bald in the novel). They take Perth, in the book the ship's blacksmith and an interesting minor character whom Ahab subjects to philosophical monologues, and transform him into a rowdy, grog-loving sailor who falls to his death off the rigging. In this version of *Moby-Dick*, the enigmatic Bulkington, whose willingness to put to sea again almost immediately after his last voyage perplexes Ishmael ("The Lee Shore," Chapter 23), inexplicably steals one of the ship's invaluable long boats and takes off for home and family – with Starbuck's permission!

Starbuck, himself, as played by Levine, best known as the serial killer in *Silence of the Lambs* (1991), is both more conspiratorial – he is convinced that Ahab has sold his soul to Satan and is guilty of the crime of "usurpation" – and antagonistic. Roddam and Diether even have Ishmael and Starbuck sit down for a preposterous heart-to-heart about the fate of the ship. In the end, they have the First Mate stay behind with *The Pequod* during the final pursuit of Moby Dick, and the ship goes to the bottom after being consumed in a fire, not sucked below, as it is in both the novel and the Huston/Bradbury version, in the whirlpool of the white whale's wake.

Like the Huston/Bradbury version, this *Moby Dick* also alters the ends of both Queequeg and Ahab. This time Queequeg's resignation to his own death follows Ahab's refusal to assist *The Rachel*. Disavowing his Captain's obsession, he is tied, catatonic, to the mast and nearly washed overboard in the storm scene (from "Candles"), coming back to life after Ahab tames the St. Elmo's Fire, groveling at his feet, and proclaiming him his god. Ahab's demise owes more to the 1956 film than to the novel. Indeed, Roddam and Diether must have been impressed with Bradbury's alternate ending, for they, too, have Ahab die entangled in harpoon lines and drowned by his nemesis, though this time Ahab later floats free.

To its credit, the Hallmark version does offer us in an early scene a glimpse of Ahab's briefly mentioned young wife and child ("The Ship," Chapter 16); does restore Fedallah and his men to the crew of *The Pequod*; does cast Pip, Ahab's black cabin boy, overboard ("The Castaway," Chapter 93) and show his later madness. It even includes a taste of some of Ahab's Shakespearean speeches: his "swerve me" railing at the gods ("Swerve me? Ye cannot swerve me, else ye swerve yourselves!" ["Sunset," Chapter 37]), for example; and Ahab's description, in conversation with the carpenter, of the perfect man ("fifty feet high in his socks . . . a quarter of an acre of fine brains . . . a sky-light on top of his head to illuminate inwards" ["Ahab and the Carpenter," Chapter 108]).

Despite the claims of superiority on "'Thar She Blows!,'" the whaling scenes, however, are especially unsatisfactory.[16] Every time we see a "whale" when a harpoon or lance pierces it and unconvincing blood spews, we are immediately aware of the artifice. Whether it is the faux whale models we watch or the CGI Moby Dick who breaches Fedallah's boat before crushing it and smashing into *The Pequod*, we are never for a moment able to suspend our disbelief.

The unmade *Moby Dick*

Will there ever be a faithful movie version of *Moby-Dick*? Putting aside the obvious, and perhaps grave, problem of the commercial viability of such a film, we can nevertheless stipulate some essential prerequisites.

It must be humorous. Although many readers, including Bradbury and Roddam and Diether, seem oblivious to Melville's sense of humor, the book is in fact filled with hilarious, often scatological, sometimes sacrilegious, comic touches never capitalized on by either the 1956 or 1998 films. The ideal movie *Moby Dick* might focus greater attention on the "marriage" of the "cosy loving pair," Ishmael and Queequeg, with which Melville has a great deal of fun ("A Bosom Friend," Chapter 10). It would not spare us, as both films do, any knowledge of the flatulence of our fellow mammal the whale, hilariously depicted in "The Pequod Meets the Virgin," (Chapter 81). It might even want to include some reference to Ishmael's discussion, in one of those cetology chapters

("The Cassock," Chapter 95) that students and screenwriters skip, of the use of the skin of a whale's penis as a much-prized, waterproof rain garment or, as our "wicked" narrator suggests,[17] in one of literature's greatest puns, as a liturgical garment for an "Archbishoprick." It is true that the censors of the 1950s or at the Hallmark Hall of Fame might well never have permitted such ribald humor, but was not Melville himself able, in the heart of Victorian America, to include just such obscenities in a book he himself knew to be blasphemous.[18]

It must make Ishmael a prominent character and tell the story from his point of view. As critics such as Robert Zoellner (and before him Charles Olson) have definitively shown, *Moby-Dick* is really Ishmael's tale, told by him and, ultimately, about him. Although both films retain Ishmael, at least in a cursory fashion, as the story's narrator, in neither film do we see through *his* point of view. What French says of the Huston/Bradbury version is true of both: "[Ishmael's] role as the mediating consciousness, which can accommodate contradictions and identify paradoxes, is eliminated along with most of his charm, wit and humor" (French "Lost at Sea," 57). She continues:

It is as if Melville is striving to create a new language out of the old one by means of contradictory juxtapositions, a language in which paradox is the central fact, the rule, a language which accommodates Melville's vision of the universe. Huston, in the film version of *Moby Dick*, provides no equivalent for this dialectic. And without Ishmael, without a universal language, whatever contradiction and complexity Bradbury chooses to retain in his script seems forced, heavy-handed, out-of-place, ideas spoken but not visually nor even narratively intrinsic. (58)

Did the screenwriters, perhaps mistaking them for more cetology, skip over as well all those passages in which Melville with great care and brilliant prose delineates Ishmael's growing disillusionment with Ahab's vendetta? That astonishing scene, for example ("A Squeeze of the Hand," Chapter 94), in which Ishmael joins his shipmates in the task of squeezing the lumps out of a large tub full of whale sperm:

as I bathed my hands among those soft, gentle globules of infiltrated tissues, woven almost within the hour; as they richly broke to my fingers, and discharged all their opulence, like fully ripe grapes their wine; as I snuffed up that uncontaminated aroma, – literally and truly, like the smell of spring violets; I declare to you, that for the time I lived as in a musky meadow; I forgot all about our horrible oath; in that inexpressible sperm, I washed my hands and my heart of it. (322)

Were they not even tempted to include it, at least for its visual potential if not for what it tells us about *The Pequod*'s sole survivor? That amazing flashback in "A Bower in the Arsacides" (Chapter 102), in which Ishmael recalls his epiphanic visit years ago to the enormous skeleton of a whale hauled ashore and left to rot, overgrown with jungle vegetation on a South Sea island in which he finds the imaginative means to see beyond "the material factory" of nature and transcend the fear of death, would have made for visually astonishing cinema while giving us an unforgettable entrance into the mind of Ishmael. And that moment, just before the final, lethal, chase of Moby Dick ("The Symphony," Chapter 132) when Ishmael imaginatively marries, as prelude to his own survival, the "firmaments of air and sea," "the gentle thoughts of the feminine air," and "the strong, troubled, murderous thinkings of the masculine sea":

But though thus contrasting within, the contrast was only in shades and shadows without; those two seemed one; it was only the sex, as it were, that distinguished them.

Aloft, like a royal czar and king, the sun seemed giving this gentle air to this bold and rolling sea; even as bride to groom. And at the girdling line of the horizon, a soft and tremulous motion – most seen here at the Equator – denoted the fond, throbbing trust, the loving alarms, with which the poor bride gave her bosom away. (404)

How could they not have included that as well?

It must be faithful to Moby-Dick's *metaphoric structure.* As any careful reader of the novel knows, the novel is an intricate weave of fact and imagination. It begins with a chapter called "Loomings"; when Pip is thrown overboard and plunges to the bottom of the sea he sees "God's foot upon the treadle of the loom, and spoke it; and therefore his shipmates called him mad." The word "loom" appears no fewer than forty times in the book. And when, as we have just seen, Ishmael recalls his transcendent moment in the presence of that whale skeleton in "A Bower in the Arsacides," only a weaving metaphor will do:

Now, amid the green, life-restless loom of that Arsacidean wood, the great, white, worshipped skeleton lay lounging – a gigantic idler! Yet, as the ever-woven verdant warp and woof intermixed and hummed around him, the mighty idler seemed the cunning weaver; himself all woven over with the vines; every month assuming greener, fresher verdure; but himself a skeleton. Life folded Death; Death trellised Life; the grim god wived with youthful Life, and begat him curly-headed glories.

Moby-Dick is a book, a poem really, with a 500-plus-page controlling metaphor. The films made from it are prosaic, literalist glosses.

Moby-Dick has not fared well at the movies. In hindsight, one of its adaptors, John Huston, would write, "Looking back now, I wonder if it is possible to do justice to *Moby-Dick* on film."[19] Moby Dick, it seems, could not be killed; but we should not so readily conclude that *Moby-Dick* cannot be adapted by some future imaginative writer/director with a more expansive conception of film's possibilities, who has actually understood the book, and is ready to proclaim "Call me Ishmael."

NOTES

1. Roland Barthes, *The Pleasure of the Text*, trans. Richard Miller (New York: Hill and Wang, 1975), pp. 10–11; italics in original.
2. I should note that I have not been able to screen either of these early versions of *Moby-Dick* and am indebted to Cahir's and Tibbetts's account of the films for my comments here. Their bad-faith distortions make them mainly of historical interest anyway.
3. Charles Feidelson, quoted in Brandon French, "Lost at Sea," in Gerald Peary and Roger Shatzkin, eds., *The Classic American Novel and the Movies* (New York: Ungar, 1977), p. 54. Further quotations from French will be cited parenthetically in the text.
4. Arthur Knight, "The Director," *Saturday Review*, June 9, 1956, p. 29.
5. As Scott Hammen observes, responding to the wishful thinking of those critics of Peck's performance that Huston had made *Moby Dick* a family affair, "if Huston had shot *Moby Dick* before his father's death [1950], he would have done it at a time when he was under strict studio supervision and not a freewheeling international celebrity, able to marshal the resources of many nations to his personal ends" (Hammen, *John Huston* [New York: Twayne, 1985], pp. 77–78).
   Peck's performance was often singled out by critics as the film's weakest link, and the influential *auteurist* critic Andrew Sarris would suggest that Huston himself should have played the part, with Orson Welles, who has a small but significant role in the film as Father Mapple, directing (cited by Thomas Atkins, "An Interview with Ray Bradbury," in Gerald Peary and Roger Shatzkin, eds. *The Classic American Novel and the Movies* (New York: Ungar, 1977), p. 3. Further quotations from Atkins will be cited parenthetically in the text.
6. Bradbury and Huston would later battle over Huston's request for a screen-writing credit, Bradbury insisting that the director contributed nothing. The Screen Writers Guild found on behalf of Huston.
7. Herman Melville, *Moby-Dick*, ed. Hershel Parker and Harrison Hayford, 2nd edn, Norton Critical Edition (New York: W. W. Norton, 2002), p. 108. Further quotations will be cited parenthetically in the text.
8. Although French may well be right about the wording in the script, which she had evidently examined first hand, I see no evidence whatsoever in the film itself that Moby Dick has been killed.
9. "I ran half way across London to Huston's hotel and I threw the script [with the new ending] at him. I said, 'There. I think that's it.' And he read it and said, 'Jesus Christ, Ray! This is it. This is the way we'll shoot the ending'" (Atkins, "An Interview," p. 46).

10. Linda Costanzo Cahir and John C. Tibbetts, "*Moby-Dick* (1851)," in John C. Tibbetts and James M. Welsh., eds., *Novels into Film: The Encyclopedia of Movies Adapted from Books* (New York: Checkmark Books, 1999), p. 154.
11. Knight, "The Director," p. 29.
12. As French observes, "whether Moby Dick is good or evil is not clear in the film any more than it is in the novel. The difference is that this ambiguity is largely ignored as unimportant in the movie, whereas it is the central focus of the novel" ("Lost at Sea," p. 54).
13. The book suggests that Ahab is in his late fifties, as was Stewart (born 1940) at the time of filming. Peck (1917–2003) was only forty when he played the role for Huston.
14. John Huston, *An Open Book* (Boston: Knopf, 1980), p. 258.
15. "'Thar She Blows!': The Making of *Moby Dick*," written and produced by Russ Patrick, *Moby Dick* DVD, Hallmark Home Entertainment, 1998.
16. The 1956 version, as mentioned above, was of course able to make use of actual whaling footage, while the 1998 *Moby Dick* had to rely solely on special effects.
17. "I have written a wicked book, and feel spotless as the lamb," Melville wrote to Nathamel Hawthorne on November 17, 1851 (Melville, *Moby-Dick*, p. 545).
18. "This is the book's motto (the secret one), – Ego non baptiso te in nominee – but make out the rest yourself," letter to Hawthorne, June 29, 1851 (ibid., p. 542).
19. Huston, *An Open Book*, p. 251.

Marcia L. Pentz-Harris, Linda Seger, and R. Barton Palmer

"The best books live by the appeal they make to the heart, even more than by the appeal they make to reason . . . [T]hey trouble the waters of sympathy within us, and keep them from stagnation."
– W. J. Dawson, *The Making of Manhood* (1890)

Just such an appeal to the heart has made former Union General Lew Wallace's novel *Ben-Hur* a literary, stage, and film phenomenon for more than 120 years. In fact, as the historian Victor Davis Hanson observes, this was a book like no other previously published in America:

Wallace's novel began the strange nexus in American life, for good or ill, between literature, motion pictures, advertising, and popular culture. The novel led to the stage and then to the movies, but in the process it spun out entire ancillary industries of songs, skits, ads, clothes, and fan clubs, ensuring that within fifty years of its publication, nearly every American had heard the word "Ben-Hur" without necessarily ever reading the book.[1]

When published in 1880, however, and long before it became a cultural phenomenon, *Ben-Hur* astounded and inspired readers with its pious affect. For many, it was probably the first and only novel they ever perused; such readers in fact considered it less an entertaining fiction and more a devotional text with which they could, and did, connect in a spiritually uplifting fashion.

Wallace's novel superficially resembles other nineteenth-century historical novels that take as their subject Roman culture of the early empire and the beginning of Christianity, the most famous of which are Henryk Sienkiewicz's later *Quo Vadis?* (1896) and Edward Bulwer-Lytton's earlier *The Last Days of Pompeii* (1832). But *Ben-Hur* differs from them in its deep engagement with the conventional elements of Christian pietistic or "sentimental" fiction. The book's narrative melded two different forms – the historical adventure (derived from Sir Walter Scott, whose influence on Wallace (1827–1905) is apparent in all his fiction, including the less famous *The Fair God* [1873] and *The Prince of India* [1893]) and the sentimental novel, the feminine form *par excellence* of the era. With this generic restructuring, Wallace established a tradition that lasted well into the next century, inspiring such notable bestsellers as Thomas B. Costain's *The Silver Chalice* (1952) and Lloyd C. Douglas's *The Robe* (1942).

In fact, *The Robe*, which itself enjoyed phenomenal sales of more than six million copies, depends heavily on Wallace's novel; the main character is a Roman soldier named Marcellus who comes into possession of Christ's robe after the Crucifixion and subsequently follows in the path of Wallace's Ben-Hur, seeking out a deepening knowledge of Jesus that eventually leads to his dramatic conversion from worldliness to spirituality. Douglas was one of the most popular novelists of the first half of the twentieth century. An ordained minister turned professional writer, he was deeply influenced by Wallace's fictional methods and spiritual themes. Perhaps his best-known book is *Magnificent Obsession* (1929), an updated version of the nineteenth-century sentimental novel that features the same kind of "manly" conversion as *Ben-Hur* (it was turned twice into successful Hollywood films, by John Stahl in 1935 and Douglas Sirk in 1954). Douglas's other well-known work, *The Big Fisherman* (1948), is a prequel to *The Robe* that turns Peter, the "rock" of the apostles, into a flawed, masculine figure who, once again in the manner of Ben-Hur, searches successfully for the full spiritual meaning of his experience with Jesus. Through Costain, Douglas, and other writers of religious historical novels, Wallace exerted a profound influence on the course of middlebrow fiction in the twentieth century.

Immense as well was the power that these novels brought to bear on the Hollywood film industry, especially during the 1950s when, in the phrase of one observer of the religious scene, America was experiencing a "surge of piety," with a renewed emphasis on those matters of individual conscience and faith that are so central in *Ben-Hur*.[2] In addition to William Wyler's remake of *Ben-Hur* (1959), *Quo Vadis?* (Mervyn LeRoy, 1951), *The Robe* (Henry Koster, 1953), *The Silver Chalice* (Victor Saville, 1954), and *The Big Fisherman* (Frank Borzage, 1959) were all transformed into successful Hollywood productions during the period, with Douglas's epic proving so popular that an original screenplay sequel, *Demetrius and the Gladiators* (Delmer Daves, 1954), was made and released, with excellent box-office returns. Of course, this was an era that, for a variety of institutional and cultural reasons, proved receptive to extravagant religious superproductions (including remakes of two of the late silent era's most profitable epics of this kind, *The Ten Commandments* [Cecil B. de Mille, 1923, 1958] and *King of Kings* [Cecil B. de Mille, 1927; Nicholas Ray, 1961]).

But Wallace's novel and Wyler's acclaimed film version must be counted as essential, formative influences on both the literary and cinematic flourishing of the hybrid genre that the former Union general almost single-handedly popularized. Even ostensibly secular entrants in the series (such as Stanley Kubrick's *Spartacus* [1960] based on the novel by Howard Fast, whose message is political rather than religious) demonstrate indebtedness to Wallace's imagining of his hero's martial adventures as simultaneously a journey of spiritual progress. And the at least indirect influence of Wallace on the Hollywood classical epic continues. The late-century revival of the sword-and-sandal genre (including such films as the 2004 releases *Troy* [Wolfgang Petersen] and *Alexander* [Oliver Stone]) owes much to Ridley Scott's highly profitable and much-acclaimed *Gladiator* (2000), which, if a remake in some sense of the earlier *The Fall of the Roman Empire* (Anthony Mann, 1964), also betrays, with its foregrounding of the masculine struggle between the hero and an evil-minded Roman former friend, now deadly rival, who destroys his family, a deep connection with *Ben-Hur*, whose hero, we might remember, also makes a name for himself as a gladiator.

Phenomenally popular in the expanding market for popular fiction of the era, *Ben-Hur* sold in the millions within a few years, making bestseller lists well into the twentieth century. Even in the early part of the twenty-first century, it continues to be in print. In fact, its closest competitor in overall sales for several decades was *Uncle Tom's Cabin* (both books were eventually surpassed by Margaret Mitchell's *Gone With the Wind*), yet even Harriet Beecher Stowe's sensationally popular novel cannot match the million-copy order placed by Sears for the first inexpensive edition of *Ben-Hur* some thirty years after initial publication.[3] Besides *Uncle Tom's Cabin*, among American novels only Owen Wister's *The Virginian* (1902), because it furthered the establishment of the western genre, can be said to have exerted so much influence on middlebrow and popular culture as did *Ben-Hur*.[4] The book's popularity was immediate and soon widespread. The public could not get enough of Wallace's exciting and edifying tale, and not long after it appeared in print, local amateur acting groups were "enacting" the story, producing their own, unauthorized performance versions. After his novel had enjoyed twenty years of steadily increasing sales, Wallace, collaborating with William Young, adapted it for the stage. Debuting on Broadway and enjoying an impressive run there and then around the country for two decades, the play brought Wallace's themes and characters to an estimated 20 million people nationwide, as well as many millions more reached by traveling companies in countries as far off as Australia.[5]

Eventually, *Ben-Hur* conquered its third medium, with screen adaptations released in 1907, 1926, and 1959, the latter two of which were prestige productions tailored for eras in which the Hollywood epic film enjoyed widespread popularity. These grandly produced adaptations had millions of filmgoers of two different eras cheering Ben-Hur in the chariot race, in what has become the best-known action sequence in film history. At present, 126 years after its publication, the public appetite for Wallace's tale has evidently not waned, as is proved by the recent successful television broadcast of a cartoon version (William Kowalchuk, 2002) in which Charlton Heston reprises, if only vocally, his performance of nearly fifty years earlier as the title character. Rather than Fred Niblo's 1926 version, which was astoundingly popular in its day, it is the 1959 William Wyler film, starring a muscular, ruggedly handsome, and charismatic Heston, that now dominates our current cultural memory of Wallace's delicately balanced tale of religion and adventure.

When we think of *Ben-Hur*, we tend to think of one thing: the race. Lew Wallace, the playwright William Young, and movie directors Niblo and Wyler with each of their adrenaline-pumping renditions, indelibly etched the image of Ben-Hur's chariot race on the American consciousness. The novel's first readers wrote to Wallace to praise the race episode, which they found so compelling that they were kept reading long into the night. For decades, no Sunday school recitation was complete without a stirring rendition of the passage recounting Ben-Hur's triumph over his enemy in the grueling and dangerous contest. Both stage and screen adaptations plumbed the race and the novel for all the spectacle they could provide – including a treadmill-bound, live horse race for the stage version, and, for the films, huge elaborate sets that dominated the performers, human and animal alike.[6]

Wallace's sprawling Christian epic reflects influence from a myriad of late nineteenth-century cultural forms: not only the dominant literary traditions of historical romance and sentimental fiction, but also toga melodramas, lavishly illustrated bibles, illustrated magazine articles, travel diaries about the Holy Land, and the anecdotal style of preaching then in fashion. Each of these informs the context and content of this expansive novel, which connected to so many discrete theological and intellectual currents. *Ben-Hur* succeeded in its own time largely because Wallace combined the socially acceptable elements of cross-denominational evangelical writing (including history, memoir, and doctrinal speculation) with the exciting adventure of historical romance and the emotionally charged dramatic encounters of sentimental fiction.[7] When first published, his romantically pious narrative spoke not only to secular "dime novel" readers and the admirers of Sir Walter Scott (perhaps the era's most popular writer of historical fiction), but also to the deeply religious women and men, young and old alike, many of whom would hardly have thought of themselves as novel readers at all.

A tale of two main characters

Wallace's novel begins with a familiar scene oddly forgotten by most readers: a lengthy introduction to the three wise men and their arrival at the birth of Jesus. The figure of Jesus, whose own story is so well known to Wallace's readers, shadows the main events of Wallace's plot. The central action begins when Ben-Hur, a fatherless Jew of royal blood, reunites after several years of separation with his boyhood friend Messala, now a Roman soldier. The meeting goes poorly because Ben-Hur now realizes that Messala's loyalty to the Roman regime sets them at odds. Their conflict accounts for Ben-Hur's resulting crisis of manhood as he realizes from Messala's new conviction that he, too, must choose a path to follow; and, most important for the plot, their conflict leads to Messala's betrayal of Ben-Hur to the authorities after his accidental dislodging of a rooftop tile that, falling to the street below, nearly kills the new Procurator of Judea, Valerius Gratus, who, as mischance would have it, happens to be passing by. The authorities, not surprisingly in a province filled with rebels and the disgruntled, believe it was no accident, and the wrath of Rome descends upon the Hur family.

Messala refuses to intervene to save his childhood friend, and, after his family is sent to prison, Ben-Hur is led off in chains to serve a long sentence as a Roman galley slave, meeting Jesus on the road before his confinement begins. The hero is toughened by the three years he passes as a galley slave and oarsman in the flagship of the Roman fleet, where he draws the eye of the Roman tribune, Quintus Arrius. In a battle against pirates, Ben-Hur saves Quintus Arrius from drowning after their ship is sunk and prevents the patrician from committing suicide when he believes, incorrectly as it turns out, that his fleet has been defeated. Victorious, Quintus Arrius adopts Ben-Hur in gratitude, releasing him from bondage and introducing him to the life of the rich and powerful in Rome. Having found a new father and a new world in which his virtues (strength, courage, intelligence, and good looks) are duly appreciated, Ben-Hur prospers.

Although he is wealthy and educated, Ben-Hur finds himself orphaned and set adrift, culturally speaking, when his benefactor dies. He heads back to Jerusalem, there to search for his mother and sister Tirzah, who are missing. Stopping over in Antioch, he overhears a conversation that leads him to meet Simonides – his dead (biological) father's slave, who has secretly kept the family riches out of Roman hands. Simonides has a dutiful daughter named Esther. Having proved himself worthy, Ben-Hur receives the family riches from Simonides, and this makes him one of the wealthiest men in the world. Ben-Hur's mission to find his mother and sister is interrupted when he once again encounters Messala, on whom he wishes to revenge himself. Learning that his former friend will compete in the chariot race in Antioch, Ben-Hur positions himself to be chosen as the driver of Sheik Ilderim's famous team and thus enters the race. During the preparation for the race, Ben-Hur is befriended by Sheik Ilderim, by the aging wise man, Balthasar, and by his comely daughter, Iras.

The chariot race is a vital event in the narrative, yet it comes only halfway through the novel. While an exciting episode, it is neither Wallace's focus nor the climax of his story. Ben-Hur wins the race and bankrupts Messala, who is also crippled when his chariot crashes. The humbled Roman is now an enemy for life. The race won and vengeance achieved, Wallace turns to the second and more spiritually powerful – if less memorable because of the lack of compelling action – half of his narrative. The pace slows, despite subplots of political intrigue, including assassination attempts and an incipient rebellion against the Roman occupiers, as the situation in Palestine becomes more troubled. While Ben-Hur begins to find the lovely Iras attractive, if dangerous, the emotional center of this part of the novel is not their romantic liaison, but Ben-Hur's increasing fascination with and vision of the messianic king whom Balthasar had described to him.

Jesus and Ben-Hur meet again, and Ben-Hur starts to question what role this new king might play, even as his own political sense of duty grows. After Pontius Pilate arrives in Jerusalem, Ben-Hur's mother and sister, having spent ten years walled up in a prison cell, reenter the tale as outcast lepers. Iras rejects Ben-Hur for Messala, and finally Esther overcomes her shyness enough to catch Ben-Hur's eye with her purity and simplicity. Building to the climax, the novel focuses on the latter days of Jesus's life. Ben-Hur spends three years as his peripheral disciple and bodyguard and witnesses Jesus healing his mother and sister as he makes his way to Jerusalem. Yet despite this demonstration of healing power, Ben-Hur's faith wavers. Nearly until the moment of the crucifixion, Ben-Hur longs for a worldly savior to save his people from Roman oppression. However, the crucifixion that Wallace describes as the "stupendous"[8] climax of the novel finally ends Ben-Hur's doubt and begins his "faith and love and clear understanding of the role of Jesus in the new spiritual order."[9] The novel ends on an infamously melodramatic note. Five years after the crucifixion, Ben-Hur and Esther, now equal in piety, have married, have two small children, and have established a home in Italy "by Misenum" where "everything in the apartment was Roman" (485). Into this last domestic scene comes a dissipated Iras, who visits to reveal that she has murdered Messala. This mission accomplished, she discreetly kills herself. In the novel's final scene, Ben-Hur determines to spend his vast wealth to help the emergent Christian church face the expected persecution by the Romans.

A muscular and sentimental hero

Despite an encyclopedic profusion of detail (which often slows the pace of the narrative) and the patently contrived melodramatic denouement, rarely, if ever, has a novel aroused such passion in the American public. Contemporary reviewers, however, were hardly unanimous in their praise. H. E. Scudder, in an oft-quoted early review of the novel for *Atlantic Monthly,* points out "the imminent danger which the book is always in of dropping into the habits of the dime novel," but concedes that the novel has "irregular power" as well as "merits by no means inconsiderable."[10] A *New York Times* reviewer was much more positive, calling *Ben-Hur* "startlingly new" and observing that the novel "[has] a rare and delicate appreciation of the majesty of the subject with which it presumes to deal" – meaning Jesus.[11] By the mid-twentieth century, Stewart Holbrook, writing for a *New York Times* series on "past best-sellers," quotes the critic Carl Van Doren saying that "*Ben-Hur* positively won the ultimate victory over village opposition. It was read by thousands who had read no other novel except perhaps *Uncle Tom's Cabin,* and they hardly thought of either book as a novel."[12]

Indeed, *Ben-Hur*'s overt appeal to "sympathy" and "quickened emotions" added to, rather than detracted from, its pietistic and doctrinal focus, helping to make it an enduring American literary icon. Unfortunately, *Ben-Hur*'s sentimental aspects, and the very popularity they garnered, also led to the novel's later critical dismissal and its subsequent absence from the American literary canon. Many believed, and with good reason, that *Ben-Hur* enlists the same sentimental tradition, "halfway between sermon and social theory" for which, as Jane Tompkins has argued, critics in the late nineteenth century and since have excoriated popular American women novelists.[13] Wallace wanted his story to attain "popularity" (*Autobiography,* 933), and thus he chose the dubious but lucrative path of the "scribbling" women and the genre they had made their own, the sentimental novel.

With no little paradox, Wallace uses literary tools supplied by the sentimental tradition to offer a manly Jesus. Such a portrait of the Savior is in direct opposition to the extremely feminized visions of Jesus that dominated the popular evangelical fiction of the period. Instead, Wallace makes use of emotional and narrative male pulpit oratory styles from the mid- to late nineteenth century that according to the historian David

Reynolds connect fully with the "masculine world of action."[14] With his use of sentimental tropes, Wallace advances an agenda that is consistently masculine as it works to break down the cultural opposition between manliness and godliness that Stowe and like-minded authors had so successfully established. Indeed, the overwhelming popularity of *Ben-Hur* in novel, stage, and film forms can be explained at least in part by Wallace's merging of what Ann Douglas discusses as male and female gendered qualities of historical romance and sentimentalism respectively. However, Wallace eschews completely the "tone of apology" and "attitude of humility" that Douglas claims for male secular sentimentalists.[15] Instead, Wallace uses both his own strong sense of purpose, and the intrinsic power of the framing religious narrative, to craft a powerful combination of adventure and piety.

During the latter half of the nineteenth century, more than thirty percent of Americans claimed some form of evangelical Christianity as their church affiliation, and there is no doubt that the evangelical community saw this novel as important to what Candy Gunther Brown argues they viewed as their proselytizing mission.[16] And there is also no doubt that Wallace understood his audience. In his *Autobiography* he recognized "the importance to a writer of first discerning a body of readers possible of capture and then addressing himself to their tastes [which] was a matter of instinct with me" (63). And that audience, as Wallace goes on to explain, "would not tolerate a novel with Jesus Christ its hero" (933). Thus Jesus is not a main character, at least in any traditional sense, but instead a dominating figure developed indirectly through his encounters with and effect on others, specifically Ben-Hur.

In order to combine the two fictional and ideological traditions, Wallace conflates Jesus with Ben-Hur, providing a hypermasculine rather than feminine conduit to Jesus. Specifically, he suggests that a manly savior can be worthy of the adoration of a strong man, who need fear neither indecision nor submission to an equally strong male figure. The text transforms Jesus into someone with whom Ben-Hur, who is the clear hero of the romantic portion of this tale, can plausibly and satisfyingly enact the emotional submission that was an essential element of sentimental narratives. Ben-Hur's final conversion, and possibly the reader's, takes place via a powerfully sentimental moment. Wallace's showcasing of male sentimental submission is central to understanding the novel's complex appeal. His imaginative, detailed rendering of Palestine and the time period locates his novel at the center of an evangelical textual milieu that not only allowed a flourishing of evangelical publishing, but, Brown argues, also encouraged a sacred reading of secular texts.[17] At the same time, Wallace's male-centered sentimentalism helps to pave the way for later Social Gospel articulations of Jesus as representative of what the historian Susan Curtis terms the "masculine ideal" of Christ as literal "peer" to those enraptured by his message.[18] Wallace, a man of action in both war and business, wrote for the emerging group of nineteenth-century Christian men who wanted and needed a "personal" Jesus. Their Jesus needed to act, or at least seem to act, like a man's man, not the feminized, weepy figure who was associated with Sunday school fiction and tract society pamphlets.[19]

Making Christ manly

Increasingly in the nineteenth century, becoming a man was conflated with becoming a Christian, so Wallace pitches his novel to a manly Christian audience. Making his main character a Jew of the royal line, Wallace elides the Old Testament hero, a noble and sophisticated Jew who is also connected to classical culture by his dominating physicality, his worldliness, and his political aspirations, with the New Testament Jesus. Such a move clearly resonated with the attempt of readers, living in an industrializing, urbanizing, and secularizing America, to come to grips with a meek Savior who is nevertheless appointed as their "leader." Conflating Ben-Hur with Jesus helps Wallace to imagine a Jesus who is no stranger to the sentimental (with his humility, womanly sad eyes, and ready tears) even as he is paired with the ultimate figure of manhood, the brave, aggressive, savvy, and successful Ben-Hur. Millions of readers raised on dime-novel and middlebrow fiction found in Ben-Hur the man who could bring them to Jesus.

Wallace was part of a strong trend in American religious life. In 1876 Nelson Sizer argued in *Choice of Pursuits* that "The most eminent men have bodies as well as brains . . . 'MUSCULAR CHRISTIANITY' . . . has a hundred times more philosophy in it than most men believe . . . Men who have broad shoulders and deep chests are the ones who lead . . . They have the throbbing heart, bounding pulse, and earnest energy that drives home their utterances."[20] But it is Ben-Hur, not Jesus, who has all the characteristics that Sizer argues a leader, especially a religious leader, should possess. Because in the world of the novel Jesus and Ben-Hur are both "just" men, Wallace can use their temporary equality to elide his characters in order to make Jesus appear more manly.

Not every critic saw this move as either wise or effective. For example, Irving McKee, one of Wallace's biographers, terms the "juxtaposition of Ben-Hur with the great Martyr . . . [a] palpably inappropriate paradox."[21] Far from "inappropriate," however, Wallace's linking of Jesus and the hero Ben-Hur has been indispensable to the novel's popularity.

Wallace explains that he felt "required to keep Him before the reader, [without] sermonizing . . . [H]e should be always coming" (*Autobiography*, 933). He accomplishes this balancing act by placing Ben-Hur's *quest* for Jesus, rather than Jesus himself, before the reader. Simple structural parallels have both Ben-Hur and Jesus raise "armies" of followers; both are identified as "riders" into Jerusalem; and the followers of each speak of them as the salvation of their people or the worldly answer to a host of problems. Finally, both are "abandoned" by fathers they will see – only thanks to the world-redeeming sacrifice of the one – in death.

The language that Wallace uses for both their stories also serves to conflate the two characters. Consider the ambiguity in this passage, which describes the experiences of Jesus and Ben-Hur in the Garden of Gethsemane, as the Roman soldiers, guided by Judas, come to make an arrest. The narrator of Wallace's novel comments, "A man may not always tell what he will do until the trial is upon him" (461). Both characters are present, but, given the context, the expectation is that the "trial" in question is the arrest and betrayal of Jesus. However, the next line effects a startling reversal, revealing that it is Ben-Hur's spiritual trial on which the narrator comments and the narrative will focus. Similarly, Wallace writes, "Ben-Hur had [not] publicly assumed ownership of the property [his father's house]. In his opinion, the hour for that was not yet come. Neither had he yet taken his proper name" (417). The prophetic tone of this description highlights the similarities between the two characters. Jesus, of course, also expects to claim his father's house, waits for "the hour that was not yet come," and has not yet assumed his proper name.

The most telling conflation of Jesus with Ben-Hur occurs in the mother's revelatory dream, which she discusses with her daughter. Tirzah says, "I do so want to live for you and my brother . . . I wonder where he is?" Her mother responds, "I dreamed about him last night, and saw him plainly . . . just before the Gate Beautiful" (354). However, the figure she sees is not her son, but the Son. In this way, she conflates the two sons – and two saviors – of the novel, modeling what Wallace wants his reader to do. The association with Ben-Hur confers on Jesus a manly strength that explains Ben-Hur's ultimate submission to God's will.

Manly sentimental power

Most critics refer to Wallace's sentimentalism purely in terms of the novel's Victorian "domestic" denouement and the feminized language in which the novelist sometimes describes Jesus. But Wallace puts sentimental power to work for the novel's masculine agenda in three important ways. First, he changes the range of emotions involved in order to admit those considered more masculine; second, he casts the requisite sentimental subordination of self to other within a male hierarchy whose only "other" is Jesus; and third, he figures Jesus's own submission as a show of strength rather than weakness.

God and exciting adventure make a strongly attractive combination. Wallace certainly understood the power of emotion, but rather than the affective force of tears, he emphasizes more "manly" feelings. Instead of scenes that emphasize sacrifice and surrender to tears, Wallace uses the adrenaline-charged excitement of chariot races in a packed coliseum as well as the dangers and narrow escapes of a battle at sea to connect more deeply with male readers. Just as weeping characters famously elicit sympathy from Stowe's readers, so, too, events that feature danger and adventure evoke a similar sympathetic response from Wallace's audience.

Wallace teaches his readers to feel correctly, that is, to convert the rush of adrenaline – even that produced by a sense of horror – into a *sympathy* that leads to deeper piety and hence to a more profound and personal sense of faith. When Balthasar the wise man first mentions Jesus, Ben-Hur's response is visceral rather than intellectual: his "imagination was heated, his feelings aroused, his will all unsettled" (246). These are the same manly emotions that he had experienced in his conflict with Messala and during the battle at sea, and Wallace suggests that it is the strength of his adrenaline-stoked feelings that sets Ben-Hur on the path to belief.

Wallace adopts the didacticism of sentimental fiction to instruct his readers not only how to feel correctly – to convert worldly to pietistic excitement – but also when to sympathize, with whom, and why. For example, when Ben-Hur's mother steps out of her prison cell suffering visibly and horribly from leprosy, rather than develop that scene with suspense, the narrator directs the reader to be "kind, tender of heart . . . [and so to] be melted with much sympathy"(351). Later in the novel, Wallace shows that he understands fully the emotional appeal of sentimental fiction, whose effect on readers he enthusiastically endorses: "The knowledge we gain from much sympathy with others passing through trials is but vaguely understood; strangely enough, it enables us, among other things, to merge our identity into theirs often so completely that their sorrows and their delights become our own" (440).

Such an identification with and sympathy for others – even fictional characters – is what achieves Wallace's successful conflation of Jesus and Ben-Hur for his sentimental ends. However, as the critic Glenn Hendler argues about the nature of sympathy, the very sympathetic "merging" that Wallace figures earlier becomes markedly more problematic with Jesus as the object of sympathy.[22] Indeed, at the end of the novel, sympathy leads Ben-Hur to a kind of confusion as he lapses into a stupor observing the events on Calvary: "Ben-Hur became anxious; he was not satisfied with himself" (463); he "cried out" (469); he doubts himself (470); "a confusion fell upon him" that is "helpless – wordless even"; and Ben-Hur walks "mechanically . . . in total unconsciousness" (472–473).

The final transcendent moment of feeling elicited by this sentimental connection of sympathy works because Wallace mediates the identification of his readers with Jesus. He depicts the crucifixion through the eyes of the character with whom readers have already formed a sympathetic bond: Ben-Hur. Any conflation of self with Jesus as character would be what Hendler calls a "paradoxically narcissistic . . . self-negat[ion]" that leads, so he argues, not to sympathetic action, but rather to dissolution.[23] So it is far better for the reader to feel confused with Ben-Hur, afterward identifying with his impulse toward conversion, rather than to feel at one with a fictional representation of God. Instead, the reader experiences first an exhilarating sympathy with Ben-Hur's worldly success, pity at the spiritual confusion the hero falls into, and then ecstasy at his eventual conversion. But in order to arouse properly masculine emotions, Wallace must make Jesus manly; and he must craft the sentimental submission of Ben-Hur to Jesus in a way that does not undermine the manliness of either character.

Wallace locates the sentimental power of Jesus's final moment in the dignity he displays, a self-possession that seems more stoic endurance than passive surrender. As the novelist was later to declare,: "To me the conduct of the sufferer in the very particular of which you speak is the most conclusive proof of His divine nature . . . by the meekness with which He endured and died" (*Autobiography*, 924). Initially the reader's access to the divine presence, Ben-Hur shifts during the crucifixion to the interpreter of Jesus's pain. Certainly, the reader is asked to sympathize with Jesus's agony, but perhaps sympathizes more intensely with Ben-Hur's *confusion* over the suffering man's apparent meekness. Because Jesus accepting his fate is depicted as stoic strength, Ben-Hur submits, that is, converts, even though submission is outside the bounds of "normative" nineteenth-century masculinity. If this strong man doubts and then sees Jesus's meekness as strength and submits, then so may the reader.

Earlier in the story, Ben-Hur is the "hero in the midst of stirring scenes" (466). But when Jesus cries out, "It is finished!" and the narrator comments, "So a hero, dying in the doing of a great deed" (482),

Wallace successfully sublimates the heroic status of Ben-Hur to the heroic status of Jesus. Yet even here Wallace will not admit a total subordination of Ben-Hur; he retains his worldly authority, and it is he who makes the final pronouncement that "the Nazarene is indeed the Son of God" (477). Although faced with a crisis that calls upon him to submit, Ben-Hur nevertheless succeeds in becoming a strong "Christian" in a sense that his readers would understand and approve.

Ben-Hur is an action-adventure novel that leads to a sentimental conversion, as Wallace attempts to refigure the life of Jesus so as to bring him to men even as men are brought to him. At the end of the novel, not only do Ben-Hur and his family convert to the new faith; Jesus is in a sense "converted" as well. The novel transforms him into a savior whom men can admire, love, and follow – and, most important, one to whom they can reasonably submit. If Jesus becomes manly through his association with Ben-Hur, the characters do remain distinct in the novel, with Ben-Hur's strength, courage, and physical dominance remaining qualities that the savior of mankind can acquire only indirectly. By the end of the century, however, the Social Gospel movement had begun to imagine a muscular and physically dominating Jesus who, striding across the Holy Land, "turns again and again on the snarling pack of His pious enemies and made them slink away."[24] A generation after *Ben-Hur* bursts onto the cultural scene to such widespread acclaim, Jesus in a sense *became* Ben-Hur, as American Christianity embraced a cult of the body, as well as an admiration for traditional masculine virtues, that might have struck St. Augustine or even Martin Luther as more than a little "pagan."

Ben-Hur, formed by the physical and mental trials of adventure, is never forced to abandon the masculine code that the circumstances of his birth and life have made his own. Given the changing nature of American life, increasingly masculinized by a variety of cultural forms (including the western, then emerging as a dominant fictional genre in opposition to the sentimental novel), it is hardly surprising that twentieth-century versions of *Ben-Hur* on stage and screen found the classical virtues of its rough-and-ready hero more interesting than his deeply spiritual conversion to submissive piety.

A religious epic becomes secular melodrama

Almost as quickly as Wallace's novel gained a foothold in the American imagination, there were those who wanted it on the stage. Wallace did not. However, not long after it was published, the novel was, in a sense, "performed" in public. Wallace criss-crossed the nation on book tours throughout the late 1880s and early 1890s, lecturing on and giving "at special request" dramatic readings of selected passages from *Ben-Hur*.[25] Other early semi-professional – and not quite legal – adaptations included such performances as "tableaus [*sic*] and readings from *Ben-Hur* . . . for the benefit of the Society for Aiding Self-Supporting Women,"[26] as well as a production sponsored by a Mrs. Ellen Knight Bradford that featured seventeen "actors" and twenty-one distinct (thirty-four total) tableaux.[27] Another version resorted to "visual aids" in order to create the right atmosphere. Just before the turn of the century, the Reverend Dr. Rogers gave multiple readings of scenes from the novel that were "illustrated by 145 richly colored lantern slides under the direction of Prof. B. P. Murray."[28] Not all versions of the story were approved by Wallace. In 1901 the novelist went to court for redress, "wishing to protect 'Ben-Hur' from the travesty and burlesque at the hands of Billy Cleveland and his 'Polite Minstrels.'"[29]

Some of the more interesting amateur (and unauthorized) stage versions of the novel continued to be performed even after the eventual Broadway adaptation opened. For example, Mrs. Gurley-Kane's scenes from *Ben-Hur* at the New Willard Theater in Washington, D. C. in 1912 helped to raise funds for victims of the *Titanic*.[30] She reprised this highly successful one-woman show many times; in it she impersonated "practically all of the characters in the story," from shepherds to Tirzah to Ben-Hur to Messala to Iras as well as *fourteen* other characters.[31] The two-hour production included songs from church choirs and musical accompaniment from the Marine Band. Under pressure from such unauthorized stage tableaux, Wallace composed his own (less than stellar) libretto for tableaux in 1891,[32] but ultimately he entered into negotiations with the theatrical firm of Marc Klaw and Abraham Erlanger. When Erlanger promised Wallace that he could stage *Ben-Hur* without depicting Jesus in person, Wallace assented.[33]

Treading the boards with horses and Jesus

As is the case with Stowe's *Uncle Tom's Cabin* and Wister's *The Virginian*, both of which were also adapted for the stage in productions that enjoyed years of popularity, the film versions of *Ben-Hur* owe much to Klaw and Erlanger's 1899 production, which excited the American imagination as intensely as the original novel. To say that the play was a success would be a wild understatement. The official stage version of *Ben-Hur* ran for more than nineteen years on Broadway and also in roadshows similar to the popular traveling stage versions of *Uncle Tom's Cabin*. In fact, the *Ben-Hur* "roadshow" version played for forty weeks each year for a decade and a half with a weekly average gross of $16,000. In addition, Klaw and Erlanger mounted a show for London's Drury Lane Theatre in 1902 and assembled another production company to tour Australia. Clearly a very special theatrical event, the stage version was part play, part circus, and all spectacle, routinely selling out the largest venues. While the elaborate and eye-popping stage effects were not particularly innovative, the sheer scope of the production, with its camels, horses, enormous mechanized and copyrighted treadmill, and moving panorama, not to mention hundreds of actors and extras, plus a reportedly "25,000 candlepower light" serving to depict Jesus, made it the first theatrical extravaganza overtly devoted to a religious theme.[34]

In each adaptation, either professional or amateur, the parties involved worked to preserve the religious piety of the text, even as they brought it to the worldlier medium of the stage. Critics hailed co-author Young for the "sincere and delicate appreciation of the danger of intrusion upon a sacred theme."[35] Robert and Katherine Morsbergers' biography of Wallace includes Wallace's comments on the Christian potential of the play. To Klaw and Erlanger, he writes that "you have now a subject which, properly outfitted, will last your lives, longer in fact than Uncle Tom, a stage interest to go hand in hand with Christianity."[36] In part, a concern for the novel's religious themes helped to shape its film adaptations. Yet the depiction of religious experience necessarily changed from one medium to the other. The melodramatic, adventure elements of *Ben-Hur* were simply more acceptable and presentable on stage than a focus on the internal struggle toward faith that was undoubtedly an essential part of what many readers found most attractive about the novel.

Staging Christian manliness

In Young's stage version the manliness of Jesus, who is not "played" by an actor, is naturally suppressed, while the crucifixion – and Ben-Hur's sentimental submission – are omitted. The sentimental tropes of melodrama were too deeply ingrained in stage culture as essentially feminine at this point, while male conflict, vengeance, and aggression were too much a staple of late nineteenth-century theatre to admit the submission of Ben-Hur on stage. With the play, and later with the films, the need for a commercially viable worldliness came to trump the novel's emphasis on piety.

With the exception of the prelude and epilogue, the staged "Tale of the Christ" only obliquely mentions the Messiah.[37] In the play Ben-Hur does not experience confused feelings at his first sight of Jesus. Instead, he is bitterly disappointed: "There will be no swords drawn. Here is no King. No! meek, with the meekness of a woman! . . . The face of one born not to rule, but to suffer and, I fear, to die" (VI:i, 278). While audiences would have understood Ben-Hur's statement in a religious context, what he says comes close to the blasphemy that Wallace and Young otherwise struggled to avoid. Young simply does not provide time enough to "heal" Ben-Hur of his skepticism about Jesus's status as a Messiah "whose kingdom is not of this earth." As a result, the play loses much of its original sentimental power and becomes more like a simple costume melodrama. While Ben-Hur's conversion is staged, it is drained of its spiritual and psychological force and becomes in fact a kind of miracle like the healing of the lepers, the scene in the play with which it is most closely connected.

Young sensationalizes and masculinizes *Ben-Hur* throughout. Male relationships become paramount, and they clearly partake of emerging muscular Christian emphases on male physicality and beauty. From the galley scenes to the chariot race to Iras's betrayal, men are in the foreground of the play. Certainly, Ben-Hur's important relationships are with men. To Simonides, he is "master," while to Quintus Arrius, Ilderim, and Balthasar he becomes "son." Young presents Ben-Hur in an even more muscular light than does Wallace, who hardly neglects his hero's impressive physicality. In the play the thrilling sea-battle scenes from the novel are augmented with sensational violence. Ben-Hur, rather than grabbing Quintus Arrius out of a savior-like instinct as the tribune starts to sink beneath the water (141–142), instead "breaks off an oar" and kills a pirate intent on murdering the tribune (II:i, 223). While Wallace sought to marry manliness and godliness, Young privileges manliness over godliness, establishing a precedent for succeeding adaptations.

For Young, and later Niblo and Wyler, the theme of submission is more political than spiritual and has little to do with the hero's acceptance of God's overlordship. Ben-Hur worries about his country's submission to Rome; Messala, in his eagerness not to appear to submit to Sanballat, wagers his fortune and sets himself up for ruin; Ilderim enters the chariot race in order to undercut his forced submission to Rome. In Young's version submission to other men is something that must be fought, literally to the death. Therefore Young asserts Ben-Hur's manliness, never showing him submitting to anyone, even to Jesus. In the final act the focus shifts not toward God, as Wallace would have it, but toward the very figures that Wallace depicts enslaved and immured in a stone wall for ten years: the women of Ben-Hur's family.

Initial tableaux renditions of the story mostly all ended with the healing of the lepers, a highly suitable scene for this kind of performance. The scene that dramatizes the healing of the lepers in the novel is powerful, but it does not compare with the sympathetic, sentimental climax of the crucifixion. Yet the emotional episode with Ben-Hur's mother and Tirzah became the finale of both stage and screen adaptations. No doubt, it is the novel's most feminine and sentimental moment, easily moving readers, playgoers, and filmgoers to tears. For nineteenth-century audiences, the return to domesticity figured by the healing of the mother and Tirzah, and the now-strong relationship between Esther and Ben-Hur, concluded the story in accord with feminine codes of the "sacrosanct." In other words, the play returns religion to the place where audiences expected it – into the domestic space presided over by women.

Opting for a different finale, Young misses the opportunity to deploy sentimental power, as Wallace understands it, and instead privileges female melodrama over masculine sensationalism. Healed of their terrible disease and invigorated with the new faith, Tirzah and her mother become strong Christian women who can guide and support Ben-Hur. Like the hero himself, moreover, Esther, his presumed bride, proves herself in a difficult adventure. Filled with love and concern, she makes a daring dash into the Vale of Hinnom, risking disease, exile, and death, in order to reunite the family of the man she loves. In the closing chapters of the novel, Esther displays a Ruth-like willingness to follow Ben-Hur wherever he leads, exhibiting a willingness to subordinate herself to her beloved in a manner that nineteenth-century audiences would immediately have recognized and approved. Ben-Hur finds not just mother and sister but, through them, God the Father. When he closes the play by exclaiming, "O day of gladness – thrice blessed – that giveth me mother, and sister and thee!" (VI:ii, 289), Ben-Hur looks at Esther, but the implication is also that he is speaking to God. His conversion is experienced through a sense of the reconstituted family. In fact, the Victorian family rather than God is resurrected in Young's final scene, which means that the hero is delivered to the power of the feminine. While Ben-Hur may rule the house, he is also surrounded by women who define his identity. While the hero's emerging faith drives the story, the faith of the women who love him provides the miracle that leads to his conversion. The play eliminates Ben-Hur's solitary spiritual awakening, which, in the novel, is experienced at the feet of Jesus, not in the bosom of his family.

From stage to reel – racing into movie history

Each of the film adaptations of *Ben-Hur*, the Kalem production in 1907 (consisting largely of tableaux based on the play), the feature-length

M-G-M versions of 1926 and 1959, and to a much lesser degree the recently released cartoon version, have followed Young's lead by making extensive changes to the story.[38] The Niblo and Wyler epics, like the play, emphasize the hero's manliness and the exciting adventures he is caught up by. In accordance with the Social Gospel movement, these films assume that men need to follow manly leaders. And, in both cases, Jesus is not presented as a manly leader, but is portrayed in that more feminized fashion that Wallace struggled so successfully to revise. Jesus, in fact, is almost absent from these two films. The play's producers, Klaw and Erlanger, used light to portray Jesus, while Niblo literalizes the "hand of God" metaphor rather ingeniously, showing only Jesus's hands throughout the movie. In the Wyler version only the hand or, in the crucifixion sequence, the back of Jesus is visible in the frame. Wallace's argument for a masculine relationship with a Jesus necessarily made manly by juxtaposition with a strong protagonist disappears. In the films the manliness, the strength, and the ascendancy of Jesus are never at issue. Rather than emphasize the sentimental submission of a worldly, masculine man to a God who is also acceptable in his manliness, the screen versions foreground Ben-Hur's pursuit of vengeance against Messala and, like the stage play, highlight the important role that women play in religion and family life. The films both expand the secular aspects of the story and provide an alpha male figure on whose story – and body – the viewer can focus. Niblo stresses the political oppression of Israel as well as Ben-Hur's thirst for vengeance against Rome. In the Wyler version these political themes (prominent in the novel as well) have disappeared, with the plot being recentered entirely around the conflict between Messala and Ben-Hur. All the films, including the 1907 one-reeler, privilege the secular, use some version of the popular healing scene as their climax, and expand the role of Esther in bringing Ben-Hur to Jesus.

M-G-M's first *Ben-Hur* – Niblo's 1926 extravaganza

Niblo's epic version of Wallace's novel starred two of the most popular male heartthrobs of the era, Ramon Navarro as Ben-Hur and Francis X. Bushman as Messala; such casting revealed the filmmakers' recognition that they were filming an essentially male "property." An immense undertaking, the film took four years to make, with shooting in both Italy and America requiring the service of tens of thousands of extras and the full talents of M-G-M's production designers. It was an immediate success with filmgoers and critics alike; the contemporary reviewer Mordaunt Hall, writing for the *New York Times*, hailed the film as "a stupendous spectacle" and "a masterpiece of style and patience" in which "the famous chariot races . . . depicted so thrillingly . . . evoked no little applause."[39] Although the movie cost almost $4 million to make (an immense budget that few productions of the era enjoyed), it more than repaid studio hopes for financial success, grossing an astounding $9 million on its initial release. With an added soundtrack that updated it for the "talking picture" era, the film was put into circulation again two years later, once again earning huge profits for the studio.[40]

Although the Niblo version secularizes Wallace's story, it is in many ways a fairly faithful adaptation. The scriptwriters relied primarily on the play for the structure of the narrative, but also included scenes from the novel that were either left out of the play (such as Jesus's actual ride into Jerusalem, his carrying the cross up Calvary, and the gathering of legions to fight for the coming king) or omitted in the 1959 version (particularly Ben-Hur's romance with Iras). The Niblo adaptation takes up the secular focus, but, more than the play and the screen remake, it pays attention to the religious context of Ben-Hur's tale.

The film offers a series of religious tableaux that evoke key moments in Christian history. Niblo depicts in detail the arrival of Mary into Bethlehem, demonstrating her holiness through reaction shots of those who assemble to honor her child. Well-known events from the life of Christ such as the crowd's stoning a prostitute and his arrival in Jerusalem find a place in the film. Niblo even stages the Last Supper in what was to become its best-known screen rendition. Because these scenes develop in more depth the events of Jesus's life, they build credibility for Ben-Hur's conversion, framing the worldly events with those of timeless religious import. Yet the center of the film is still the human world of conflict.

The film abounds with scenes of torture and spends much time on the sea battle (including a gruesome scene depicting how a Roman slave captured by pirates is used as a human battering ram). With subjective camera techniques and action close-ups, the viewer is dropped right into the chaos of the chariot race. The film, in fact, finds room for all kinds of spectacle. Nearly naked women trip across the screen as slaves and dancing girls, while Iras becomes a scantily clad double agent in Messala's employ who tries to ply Ben-Hur with aphrodisiacs. Although they did not escape the condemnation of religious authorities at the time, who were becoming appalled by what they saw as the growing immorality of Hollywood film, these details certainly establish the decadence of Roman culture, indicating, as Wallace himself observed, the need for the spiritual and ethical reformation that Jesus was to bring (*Autobiography*, 931).

To that same end, Niblo also emphasizes the martial aspects of Wallace's tale. The chariot race, while clearly personal and staged with manly posturing between Messala and Ben-Hur, also symbolizes the brewing clash between Roman and Jew, because all parties involved recognize the larger implications of Ben-Hur's win as they are immediately borne out with Balthasar's arrival after the race. After Ben-Hur's victory, Balthasar – absent from the movie entirely until that point – appears in order to announce the coming of the king. Ben-Hur immediately pledges to his loyalty this new ruler, offering him "money, lands and life itself," as he proclaims that he will "follow him unto death."[41] Although he is clearly elderly, Balthasar suggests that they "make haste" in the gathering of legions. And it is Balthasar – not Ben-Hur – who speaks to these assembled forces, claiming that Jesus has asked them to put away their swords and follow the path of peace.

Esther's role, moreover, is enhanced, and the power of the word of Jesus – of religion – again comes to rest with women. The servant woman, Amrah, convinces Esther that she has seen the Messiah and that he has performed miracles. So Esther seeks out Ben-Hur's mother and Tirzah in the valley of the lepers so that Jesus can heal them in Jerusalem. As in the stage version, in the film a simple and deep faith is to be found only in the female characters. Reunited with his family and in the presence of Jesus, Ben-Hur is strongly infused with faith, and that conversion is solidified by a miracle, as Jesus heals his mother and sister of their affliction. At the end, the word of Jesus is passed on and believed first by women, but Niblo returns to the spirit at least of Wallace's *Ben-Hur* when he gives Ben-Hur the movie's final comment. Embracing his mother and Tirzah, he assures them that Jesus is "not dead. He will live in the hearts of men forever."[42]

The Academy's darling – William Wyler's 1959 *Ben-Hur*

Wyler worked on the 1925 film as an assistant director, so he was an obvious choice to direct the remake that M-G-M hoped would be even more successful than the original adaptation. Starring Charlton Heston as Ben-Hur and Stephen Boyd as Messala, this project turned out, first, to be one of the most expensive adaptations in film history and, subsequently, one of the most popular and acclaimed. M-G-M's costs rose to $50 million, but, like its predecessor, the film turned a handsome profit, earning $80 million in its original run. In addition, *Ben-Hur* turned out to be one of the most prestigious productions of a studio famous for quality and cinematic artistry, being nominated for an amazing twelve Academy Awards and winning eleven, a feat unsurpassed until *Titanic* (1997) and *Lord of the Rings* (2001).

Although the film alters the story dramatically, Wyler and the screen-writers stay true to at least some of the central ideas of the novel. Significantly, Ben-Hur shares the focus not with Jesus but with Messala through most of the film; yet Wyler still manages to treat notions of manliness and submission in a manner of which Wallace would surely have approved. Neither Ben-Hur nor Messala will submit to the other, and thus Wyler dramatizes the novel's central ethic: submission of any kind violates male codes of behavior. The intensity of the conflict be-tween the two characters, and the righteous violence with which it is pursued (as the chariot race becomes something like hand-to-hand combat) underscores that fact. However, at the same time, Wyler's film is also more religious – if not more Christian – than the Niblo version. While the original screen *Ben-Hur* includes additional biblical scenes, Wyler dramatizes Ben-Hur's piety convincingly throughout the film. The hero is presented, in fact, as a good Jew long before he becomes a good Christian.

As part of that Old Testament piety, Ben-Hur prays for vengeance, but he also learns over the course of the movie to submit first to God and then to the women in his life. Like Wallace, Wyler makes Ben-Hur's submission merely a step toward further success. Ben-Hur gains the attention of Quintus Arrius through his unbowed submission to author-ity, and this leads to his being freed. It is this freedom that allows Ben-Hur to feel regret for, if not forgive, his former friend when Messala, dying, summons him to his side. Ben-Hur must submit as well to the painful request of his mother to stay away. By the end of the film, he has learned the virtue of self-abnegation and is able to obey the spirit of Jesus's command and put down his sword.

If Wyler captures the essence of Wallace's religiosity, he also, like Niblo, spectacularly foregrounds the secular. Rather than the wider political conflict between Judea and Rome, he emphasizes the deeply competitive and physical relationship between Ben-Hur and Messala that culminates in a raw display of their impressive masculine prowess – the chariot race. Wyler glamorizes the often nearly naked bodies of Heston and Boyd, displaying their muscularity whenever possible. The Niblo version eroticizes the female body in order to depict the moral dangers and decadence of Roman culture, but Wyler prefers shots of Heston's well-oiled massive torso, thick arms straining at the oar. An object of triumphant suffering and victorious endurance, Ben-Hur's body is a surrogate for the body of Jesus, who is masculinized by proxy when the physically imposing hero submits to his will. Yet Wyler's film implicitly assigns the physical another value. Esther falls in love with Ben-Hur at first sight before he is sent to the galleys, and she is waiting for him when he returns years later. Despite this intensity of feeling, their love never involves the spectacular physicality of Ben-Hur's scenes with Messala, thereby suggesting a movement away from the decadence of Rome, so marked by its preoccupation with the physical, to the spiritual decorum of a chaste and pure Christian connection.

Esther plays an expanded role in another sense. The plot, centered from the beginning on the rivalry between Ben-Hur and Messala reaches a point of stasis with the latter's death after the chariot race, which comes much earlier in the film than in the novel, closing out the essentially secular story of male rivalry and revenge. Thereafter, the narrative emphasizes the love of Ben-Hur and Esther, which eventually leads to the reuniting of his family and the melodramatic climax. Esther in a sense bridges the gap between the secular and the more overtly religious parts of Wyler's story. She is the one who locates the mother and sister and gives them food, all the time keeping the secret from Ben-Hur. What then follows are scenes that diverge completely from the novel, radically transforming Wallace's emphasis on the exclusively masculine nature of Ben-Hur's conversion. Esther, not Ben-Hur, listens to Jesus speak, and afterward she is the one who encourages Ben-Hur to follow "this young rabbi" and let go of his hatred toward the Romans.[43]

As in the Young and Niblo versions, the healing of the lepers finalizes Ben-Hur's conversion. Esther plays a prominent role in the events that lead up to this climactic moment. She is the one who takes the mother and sister to safety during the crucifixion of Jesus and remains by their side when they are healed. Wyler follows Niblo's lead and delays the healing, making it a parallel climactic moment with the crucifixion. Jesus touches the lepers to heal them in the earlier versions; Wyler's approach generates more suspense. Jesus is already on his way to Calvary as they approach, and they are turned away when the mob around them scatters, yelling "Unclean!" and "Lepers!" and throwing stones before Esther draws the pair away. During the violent thunderstorm that signals Jesus's death, the despairing women shelter in a cave. Their belief is so strong that they do not need his touch, only a literal version of the redemption bought by Christ's blood in which all will share. Tirzah and her mother are cleansed by the blood that, in the rain, flows from the cross in a stream past their cave. In another highly charged religious image, the blood and water seemingly flow out into the world in a gushing flood.

Briefly imaged in the film, Ben-Hur's conversion occurs at the foot of the cross, but the plot finds its climax only when he returns home to find his mother and sister now free of disease. In Wyler's version the brawny, charismatic Jewish prince who triumphs in a deadly chariot race over the most dangerous of rivals never submits to men or even to a feminized Jesus, but rather to the Christian women in his life. The relationship he finds with the Savior is mediated by his experience of a loving family and Esther, the strong-minded woman who will become his wife and who has already proven her value as a strong and resourceful helpmate. If the film considerably modifies Wallace's masculinist agenda, Wyler still re-affirms, in a form that the novelist would likely have approved, those conservative Christian values enshrined in the tradition of the sentimen-tal novel. After all, true to Wallace's masculine vision, Wyler's Ben-Hur finds himself not in abject submission to God, but filled with reverence for the strength he has discovered in Jesus. While not feminized, he is guided carefully toward the sentimental, experiencing profound grati-tude, in that transfiguring reunion with his mother and sister, for the forms of salvation, both physical and spiritual, that he and his loved ones have taken away from their encounter with the Redeemer.

Figure 7. The raw physicality of Judah Ben-Hur (Ramon Novarro) conquers the political power of the Roman ruling class, represented by the tribune Quintus Arrius (Frank Currier), in the 1925 M-G-M production of Lew Wallace's *Ben-Hur*.

Figure 8. The 1925 M-G-M version of *Ben-Hur* exemplifies Hollywood's growing interest in elaborate, authentic spectacle.

NOTES

1. Victor Davis Hanson, *Ripples of Battle: How Wars of the Past Still Determine How We Fight, How We Live, and How We Think* (New York: Doubleday, 2003), p. 142.

2. See A. Roy Eckhardt, *The Surge of Piety in America* (New York: Association Press, 1958), who observes of the postwar period that "piety has proliferated beyond the bounds of traditional institutional effort into many areas of American life" (p. 23).

3. "Hoyns 49 Years on Harper's Staff," *New York Times*, December 29, 1933, p. 19.

4. For an interesting argument about the nascent "western" characteristics of *Ben-Hur*, see Blake Allmendinger's *Ten Most Wanted: The New Western Literature* (New York and London: Routledge, 1998). Allmendinger argues that "[a]s a 'spiritual' western, Ben-Hur functions as a transitional text in the history of American Literature" (p. 121).

5. "£14,000 Fire in a Sydney Theatre," *New York Times*, March 24, 1902, p. 9.

6. Robert E. Morsberger and Katherine M. Morsberger, *Lew Wallace: Militant Romantic* (New York: McGraw-Hill Book Company, 1980), pp. 311, 459.

7. For further discussion of theological and intellectual currents and evangelical writing, see Candy Gunther Brown, *The Word in the World: Evangelical Writing, Publishing and Reading in America, 1789–1880* (Chapel Hill: University of North Carolina Press. 2004); Paul C. Gutjahr, *An American Bible: A History of the Good Book in the United States, 1777–1880* (Stanford, CA: Stanford University Press, 1999), p. 81; Gutjahr, "'To the Heart of Solid Puritans': Historicizing the Popularity of Ben-Hur," *Mosaic* 26 (1993), pp. 53–67; Lester I. Vogel, *To See a Promised Land: Americans and the Holy Land in the Nineteenth Century* (University Park, PA: Pennsylvania State University Press, 1993), pp. 1–13; David Mayer, *Playing Out the Empire: Ben Hur and Other Toga Plays and Films, 1883–1908, A Critical Anthology* (Oxford: Clarendon Press, 1994), p. 189.

8. Lew Wallace, *Lew Wallace: An Autobiography* (New York: Harper and Brothers Publishers, 1906), p. 931. Further quotations will be cited parenthetically in the text.

9. Lew Wallace, *Ben-Hur: A Tale of the Christ* (New Jersey: Barbour and Company, Inc., 1985), p. 475. Further quotations will be cited parenthetically in the text.

10. H. E. Scudder, "The Head of Medusa and other Novels," *Atlantic Monthly* 47 (1881), pp. 710–711.

11. "A Story of the East," *New York Times*, November 14, 1880, p.4.

12. Carl Van Doren, quoted in Stewart Holbrook, "General Wallace and *Ben Hur*," *New York Times Book Review*, August 6, 1944, p.7. For additional discussions of the novel's initial reception, see H. A. B., "Fiction and Social Science," *Century* 29 (1884), pp. 153–155; Irving Mckee, *"Ben-Hur" Wallace: The Life of General Lew Wallace* (Berkeley, CA: University of California Press, 1947), pp. 173–175; and Morsberger and Morsberger, *Militant Romantic*, pp. 309–312.

13. Jane Tompkins, *Sensational Designs: The Cultural Work of American Fiction, 1790–1860* (New York: Oxford University Press, 1985), pp. 126. As Tompkins famously asserts about another misunderstood Christian sentimental novel, *Uncle Tom's Cabin*, sentimental novels were dismissed by the "male-dominated scholarly tradition . . . in a struggle to supplant the tradition of

evangelical piety and moral commitment" (p. 123). Wallace's critical reception falls victim to this struggle.

14. David S. Reynolds, "From Doctrine to Pulpit: The Rise of Pulpit Storytelling" *American Quarterly* 32 (1980), p. 485. See also Reynolds, *Beneath the American Renaissance: The Subversive Imagination in the Age of Emerson and Melville* (Cambridge, MA; Harvard University Press, 1989) p. 21.

15. Ann Douglas, *The Feminization of American Culture* (New York: Anchor Books and Doubleday, 1977), p. 238 and throughout the text.

16. Brown, *The Word in the World*, pp. 1–23.

17. Ibid., pp. 76–78, 95.

18. Susan Curtis, "The Son of Man and God the Father: The Social Gospel and Victorian Masculinity," in Mark C. Carnes and Clyde Griffen, eds., *Meanings for Manhood: Constructions of Masculinity in Victorian America* (Chicago: University of Chicago Press, 1990), pp. 72–74. Wallace uses this precise language in a story he was commissioned to write for a Christmas edition of *Harper's*. When the story's main character, Uncle Midas, explains Christ's boyhood and his own love of Jesus to his young relatives, he refers to Christ as "my brother, my friend" (p. 6). Lew Wallace, "The Boyhood of Christ," *Harper's New Monthly Magazine* 74 (1886), pp. 1–18.

19. J. Clinton Ransom, *The Successful Man in his Manifold Relations with Life* (Baltimore: Hill and Harvey Publishers, 1886), p. 292. See also Curtis, "The Son of Man," p. 72.

20. Nelson Sizer, *Choice of Pursuits; or, What to Do and Why* (New York: Fowler and Wells Co. Publishers, 1890), p. 184.

21. McKee, *"Ben-Hur" Wallace*, p. 170.

22. Glenn Hendler, *Public Sentiments: Structures of Feeling in Nineteenth-Century American Literature* (Chapel Hill and London: University of North Carolina Press, 2001), p. 4.

23. Ibid., p. 5.

24. Walter Rauschenbusch, quoted in Curtis, "The Son of Man," p. 72.

25. Lee Scott Theisen, "'My God, Did I Set All of This in Motion?': General Lew Wallace and Ben Hur," *Journal of Popular Culture* 18 (1984), pp. 33–41; "The C.C. Lecture Course," *Washington Post*, November 18, 1894, p. 7; Morsberger and Morsberger, *Militant Romantic*, pp. 352–383.

26. "Helping a Worthy Object," *New York Times*, April 24, 1889, p. 5.

27. "The Story of *Ben Hur*," *Washington Post*, April 18, 1890, p. 4.

28. "Dr. Rogers' Farewell Lecture," *Washington Post*, April 25, 1897, p. 2.

29. "*Ben-Hur* and Burlesque," *New York Times*, October 11, 1901, p. 9.

30. "For Titanic Monument Fund," *Washington Post*, May 10, 1912, p. 5.

31. "Makes *Ben-Hur* Real," *Washington Post*, February 18, 1914, p. 2.

32. Morsberger and Morsberger, *Militant Romantic*, p. 454.

33. "Experiences with *Ben-Hur*," *New York Times*, January 31, 1926, p. X5; "How *Ben-Hur* Was Made," *Washington Post*, October 2, 1926, p. SM5.

34. The play helped to create a tradition of religious spectacle still staged in American evangelical communities at places such as the Millennium Theater in Strasburg, Pennsylvania. For the details in this paragraph we have drawn from many sources: Nelson E. Bell, "Public Choices Surprise," *Washington Post*, July 10, 1934, p. 14; "*Ben-Hur* Dramatized," *Washington*

Post, November 13, 1899, p. 7; "Dramatic and Musical: *Ben-Hur* as a Play at the Broadway Theatre," *New York Times,* November 30, 1899, p. 7; "Facts About *Ben-Hur,*" *Washington Post,* April 13, 1913, p. MT2; "London Theatrical Chat: The Dramatic Critics Find Fault with *Ben-Hur,*" special cable to the *New York Times,* April 6, 1902, p. 7; Millennium Theater, Lancaster County, PA, full-page color advertisement in the *Washington Post,* March 2, 2003, p.G14. Morsberger and Morsberger, *Militant Romantic,* p. 466; Theisen, "'My God,'" p. 37.

35. "*Ben-Hur* and Its Dramatist," *The Washington Post,* April 23, 1905, p. B6.

36. Lew Wallace to Klaw and Erlanger, March 25, 1899, Wallace Collection, Lilly Library, Indiana University, quoted in Morsberger and Morsberger, *Militant Romantic,* p. 457.

37. Young makes few overt references to Jesus; the story becomes a buried subplot on stage: "When the King cometh" (I:i, p. 212); "Bethlehem ... out of thee shall he come forth . . . ," "When the King cometh, when I may see and know him, all I have is His" (III:i, p. 230); "In the name of the One God . . . ," (III:4, p. 245); "And now the child is a man" (IV:i, p. 255); "Thou knowest, Esther, I am slow of belief, but if this in truth be he of whom the prophets have spoken" (VI:i, p. 274). These brief oblique references are all the mention that Jesus accrues in the play. References here and in this chapter are keyed by act, scene and page number in reference to the reprinted version of William Young's adaptation of *Ben-Hur* in Mayer, *Playing Out the Empire,* pp. 204–290.

38. William R. Kowalchuk, dir., *Ben-Hur* (2002), (Tundra Productions Inc., and Agamemnon Films, 2003). This fourth movie adaptation is a cartoon version starring the voice of Charlton Heston. It turns the story into a Sunday school parable with Ben-Hur figured as a much younger boy and makes Jesus a more prominent character: "[Heston] said he wanted youngsters to have a tamer introduction to the story." Quoted in "Heston reprises 'Ben-Hur' for cartoon," CNN.com/Entertainment, February 14, 2003; http://www.cnn.com/203/SHOWBIZ/Movies/02/14/movies.heston.ap/ While perhaps known within the present-day evangelical American community, the film has less significant impact on the story's larger reception to date, and we choose to leave its analysis for other venues.

39. Mordaunt Hall, "The Screen: A Stupendous Spectacle," *New York Times* December 31, 1925, p.10.

40. Kevin Hagopian, "Ben-Hur Film Notes," New York State Writers Institute; http://www.albany.edu/writers-inst/fnf98n5.html. Retrieved March 24, 2003; Morsberger and Morsberger, *Militant Romantic,* p. 476; "Old Film With Sounds," *New York Times,* December 4, 1931, p. 28; David Mayer, ed., "Introduction and Notes," in Lew Wallace, *Ben-Hur* (Oxford: Oxford University Press, 1998), pp. vii, i–xxx.

41. Fred Niblo, dir., *Ben-Hur: A Tale of the Christ* (1927), (M-G-M Silent Classics: Turner Entertainment Company, 1988).

42. Ibid.

43. William Wyler, dir., *Ben-Hur: A Tale of the Christ* (1959), (M-G-M: Turner Entertainment Company, 2001).

8   John Huston's *The Red Badge of Courage*

Jakob Lothe

The challenges and processes of adaptation both resemble each other and differ from each other. On the one hand, all film adaptations of novels involve a transfer from the medium of verbal prose fiction to that of film. It is important to remember that this is a radical form of transfer – a "translation into film language,"[1] as the Russian formalist Boris Eikhenbaum put it as early as 1926 – regardless of what kind of adaptation is being made. On the other hand, one and the same literary text can, of course, be adapted in different ways according to the director's ideas, as regards both filmmaking in general and adaptation in particular. Moreover, the director's adaptation of a literary text is unavoidably marked by his or her response to, and interpretation of, that text; and as we all know, such interpretations can vary very considerably. As Robert Stam has shown, the main issue here is not an adaptation's "fidelity" to a literary text but rather a complex form of dialogue between two different media. Even though it is possible to consider the phenomenon and practice of adaptation as a translation from one medium to another, there is no "transferable core: a single novelistic text comprises a series of verbal signals that can generate a plethora of possible readings, including even readings of the narrative itself."[2]

I want to consider John Huston's 1951 adaptation of Stephen Crane's classic novel of the American Civil War, *The Red Badge of Courage*, in the light of these introductory comments. More specifically, paying particular attention to the challenge of presenting literary impressionism on film, I will discuss how Huston presents selected key scenes from Crane's literary text. But first of all a brief introduction to the novel, first published as a single volume in 1895 when its author was only twenty-three years old.

For Willa Cather, Crane (1871–1900) was "the first writer of his time in the picturing of episodic, fragmentary life."[3] Throughout his brief but varied life, Crane's stories focused, as Anthony Mellors and Fiona Robertson point out in their informative introduction to *The Red Badge of Courage and Other Stories*, on individuals in extreme situations and on moments in which selfhood is at once intensely felt and troublingly unstable. In the exemplary case of Crane's second novel and most famous work, *The Red Badge of Courage*, an untried soldier finds his heroic idealizations replaced by confusing experiences which threaten his subjective fantasies. In a genre traditionally dominated by decisive action rather than by reflection, Crane's Civil War story portrays a character whose erratic responses to battle are mediated by mistaken notions of self-identity.[4]

Incorporating and yet moving beyond a summary of the story's plot, this introductory comment pinpoints two of the most characteristic, and most significant, aspects of *The Red Badge of Courage*: a novel in the tradition of nineteenth-century realist fiction, it is also an experimental novel on the threshold of modernism. Major representatives of early modernism such as Henry James and Joseph Conrad considered *The Red Badge of Courage* a very important and highly original novel, and with hindsight we can now see that they were right. In common with novels such as Knut Hamsun's *Hunger* (1890), Thomas Hardy's *The Well-Beloved* (1892, 1897) and Conrad's *Heart of Darkness* (1899), *The Red Badge of Courage* is a seminal text marking the transition from realism to modernism. A key aspect of the novel's transitional quality is its literary impressionism.

The aesthetic term "impressionism" appears to have been put into circulation by a French journalist, Louis Leroy, to comment critically on Claude Monet's painting *Impression: Sunrise*, first exhibited in Paris in 1874. Monet's response to the criticism leveled at his painting is deservedly famous: "Poor blind idiots. They want to see everything clearly, even through the fog!"[5] This riposte highlights two characteristic features associated not only with Monet's impressionist painting, but also with Crane's literary impressionism. First, Monet draws attention to the difficulty of presenting clearly something that is intrinsically unclear, that is, something that cannot be properly seen or adequately understood. Second, without saying that the object perceived is unimportant, Monet puts emphasis on the perceiving consciousness. "In one way or another," notes Ian Watt, "all the main Impressionists made it their aim to give a pictorial equivalent of the visual sensations of a particular individual at a particular time and place."[6] As I will attempt to show, this observation can be related both to Crane's novel and to Huston's adaptation.

Conrad considered Crane "the chief impressionist of the age."[7] Indeed, the narrative discourse of *The Red Badge of Courage* applies "the basic canons of impressionistic writing: the apprehension of life through the play of perceptions, the significant montage of sense impressions, the reproduction of chromatic touches by colorful and precise notations, the reduction of elaborate syntax to the correlation of sentences."[8] And yet, as briefly indicated already, Crane's novel is also influenced by the powerful trends of realism and naturalism. The most significant historical event to which Crane responds is, of course, the American Civil War. Some Civil War veterans, most notoriously General Alexander C. McClurg, described the novel as "a vicious satire upon American soldiers and American armies."[9] Tending to disagree with such a description, recent historians of the Civil War find that the book bears the imprint of a particular battle: Chancellorsville. Ernest B. Furguson notes that "the best-known book about Chancellorsville is one in which the battle is never named: Stephen Crane's great novel *The Red Badge of Courage*."[10]

Continuing yet modifying the traditions of realism and naturalism, Crane blends naturalist and impressionist styles. As Mellors and Robertson observe, the novel's "descriptions of landscapes and events disconcertingly combine detailed observations with fragmented, symbolic image-complexes derived explicitly from the language of painting."[11] In order to discuss how Huston as film director responds to this kind of impressionist literary discourse, I first turn to the openings of the novel and the adaptation. The literary text begins thus:

> The cold passed reluctantly from the earth, and the retiring fogs revealed an army stretched out on the hills, resting. As the landscape changed from brown to green, the army awakened, and began to tremble with eagerness at the noise of rumors. It cast its eyes open upon the roads, which were growing from long troughs of liquid mud to proper thoroughfares. A river, amber-tinted in the shadow of its banks, purled at the army's feet; and at night, when the stream had become of a sorrowful blackness, one could see across it the red, eyelike gleam of hostile camp-fires set in the low brows of distant hills. (3)

Two constituent aspects of Crane's literary art are particularly striking in this opening paragraph. We first note that Crane uses a third-person narrator who introduces the reader both to "the landscape" and to characters – "the army" – positioned in that landscape. Yet although at first glance this third-person narrator appears to be knowledgeable and authoritative, the information provided already in the first sentence that the army becomes visible to him as a result of "the retiring fogs" signals a particular perspective. The narrative perspective on the landscape, events, and characters is limited and selective. This narrator is not to be confused with the author (since he is part of the fiction created by Crane); yet his narrative authority is striking as early as in this opening paragraph.

Second, although in one sense the narrator's perspective here resembles that of a film camera – capable of registering and showing what can be seen as the fog retires – we are struck by the extent to which the narrator not only observes but also interprets. This characteristic feature of Crane's narrative method becomes particularly evident in the use of personification. The army "awakened, and began to tremble," the river "had become of a sorrowful blackness," and, seeing across it, the narrator discovers the "eyelike gleam of hostile camp-fires." It could be countered that the first example is no personification since an army after all consists of men. Yet we tend to forget that an army is made up of a large number of individuals – soldiers who experience human emotions including, very understandably, fear. Thus Crane's use of the verb "tremble" in this paragraph is peculiarly suggestive.

How does Huston's film version of *The Red Badge of Courage* begin? Since, as indicated already, the media of literature and film are vastly different, in asking this question I may have embarked on a form of comparison that is critically problematic. Yet a consideration of the film's beginning can tell us something important about the dissimilar ways in which these two media operate, and it can also signal the director's attitude to the film he has chosen to adapt. A versatile artist of the cinema, Huston had a long and distinguished career which extended from *The Maltese Falcon* (1941), one of his most important films, starring Humphrey Bogart and Mary Astor, to *The Dead* (1987), an adaptation of James Joyce's short story starring Donal McGann and Anjelica Huston. "It is possible," notes Lesley Brill in *John Huston's Filmmaking*, "for a director to make a strong, original film or two without the kind of formal engagement and ingenuity that Huston brought to his art. But few directors have been able to sustain significant careers without absorbing themselves in all the possibilities of their medium."[12] This was exactly what Huston did, and he did so at different stages of film production. For instance, whether he took a screenwriting credit or not, Huston participated extensively in the production of the screenplays of all his films. Moreover, "editing was largely his responsibility; by many accounts, including his own, Huston did most of his editing in the camera during shooting."[13] Not only did Huston have overall responsibility for according priorities and coordinating the activities that are part of the production process; he also functioned creatively in relation to the screenplay and the films' thematics.

As a film author leaving his creative imprint on the films he made, Huston had a strong conception of the differences between his own medium and that of literature. Still, like other major twentieth-century directors such as Orson Welles and Francis Ford Coppola, Huston was repeatedly drawn to literary texts – both as a source of inspiration and as a possible basis for his filmmaking. While taking cognizance of the differences between the media, he did not fail to see that both literature and film are narrative forms of communication, and that filmmakers can take advantage of this point of contact. In *The Red Badge of Courage*, as in *The Dead* nearly forty years later, Huston is concerned with the narrative consequences of the literary text's features – features typically referred to by terms such as event, character, plot, and symbol. Transforming these literary features into filmic ones, Huston employs a complex combination of visual and auditory signals that combine to produce film narration, and that can be subsumed under the concept of "film narrator." This term is somewhat controversial. For David Bordwell, film has narration but no narrator: "in watching films, we are seldom aware of being told something by an entity resembling a human being . . . [Therefore film] narration is better understood as the organization of a set of cues for the construction of a story. This presupposes a perceiver, but not any sender, of a message."[14] The emphasis Bordwell puts on the viewer's active role is critically illuminating. Yet although the viewer, on the basis of an indeterminate number of visual and auditory impressions, first constructs connected and comprehensible images and then a story, it is difficult to imagine that a film is "organized" without being "sent." If, as Seymour Chatman suggests, "narration" at least partly inhabits the film, "we can legitimately ask why it should not be granted some status as an agent," and then, for films as for novels, we can "distinguish between a *presenter* of a story, the narrator (who is a component of the discourse), and the *inventor* of both the story and the discourse (including the narrator): that is, the implied author . . . as the principle within the text to which we assign the inventional tasks."[15]

In the case of the adaptation under consideration here, it is natural to link the implied author to Huston's imprint on the film: the combined result of his choices, priorities, and decisions not only as director but also as the writer of the screenplay. Yet since this particular film is an adaptation, Crane is an "implied co-author," that is, an implied author whose story, ideas, and value system Huston both represents and interprets. As regards the film narrator, it is important to emphasize his, or perhaps rather its, multiplexity. As Chatman shows in *Coming to Terms: The Rhetoric of Narrative in Fiction and Film*,[16] the film narrator is the sum of a large number of variable elements, whose narrative functions and effects typically depend on the manner in which they are combined. Unsurprisingly, Huston's adaptation features those two elements of film that perform the most obvious, and most crucial, narrative functions: moving photographic images of acting characters, and phonetic sound (voice) spoken by these characters. But to these two constituent aspects of film narration Huston adds a third: an accompanying voiceover commentary. This voiceover establishes an exceptionally direct link to the literary text since, as it informs the viewer right at the beginning of the film, "The narration you will hear spoken consists of quotes from the book itself."[17]

These three facets of narration in Huston's *The Red Badge of Courage* can all be subsumed under the concept of the film narrator. If, as Eikhenbaum argues, film spectators move "from comparison of the moving frames [of film] to their comprehension,"[18] viewers of this particular film are invited by the voiceover to link their comprehension to the commentary that accompanies the moving images projected over the screen. Most of the voiceover consists indeed of quotations from the novel, which the voiceover introduces thus: "*The Red Badge of Courage* was written by Stephen Crane in 1894 . . . From the moment it was published it was accepted as a classic study of war, and of the men who fought the war . . . Stephen Crane wrote this book when he was a boy of 22. Its publication made him a man." Listening to these words of praise, the viewer sees a large copy of Crane's novel displayed on the screen. This kind of explicit reference to a film's literary source is unusual, and the beginning of Huston's *The Red Badge of Courage* is very much the beginning of an adaptation. Yet although Huston presents his film as a film version of a classic work of literature, this act of homage does not in itself impair the artistic qualities of the production, nor does it necessarily make it less independent as film.

An illustrative example of Huston's original filmmaking is provided by the transition from the introductory comments on Crane's novel to the opening shots of the filmic action. Now there is a strong sense in which a film needs action, or at least movement approximating to action, in order to constitute itself as film. This perhaps obvious point forms the basis for my next: although Huston focuses on soldiers gathered in a military camp, he reveals how their "endless drilling" becomes an action perceived by the soldiers as nonaction – a state of waiting curiously opposed to that of being at war. By linking comments made by the soldiers to medium shots of their facial expressions, Huston shows how the strain of waiting and drilling serves to enhance the soldiers' sense of fear and doubt. Thus, although the literary qualities of the paragraph briefly considered above may appear to be missing from the film's beginning, some of these literary qualities are turned into filmic ones – and the combination of these devices and effects creates an atmosphere comparable to that evoked by the third-person narrator in Crane's literary text. As indicated already, Huston's use of the film camera plays a significant role here. If the camera is distanced from the action it registers and displays, the third-person narrator is similarly positioned at a considerable distance from the events he records. I hasten to add that, of course, no film camera can comment on what it shows in the way a literary narrator can comment on what he or she narrates. Yet we must not forget that the camera in its own way reveals much more than any narrator can possibly tell. As the plethora of visual images projected over the screen not only invites but actively furthers interpretation, there is a sense in which the literary narrator's commentary is taken over by the viewer of the film.[19]

In the opening chapters of Crane's novel, the third-person narrator's comments on the soldiers' fear of the impending fighting, and on the doubts they secretly harbor as regards their own ability to fight bravely, are related both to Henry and to the soldiers as a group. Henry is "the youth" who, tending to think of himself as a hero, wants to go to war, and yet secretly suspects he may not be up to it. They are all "untested men" (23), and when the battle eventually begins it catches them by surprise: "The din in front swelled to a tremendous chorus. The youth and his fellows were frozen to silence" (27). Before discussing how Huston presents the battle, I want to look at Crane's literary presentation of it. Consider these two passages from Chapter 5:

The men dropped here and there like bundles. The captain of the youth's company had been killed in an early part of the action. His body lay stretched out in the position of a tired man resting, but upon his face there was an astonished and sorrowful look, as if he thought some friend had done him an ill turn. (33)

The youth felt the old thrill at the sight of the emblems. They were like beautiful birds strangely undaunted in a storm.

As he listened to the din from the hillside, to a deep pulsating thunder that came from afar to the left, and to the lesser clamors which came from many directions, it occurred to him that they were fighting, too, over there, and over there, and over there. Heretofore he had supposed that all the battle was directly under his nose.

As he gazed around him the youth felt a flash of astonishment at the blue, pure sky and the sun-gleamings on the trees and fields. It was surprising that Nature had gone tranquilly on with her golden process in the midst of so much devilment. (34)

What is striking about this portrayal of war, rendered in the form of verbal fiction, is the combination of fact-oriented observation and subjective impression. On the one hand, the third-person narrator serves as a recording witness who registers and reports what happens. This facet of Crane's narrative art is evident in both quotations. On the other hand, what happens is immediately, almost irresistibly, related to the thoughts and feelings of the observer. In the second quotation these are consistently linked to the youth. But in the first one they are mainly associated with the narrator. Thus the attitudinal distance between the narrator and Henry is reduced from page 33 to page 34: although the narrator is more knowledgeable than Henry, and although he is skeptical about Henry's dreams of acts of heroism, his description of the battle reveals his human qualities. If Henry is shocked by what he experiences, the narrator, too, appears to be shaken by what he has to report. In the second quotation Henry's impressions of the battle are repeatedly related to what he and the narrator hear and see – the emblems, the din of the guns, the sky, and the sun.

One important aspect of literary impressionism is the insistent linking, in a short story or novel, of an event to the narrator's or character's perception, understanding, and interpretation of that event. In these two passages from Crane's *The Red Badge of Courage*, the narrative qualities just noted contribute significantly to the formation of the novel's impressionism. But they do so in close combination with two other facets of Crane's narrative. First, since the violent acts of the battle are shocking not just for the inexperienced soldier Henry but also for the authoritative third-person narrator, the reader, too, is more forcibly struck by them. The impressionist effect is furthered, and strengthened, by linking the same event to different perceptions of that event.

Second, the narrative discourse of both passages activates variants of the technique of defamiliarization – or, more accurately, 'enstrangement' – first described by the Russian formalists. In his classic essay "Art as Device," the Russian formalist Viktor Shklovsky starts from the premise that in accordance with "the general laws of perception," human skills and experiences become, unavoidably, habitual and automatic.[20] For Shklovsky, the essential purpose of art is to question, halt, and if possible reverse this process. Art can do so through *ostranie*: "By 'estranging' objects and complicating form, the device of art makes perception long and 'laborious.'"[21] In the passage under consideration here, one significant estranging device is Crane's technique of distorted or "fractured" perspective. Even though Henry's location is identical with that of the soldiers around him, his perspective during this early battle deviates from that of a professional soldier. His perspective is fractured in one particular sense: overwhelmed by the experience, he cannot just focus on fighting the enemy but is distracted by the sheer violence of the battle and by the contrast between the men's "devilment" and the "golden process" of nature. Yet Henry's distorted perspective is also a gain, since it enables him to look at the battle from a distance; the activity of fighting is subordinated to, or perhaps rather blends into, his own impression of the battle as a frightening, senseless activity. Thus what is a character flaw at the level of action is a strength at the level of reflection, and there is an interesting link between the inexperienced Henry's view of the battle and the skeptically observant view of the third-person narrator.[22]

When Henry in later battles has learned to fight bravely, his perspective is no longer fractured in this way. Crane's presentation of this change as both a gain and a loss indicates one of the ways in which he problematizes the romantic *Bildungsroman* in *The Red Badge of Courage*.

There is a sense in which a battle is deceptively easy to display on film. No artistic medium can compete with film when it comes to the presentation of dramatic action, yet for this very reason many war films are often remarkably one-dimensional in their character portrayals. Many directors have, of course, experimented with various ways of counteracting this tendency. For example, in *Apocalypse Now* (1979) Francis Ford Coppola makes ingenious use of sound (ranging from Kurtz's voice played on tape to the music of Richard Wagner's *The Ride of the Valkyries*) in order to invite the viewer to reflect critically on the motives for, and consequences of, the fighting shown on screen; and in *The Thin Red Line* (1998) Terrence Malick makes suggestive use of voiceover commentary in order to achieve a similar effect. Interestingly, in both these films, literature, and especially classical literature, plays a significant part. As far as Huston's filmic rendering of the battle scene in *The Red Badge of Courage* is concerned, two points can be made. Both of these are directly related to the two passages from the novel just considered, but they also apply, albeit with some qualifications, to Huston's presentation of other battle scenes.

My first point concerns, once again, narrative perspective. In Crane's novel the soldiers', including Henry's, sense of fear is enhanced by the limitation of perspective to just one of the two forces fighting each other, and Huston, too, focuses on the army in which Henry and his comrades serve. The other side, the enemy, is left largely in the dark. As regards plot progression, this choice of perspective enhances suspense, since the strength of the opposing army is not revealed. More importantly, suspense on the level of plot is closely linked to the suspense, and fear, felt by the fighting men. A notable gain of this technique, which establishes a further filmic parallel to the novel's impressionism, is the implied suggestion that the enemy's experience of the battle is not unlike that rendered here. This effect is strengthened by short episodes inserted into the film narrative. One such episode is particularly illustrative: as he is carelessly standing in the moonlight during his night watch, one of the soldiers is spotted by an enemy soldier. Rather than shooting him, this soldier asks the other one to step into the shadow. Individual solidarity momentarily triumphs over the brutal mechanics of war.

Second, proceeding from the point just made, I want to call attention to the way in which Huston positions the soldiers in the landscape. He shows many soldiers fighting, and the large number of men who are shot testifies to the violence and brutality of the war. Yet in most of the battle scenes, the fighting soldiers occupy just a small portion of the frame. Huston repeatedly situates his soldiers in beautiful scenery – complete with rivers, trees, and plains of grass. There is a strong suggestion that the fighting men not only disturb nature but commit an act of violence against the beautiful landscape. The contrastive function of nature's beauty, harmony, and permanence is as striking in the film as in the novel. Consider this short passage from Chapter 12: "The blue haze of evening was upon the field. The lines of forest were long purple shadows. One cloud lay along the western sky partly smothering the red" (63). "Haze" is a favorite word of literary impressionism; it plays a significant role, for instance, in the first paragraph of Conrad's *Heart of Darkness*. Haze is not just a quality of the physical surroundings, however. Since the word draws attention to the difficulty of seeing clearly, it highlights the role of the observer. In Crane's novel this problem of perception, of ascertaining what is happening and what the incidents mean, is primarily related to Henry, but it is also linked to the narrator and to the other soldiers. In Huston's film, too, it is essentially Henry who represents, and in one sense personifies, the problem of perception. Yet by using, and suggestively combining, a number of filmic techniques, Huston shows how disorienting and confusing war is.

For example, on two occasions Huston presents an image of rays of sunlight seen through the leaves of a tree. The filmic technique is simple – the camera, positioned close to the ground, is directed upward toward the light – yet the effect is remarkable. It is as though Henry, and by implication the other soldiers as well as the viewer, are momentarily blinded by the light. This light is not just disorienting, however. Although the shot of the rays of sunlight halts plot progression for just a few seconds, it has a distinctly estranging effect. For me, the contrast between the rays of sunlight and the fighting makes the latter appear absurd. The effect is dreamlike, yet this dream is the brutal reality of war. This brief segment of Huston's film is both an integral part of the film's action and a comment on that action. Capturing the tension between participating in a war yet being a spectator of it, the segment offers a succinct filmic illustration of a major conflict dramatized in Crane's novel.[23]

A further constituent aspect closely related to that just discussed is Huston's presentation of the soldiers' facial expressions. I have already drawn attention to the different ways in which Crane and Huston limit the soldiers' perspective, as well as those of the reader and viewer, to just one side of the fighting armies. Whereas Crane uses the narrative instrument of the third-person narrator to establish this limitation of perspective, Huston makes effective use of the film camera. Sometimes he places it behind Henry and the other soldiers, in a position approximating to that of the commanding general. This variant of filmic perspective is combined with that of positioning the camera just in front of the soldiers, thus focusing on their facial expressions. These expressions vary very considerably. The ways in which we interpret them will inevitably differ from viewer to viewer, but for me they range from amazement and wonder via fear to determination and courage. While these expressions change in accordance with the film's plot progression, on a different yet related level they change according to the soldier's feelings, thoughts, and impressions at a given moment. Thus Huston establishes a thematically productive connection between medium and close shots of different facial expressions and other filmic effects such as that of the rays of sunlight striking the men from above.

Even though there are, of course, many different ways of adapting Crane's *The Red Badge of Courage*, I hope to have indicated some of the main reasons why, in my judgment, Huston's film version is not just an interesting film but also a fine adaptation. As Stam has observed, an

Figure 9. World War II's most decorated soldier, Audie Murphy, stars as the soldier in the 1951 M-G-M production of Stephen Crane's *The Red Badge of Courage*.

adaptation "is less an attempted resuscitation of an originary word than a turn in an ongoing dialogical process."[24] Activating and innovatively combining the modest filmic means at his disposal, Huston manages to present filmically, in remarkably condensed form, several of the novel's features. These include a strong and persistent sense of disorientation, an equally strong sense of being tested, and a sustained focus on the individual's subjective impression of war as absurd yet formative because, at least for Henry, it serves to create a kind of invented or willed identity. Crane's novel and Huston's film provide an example of how fruitful the relationship between two very different media can be, and it seems appropriate that, unusually, the film ends by paying homage to, and referring the viewer back to, Crane's literary masterpiece.

NOTES

1. Boris Eikhenbaum, "Literature and Cinema" (1926), in Stephen Bann and John E. Bowlt, eds., *Russian Formalism: A Collection of Articles and Texts in Translation* (Edinburgh: Scottish Academic Press, 1973), p. 123.
2. Robert Stam, "Beyond Fidelity: The Dialogics of Adaptation," in James Naremore, ed., *Film Adaptation* (New Brunswick, NJ: Rutgers University Press, 2000), p. 57.
3. Willa Cather, "When I Knew Stephen Crane," in Maurice Bassan, ed., *Stephen Crane: A Collection of Critical Essays* (Englewood Cliffs, NJ: Prentice-Hall, 1967), p. 17.
4. Anthony Mellors and Fiona Robertson, "Introduction," in Stephen Crane, *The Red Badge of Courage and Other Stories*, ed. Anthony Mellors and Fiona Robertson, Oxford World's Classics (Oxford: Oxford University Press, 1998), p. vii. Further quotations are from this edition and will be cited parenthetically in the text.
5. Quoted by Ian Watt in *Conrad in the Nineteenth Century* (London: Chatto & Windus, 1980), p. 170.
6. Ibid., p. 170.
7. Joseph Conrad, *Tales of Hearsay and Last Essays* (London: Dent, 1972), p. 111.
8. Sergio Perosa, "Naturalism and Impressionism in Stephen Crane's Fiction," in Bassan, ed., *Critical Essays*, pp. 84–85.
9. Quoted by Lee Clark Mitchell, "Introduction," in Mitchell, ed., *New Essays on The Red Badge of Courage* (Cambridge: Cambridge University Press, 1988), p. 6.
10. Ernest W. Furguson, *Chancellorsville 1863: The Souls of the Brave* (New York, 1993), p. xiv.
11. Mellors and Robertson, "Introduction," p. xii. Mellors and Robertson also point out that although many commentators have stressed the links between Crane's narrative method and French Impressionism, they have tended to neglect the context provided by American art of the period. For instance, "emblematic works such as George Bower's paintings of New York

cityscapes and boxing matches deploy impressionist techniques to heighten the sense of chaotic movement" ("Introduction," p. xii).

12. Lesley Brill, *John Huston's Filmmaking* (Cambridge: Cambridge University Press, 1997), p. 10.
13. Ibid., p. 11.
14. David Bordwell, *Narration in the Fiction Film* (Madison: University of Wisconsin Press, 1985), p. 62.
15. Seymour Chatman, *Coming to Terms: The Rhetoric of Narrative in Fiction and Film* (Ithaca: Cornell University Press, 1990), pp. 126, 133; italics in original.
16. Ibid., pp. 134–135. See also my *Narrative in Fiction and Film: An Introduction* (Oxford: Oxford University Press, 2000), p. 31.
17. *The Red Badge of Courage* (1951). Director, John Huston; screenplay, John Huston; production, Gottfried Reinhardt and John Huston; starring Audie Murphy, Bill Mauldin, et al. A M-G-M Picture; Warner Home DVD.
18. Eikhenbaum, "Literature and Cinema," p. 123.
19. See Stam, "Beyond Fidelity," pp. 57–63.
20. Viktor Shklovsky, "Art as Device," in Shklovsky, *Theory of Prose*, ed. Gerald L. Burns, trans. Benjamin Sher (Normal, IL: Dalkey Archive Press, 1998), p. 4. See also Jakob Lothe, "Short Fiction as Estrangement: From Franz Kafka to Tarjei Vesaas and Kjell Askildsen," in Mats Jansson, Jakob Lothe, and Hannu Riikonen, *European and Nordic Modernisms* (Norwich: Norvik Press, 2004), pp. 97–115.
21. Shklovsky, "Art as Device," p. 6.
22. Crane's narrative modulation of perspective resembles Conrad's presentation of a battle scene in his novel *Nostromo* (1904). Conrad, too, uses a third-person narrator, but the narrator's description of the battle is linked to the perspective of a minor character, Giorgio, who arrives too late to participate in it. Seen from a distance, the soldiers' desperate fighting seems absurd to Giorgio, and the battle itself reminds him of a game of chess. While in *Nostromo* the perspective is related to physical distance and nonparticipation, in the case of *The Red Badge of Courage* it is a matter of the character's senses being swamped so that only selected impressions can be decoded and presented to the reader. See Joseph Conrad, *Nostromo: A Tale of the Seabord*, ed. Keith Karabine, Oxford World's Classics (Oxford: Oxford University Press, 1984), pp. 26–27.
23. For a viewer familiar with Crane's poetry, the interest and interpretative potential of this filmic segment are further enhanced by the manner in which it echoes sense impressions and unresolved tensions in a collection of poems such as *War is Kind* (1899). As John Berryman has noted, Crane's poetry has "the character of a 'dream,' something seen naïvely, in a new relation." See John Berryman, "Crane's Art," in Bassan, ed., *Critical Essays*, p. 38.
24. Stam, "Beyond Fidelity," p. 64.

Translating *Daisy Miller*

Douglas McFarland

Near the beginning of Henry James's *The Portrait of a Lady* (1881) we learn that the brother-in-law of Isabel Archer is at a loss to understand her. She is, he observes, "written in a foreign tongue; I can't make her out." Ludlow goes on to confess, "Well, I don't like originals; I like translations."[1] The inability of others to take Isabel on her own terms and the need for a familiar context in which she might be placed speak to James's interest in women, especially American women in a European culture where they are often as misunderstood as they might have been in America. But it also speaks to the subject of my essay: the translation of nineteenth-century American originals into the contemporary medium of film. Ludlow would no doubt prefer a two-hour film version of Isabel to the six hundred pages of often dense prose which James (1843–1916) devotes to her. But I also suspect that he might very well be bored if he were to sit through the 126 minutes of Jane Campion's film version of the novel. The point I am making is that the translation of a novel into a film is a much more complicated process than Ludlow might imagine. For my purposes, let me put it another way: translation is not in the service of an audience which cannot decipher an original, but rather, as Walter Benjamin asserts, "Translation marks their stage of a con- tinued life . . . a transformation and a renewal of something living."[2] We might call this metamorphosis rather than translation, a process in which there is no inherent sense of nostalgia or loss, no shadow of an original haunting and silently passing judgment on a copy, no accusations of infidelity and reduction, but rather the release of a set of thematic, formal, and cultural forces into another context both within and beyond the conscious control of the so-called translator. This results not only in a renewed existence of an original but also in the expansion of the formal and cultural properties of the medium of translation. This last point is crucial. Although a meaningful translation does not primarily serve an audience requiring access, it does challenge that audience to expand its capacity for formal expression while concurrently prodding the audience to deepen its own cultural self-awareness.

Peter Bogdanovich's 1974 film version of Henry James's *Daisy Miller* (1879) offers an example of the possibilities and pitfalls inherent in this process. The director's overt and self-conscious strategies of translation succeed in creating an artifact whose formal sophistication far surpasses that of its source material. In a much more subtle manner, as James's novella is translated into the medium of film, it comes under the influence of traditional structures of cinematic narrative and the typologies of character and scene which that tradition generates. This in turn opens the way for the inevitable intrusion of contemporary social perspectives and audience expectations.

I

The formal characteristics of *Daisy Miller* seem particularly well suited to film adaptation. The relatively short length of the novella is well within the scope of a ninety-minute film. The action unfolds in realistic landscapes, made up of a series of set pieces, first at a resort in Switzerland and then in Rome. Within each set piece there is a preponderance of dialogue. Although James does provide a first-person narrator capable of ironic commentary, his voice is undeveloped and his irony muted. The filmmaker is not confronted, therefore, with the relentlessly probing narrator of James's later works, nor with the complex and difficult syntax which that narrator uses. The premodernist form of *Daisy Miller* meshes well with the bias for realism of traditional filmmaking. Indeed, as several critics have pointed out, Bogdanovich takes advantage of these characteristics to make an ostensibly faithful adaptation of James's novella, one which does not stray from narrative sequence, period setting, locations, or for the most part the original dialogue.[3]

Fidelity to a classic work by the so called "master," Henry James, would, however, seem to contradict what we know of Bogdanovich's own understanding of himself as a filmmaker. One may or may not subscribe to the *auteur* theory, but it is certainly the case that Bogdanovich, in the tradition of Orson Welles, Alfred Hitchcock, and Howard Hawks, defines himself as an *auteur*. One would expect an *auteur* to be wary of adapting a so-called classic lest his own work, or perhaps what we might call the signature of his work, be relegated to a secondary status. The New Wave of French *auteurs* tended to avoid so-called high art as a source for adaptation. François Truffaut's *Shoot the Piano Player* (1960), for instance, is based on a novel by the American pulp writer David Goodis. This noir fiction does not resist the imprint of the director. When Truffaut does turn to canonical literature, he does so with the intention of asserting himself over the material. Although

Truffaut's *The Green Room* (1978) is based primarily on a Henry James short story, the director draws on a number of other works by James to the extent that he credits "Themes of Henry James" and not a specific text as the basis for the screenplay. Moreover, the story is relocated to France in the years following World War I and draws heavily for its treatment on that particular historical moment. Finally, Truffaut himself plays the leading role, a literal sign of the director's presence in the film.[4] In choosing *Daisy Miller* and making an apparently faithful adaptation of this classic, Bogdanovich would seem, therefore, to have relegated himself to a secondary status, thereby relinquishing his role as *auteur*.

Bogdanovich proves, however, quite unfaithful to the "master" through his decision to strip his source material of its cultural context. Fidelity to setting, content, and dialogue is countered by an infidelity to the social and ideological underpinnings of James's representation of the American girl, Daisy Miller. As Bogdanovich himself asserted at the time of the film's release, "What James meant to say with the story doesn't really concern me . . . I think all that social stuff is based on some kind of repression anyway."[5] Bogdanovich's strategy is to take from James what he perceives to be a timeless and universal theme: the missed opportunity between two individuals who might have made a life together. The ensuing tragedy will not hinge on social barriers but rather on the decontextualized character of the two individuals. This maneuver opens the way for the director to assert his authority over this "classic novella."

I will comment later on Bogdanovich's ultimate inability to cast out cultural context from his film, but for now let me point out a different kind of authority which hovers about Bogdanovich's notion of himself as an *auteur*, one that is pivotal in understanding the formal achievements of his work. I am referring to Bogdanovich's indebtedness to the very concept of *auteur*. The self-perception of many French New Wave directors as the authors of their films derives from their understanding of a group of American filmmakers of the 1930s and 1940s such as Welles, Hawks, John Ford, and Raoul Walsh. Although made for particular studios, the work of these filmmakers bore their personal stamp. This provided many New Wave directors with a model of how they might approach their own filmmaking. There is, however, a crucial distinction in the way in which Bogdanovich expresses himself as an *auteur*. He does not simply emulate the authority of directors such as Ford and Hawks over their films; he also, at least before *Daisy Miller*, adopts their specific styles and themes. In short, he confuses imprinting his own style on his work with paying homage to other filmmakers. Consider *The Last Picture Show* (1971). It would seem as if Bogdanovich might easily put his mark on the source material, a novel written by Larry McMurtry, but instead he imitates Welles and Ford. The opening shot of *The Last Picture Show* unequivocally refers to the opening of Ford's *The Grapes of Wrath* (1940), and the theme of the film, the transition from movie house to television set, echoes that of Welles's *The Magnificent Ambersons* (1942), the transition from carriage to automobile. His indebtedness to others is even more pronounced in his next film, *What's Up Doc?* (1972). Buck Henry may have written the script, but the real source material is Hawks's screwball comedy *Bringing Up Baby* (1938), which you might say is translated verbatim.

With *Daisy Miller*, however, Bogdanovich removes himself from the shadow of his cinematic masters and in so doing transforms his source material into something which becomes his own, something whose formal characteristics reflect his maturity as a filmmaker. The modernist style left undeveloped in James's novella becomes fully developed in Bogdanovich's film. The complexity of grammar and syntax which we find in James's later works is expressed by Bogdanovich through the grammar and syntax of film. James's *Daisy Miller* is translated into high modernist art. This is evident in scene after scene, from the opening long take and vertical panning shot, to the expression of multiple points of view in the gardens at Vervey, to the lighting after Daisy has contracted her illness, to the camera position as Winterbourne learns of her death, and finally to the atmospheric conclusion over Daisy's grave. But it is the first scene in Mrs. Walker's "little crimson drawing room" which may offer the most telling example of how Bogdanovich reaches well beyond James in narrative sophistication.

The scene in question marks the occasion on which Winterbourne encounters Daisy in Rome after their initial meeting at Vervey. By utilizing an array of techniques, including set decoration, lighting, music, close-ups, grouping of actors, cutting, and camera movement, Bogdanovich conveys more information and with much greater depth than his counterpart. The scene opens with a private conversation which does not appear in the novella. In keeping with the desire to remove his adaptation from the social context of James's story, Bogdanovich uses this exchange between Winterbourne and Mrs. Walker to establish a motive other than a kind of Victorian snobbery for the eventual ostracism of Daisy. The close-up of Mrs. Walker with which Bogdanovich begins the scene tells us immediately that she will take on an expanded role. Although Brian McFarlane has counted more than 200 close-ups in the film, they are not of a uniform variety.[6] Most are medium close-ups and fail to scrutinize the face or to register intimacy. The close-up of Mrs. Walker is qualitatively different from what has appeared before. She appears to be looking at herself in a mirror and adjusting a lock of hair in anticipation of conversing with the guests who are chatting and drinking tea in the background. A Haydn piano sonata is being played. The ornate room behind her is fully lit, artificially bright. All of this is juxtaposed with the risqué look on her face and the off-color riddle which she is in the process of posing to an unseen confidant. "How does a Roman distinguish between his pleasures and his sins?" she asks. After a minor pause, she answers the riddle herself: "His sins he confesses, his pleasures he enjoys." The face into which the camera peers is broad and mature, already hardening into middle age. The close-up grants access to a subtext beneath the social façade. The audience finds itself enmeshed not in social but rather in sexual politics. Mrs. Walker's room is, to use Welles's phrase, a "bright guilty world."

As the camera smoothly pulls back, we realize that the close-up of Mrs. Walker is in fact her image reflected in a mirror. The effect is disorienting and marks the first instant in which the director takes advantage of the paneled mirrors which we can now see cover several of the walls. What we thought was an entryway into another room is in fact a large mirror. As the camera pulls back further, Winterbourne comes into view, and we recognize that between him and Mrs. Walker there has been a longstanding intimacy. At first he seems to be looking away from her, but when we realize that she is looking into a mirror, we know that he is looking directly at her. Their faces meet for merely an instant as her head moves past his in one continuous motion until she faces the room. The camera has pulled back out of the close-up far enough so that we now see her in the foreground but also reflected in the mirror behind. She has assumed a different facial expression, a social mask which reflects her status as the hostess. But without looking at Winterbourne, she brings up that woman in Geneva, Madame Olga and the "singular stories about her." In the novella this phrase is used much earlier by the narrator. By assigning it to Mrs. Walker, Bogdanovich gives added emphasis to the aura of sexual intrigue. We are left with the understanding of an affair between Olga and Winterbourne, Mrs. Walker's knowledge of it, her willingness to use it in order to unsettle if not manipulate Winterbourne, and perhaps a previous affair between herself and Winterbourne. All of this is conveyed in roughly one minute of film.

This moment is quickly interrupted by the announcement of an arrival. The camera fluidly pulls back at an angle and follows Winterbourne as he follows Mrs. Walker toward the entrance to the room. The camera smoothly, almost elegantly, completes a half-oval, and when the Millers enter we look out from behind Winterbourne to see the arrivals but concurrently we can see Winterbourne's face reflected in the mirror. We now realize that nearly every wall is covered by a mirror. At this point, the first and only cut in the scene occurs, a close-up of Daisy. Her soft pastel blue and white dress stands out in the bright, intensive light of the room and in contrast to Mrs. Walker's relatively dark green dress. The close-up itself is fleeting and expresses her delight that Winterbourne is there.

In the second half of the scene, Bogdanovich makes full use of the mirrors which cover the walls. Although the camera primarily focuses on Winterbourne conversing with Daisy's mother and brother, we see multiple reflections of Daisy and Mrs. Walker as they stroll together about the room. At times, the reflection of Winterbourne enters the frame of a mirror so that he is simultaneously part of two groupings. The complexity of the choreography for this one long take never calls attention to itself. The scene concludes with a second close-up of Mrs. Walker so that her face frames the set-piece.

We are left with a sense that the scene belongs to Mrs. Walker, that Daisy and Winterbourne are contained within her risqué and hardened expression, that Winterbourne is complicit with this hardening, that a social façade covers over sexual intrigue, that this room reflects a self-conscious awareness of looking and being seen, and that Winterbourne and Daisy are caught up in multiple and complex groupings. It is not a question simply of filling in the unspoken in James's version. By utilizing film technique and craft, evocative but not derivative of Welles and Ford, Bogdanovich adds a depth which is quite simply lacking in the novella. This scene is typical of the film and demonstrates Bogdanovich's maturity as a filmmaker. The film bears the stamp of its director more than the stamp of James. The formal success of Bogdanovich is reflected in the borrowing made by a filmmaker of a younger generation: Wes Anderson has acknowledged that the final scene at Daisy's grave inspired a similar scene in *Rushmore* (1998).

II

Daisy Miller starts out as simply a girl from America traveling in Europe, a character in a nineteenth-century novella, but at some point she becomes more than that. She becomes the exemplar of a particular type. No longer "an American girl," she is "the American girl" and as such is repeatedly recast in different forms and in different eras. These later manifestations range from F. Scott Fitzgerald's Daisy Buchanan to William Faulkner's Temple Drake, and even to Madonna, whose first husband reportedly nicknamed her Daisy. Bogdanovich's adaptation of James's novella constitutes another recasting of Daisy. His understanding of her is influenced by the American girls he knows from American cinema and the particular film genres in which they are represented.

In his review in the *New York Times* of *Daisy Miller* on its release in 1974, Vincent Canby offered one of the few positive assessments, calling it an "unexpected triumph" and a "romantic comedy" in "the tradition of old-time Hollywood producers."[7] Two weeks later in the same newspaper, Michael Sragow published a scathing response to Canby in which he excoriated Bogdanovich and his film. But oddly enough, he saw it in generic terms which were similar to Canby's. Instead of a romantic comedy, he called it a "flirtatious sexual battle," and asserted that Bogdanovich had missed the "sad" implications of James's novella.[8] Both critics, in short, respond almost instinctually to the comic elements in the film, but neither knows what to do with these elements. At issue is a fundamental ingredient in the adaptation of a literary work: genre and the traditions of genre within the medium of film. This medium has a history of storytelling, a history of particular narrative structures and patterns, and these can influence the final form of the translated material. Understanding how cinema genre contributes to the way in which Bogdanovich narrates the story of *Daisy Miller* will help to clarify how the comic elements, which Canby and Sragow identify, function in the film.

For the two films he made immediately before *Daisy Miller*, Bogdanovich drew upon genres of 1930s American cinema: the screwball comedy and the road picture. The portrayals of the American girl in these films influence Bogdanovich's representation of Daisy Miller. The first of these is *What's Up Doc?*, a self-conscious remake, as noted earlier, of Hawks's *Bringing Up Baby*. Barbra Streisand plays the Katharine Hepburn role as the free spirit who initiates the one-dimensional intellectual male into a world of play and adult sexuality. This female figure is an example of what Maria DiBattista calls the "fast-talking dame," a fixture of 1930s comedies. In films such as *Twentieth Century* (1934), *His Girl Friday* (1940), and *The Lady Eve* (1941), as well as *Bringing Up Baby* (1938), this version of the American girl sees her task as "first to create herself; second, to bring the male of her choosing and delight into her sphere of life by making him a fit . . . companion for her."[9] Bogdanovich updates the role by making the Streisand character not simply flighty but also well educated: she is intellectually gifted but keeps changing her major. In Bogdanovich's next feature, *Paper Moon* (1973), a variation on this scenario unfolds. Instead of his would-be lover, the female protagonist is the daughter of the male lead. The father is a traveling conman, selling Bibles to grieving widows, and although he might be well experienced in the ways of the world, his daughter teaches him the thrill of improvisation and the camaraderie of the road. And like the typical screwball heroine, she is a fast talker.

These two roles lead naturally, almost seamlessly, into Bogdanovich's version of Daisy. DiBattista's study is again particularly helpful. Although she does not refer directly to Daisy Miller, DiBattista does trace the figure of the fast-talking dame back to Henry James. Citing his commencement address at the end of the academic year at Bryn Mawr College in 1905, DiBattista points out that for James the cultivation of language is integral to the cultivation of self.[10] James gave this address to a group of young women some thirty-five years after the publication of *Daisy Miller*, but it suggests that Daisy's "chattering" may be something more than a sign of adolescent self-consciousness.

Bogdanovich does seem to recognize the kinship between Daisy and the fast-talking women of the Hollywood comedies of the 1930s. His Daisy is not simply a victim of missed opportunities, but, like the versions of the comic heroines portrayed in *What's Up Doc?* and *Paper Moon*, she asserts herself in the world and strives to free her male companion from his apparently one-dimensional character. Daisy would become Pygmalion not only to herself but to Winterbourne as well. She would make him less "stiff." This is most apparent in Bogdanovich's filming of the excursion to the castle at Vervey. In the novella James sets the stage for the emergence of a linguistically assertive Daisy. On the trip to the castle, Winterbourne is relieved to find that she does not "talk loud" and "laugh overmuch."[11] Upon their arrival, however, she takes the "plunge" (35) into loquacious banter and gives rein to the "independence of her humor" (35). What might have been called "prattle" (35) becomes by the end of the trip playful and even sharply ironic. When she asks Winterbourne to meet her in Rome, he refers to his obligations to the woman in Geneva. Without missing a beat, Daisy playfully asks, "Doesn't she give you a vacation in summer?" (38).

Bogdanovich begins his adaptation of the scene with a burst of energy that we do not find in the novella. The scene opens with Daisy in mid-flight, racing down the steps to the boat with Winterbourne in tow. She shouts "Whoo!" in utter delight. Once on board, she asks if they should dance, and before he can answer snatches his hat and forces him to play a game of keep away. Upon their arrival, Winterbourne begins a dry lecture on the history of the castle but is interrupted by an already impatient Daisy, who commands "Come on!" Just before entering the castle, Daisy overhears Winterbourne's correction of the porter's terminology and then a few minutes later purposefully makes the same error and giggles when Winterbourne corrects her. She repeatedly plays with "*oubliette*," the name of the deep hole which in former days had been used as a dungeon. "Don't fall," he tells her as they continue the tour. "Into an *oubliette*? . . . I hope you won't forget me," she responds. A few minutes later, Daisy playfully cavorts across an elevated passageway. Winterbourne's cautioning could be that of Cary Grant directed toward Katharine Hepburn: "Now Susan, be careful." When they enter the chapel, she immediately begins to play hide and seek, popping out from behind the pulpit once Winterbourne has walked past her. None of the examples I have just given is in James and each of them adds to what becomes in Daisy's hands a comic locale. I mean by this a space set aside from the impediments which might separate a couple. In this case those impediments are less social than psychological. Yes, Daisy has separated herself and Winterbourne from her pesky younger brother and from her husky watchdog Eugenio, but it is Winterbourne's reluctance to enter Daisy's world of energy and play, an inner "stiffness," which Daisy attempts to loosen at the castle. Daisy's kinship to Bogdanovich's earlier comic heroines, grounded in the tradition of American cinema, could not be on better display than in this episode.

While Canby and Sragow were quite correct, therefore, in recognizing the comic perspective of the film, they failed to recognize that it is contained within a darker perspective. The castle is eventually subsumed by the Colosseum, the tainted parody of a comic locale where disease is contracted in the moonlight. There is something much stronger here than a missed opportunity between two would-be lovers. The elimination of Daisy is accompanied by the elimination of a generic comic role for the American girl. In the final scene of the film, which does not appear in the novella, the fast-talking Daisy has been entombed and the rambling mother silenced by her grief. The Daisy whom Bogdanovich fashions as a catalyst for comedy and then banishes into darkness is a figure he had first met in American cinema.

III

This is, however, not the whole story. As I mentioned earlier, Bogdanovich consciously attempts to purge his adaptation of any trace of what he perceives to be the outmoded and stuffy social underpinnings of James's novella. Nevertheless, he is unable to escape the cultural context of the twentieth century, the context in which the film was made and perhaps more importantly into which it was released. To varying degrees, social and material factors will inevitably assert themselves into the process of crossing over from novel to film. In this case, the intrusion of social elements is a particularly strong one. For an audience of the 1970s, a time when the status of a woman's identity was coming under intense scrutiny, Daisy Miller, and I mean the character Daisy Miller, touched a nerve. The director's unwillingness to engage contemporary concerns contributed as much as anything to its unkind reception. The failure of the film to move its audience as the director had intended and the concurrent failure of its formal achievements to be recognized set in motion the downward spiral of Bogdanovich's career. The chief culprit for the failure of what is otherwise a sophisticated and moving adaptation is a cultural subtext which simply cannot be dismissed.

As Daisy is a catalyst for the release of comic energy, Cybill Shepherd is a catalyst for the release of cultural subtext. Among the many seemingly external factors which influence film adaptation of a literary work, casting is one of the most significant. The selection of a specific actor to play a part from a novel transforms what a reader must imagine into what an audience necessarily sees. The mental representation of Daisy shaped through the reader's encounter with multiple descriptions and interactions with other characters becomes in the film adaptation much more concrete and dependent on the physical characteristics, intonation of voice, and mannerisms of, in this case, Cybill Shepherd. This speaks directly to a major issue in James's novella: Daisy's resistance to any fixed characterization. She is an amalgamation of adjectives: pretty, little, charming, vulgar, ironic, innocent, ignorant, passive, crude, exquisite, direct, uneducated, nice, childish, cynical, ruthless, strange, and, of course, flirtatious. As Winterbourne says of her at their first meeting, frustrated in his attempt at categorization, Daisy is made of "charming parts . . . that made no ensemble" (9). It becomes the need of both Winterbourne and the reader to determine whether this American girl does have an identity beneath her flirtatious surface. It is the elusiveness and teasing nature of Daisy which are threatened by the casting of a particular actress in the role.

On the other hand, it would be foolish to assume that an accomplished actor would not able to bring depth and ambiguity to a role. The issue here is not, however, the technical ability or inability of Shepherd to provide such depth, but rather the multiple cultural factors which she brings to the role through her professional and personal identity. These include her career prior to becoming an actress, her previous roles as a film actress, and her relationship to Bogdanovich himself. Because of the specific nature of these interwoven factors, Shepherd influences how an audience perceives Bogdanovich's representation of Daisy. She generates, in short, questions concerning the status of the American girl in the 1970s.

Shepherd's first film role came just three years before the release of Daisy Miller, in Bogdanovich's own breakthrough feature, *The Last Picture Show*. Before being discovered by Bogdanovich, she had been a model and former beauty queen from Memphis. In this film she plays

Jaycee, an upper-middle-class and sexually precocious teenager growing up in a dying Texas town in the 1950s. Soon after the film's release, Bogdanovich left his wife and collaborator, Polly Platt, to be with Shepherd. They paraded their relationship before the public, appearing on magazine covers and television talk shows. Some commentators have argued that resentment among audiences and critics over the couple's cloying self-absorption contributed to the negative reception of *Daisy Miller*.[12] That self-absorption is, however, part of something larger.

Shepherd brings a certain authenticity to her role as Jaycee that has less to do with her skills as an actress than with her earlier career. The transition from beauty contestant and model to Jaycee is for Shepherd an effortless one. At times, one senses that she is playing herself rather than acting. Shepherd had already established herself professionally as one who is looked at by others, one who uses her beauty and allure to manipulate an audience. The professional model is a tease, concurrently offering herself and withholding herself, creating desire yet denying intimacy. Jaycee operates in a similar manner. It is an aura of good looks, upper-middle-class status, and the material trappings of that status which empower Jaycee. She is very much about style. The rolled-up jeans, the saddle shoes, the blouse tied in a knot across her stomach, and, of course, the convertible provide Jaycee with an irresistible aura. And she knows it.

Shepherd's two previous roles, as model and as Jaycee, haunt her portrayal of Daisy Miller. By casting Shepherd, Bogdanovich opened the way for questions concerning the modern American girl. As was mentioned earlier, Daisy Miller came to represent a type that has been continuously recast. In Bogdanovich's film there is an implicit sense that Shepherd herself, as a model, as a performer, as the unabashed companion of her director, constitutes a recasting of Daisy, a twentieth-century version of James's American girl. The juxtaposition of Shepherd and the Daisy whom Bogdanovich intends to represent creates an underlying tension in the film which is never addressed by the director. I suspect that Bogdanovich saw in Daisy Miller a role which would showcase Shepherd's skill as a comic actress, but ironically it is her public and professional persona that makes her a match for the part. Bogdanovich's attempt to validate Shepherd depends on erasing this persona. His inability to do so leaves a subtext unexplored but palpable.

The tension just described is heightened by the contemporary social context of the film. The feminist movement in America had by this time become fully established, and the status of the American girl was coming under intense and often critical scrutiny in a variety of forums. James's novella was itself being reevaluated by feminist academics. In an article first published in 1969 and then reprinted in 1976, Barbara Welter examined the relationship between James's representation of Daisy Miller and the social status of women in the late nineteenth century. Daisy's "emergence as a popular national type and her cautionary tale reflected an enthusiasm for the American maiden which amounted at times to 'a girl fetish.' The girl was exalted as the symbol of the nation while the American male built his bridges and his empires." Drawing upon handbooks of etiquette, popular magazines, and popular fiction, Welter uncovers a set of attitudes from the late nineteenth century which prescribe that a young woman be "religious, modest, passive, submissive, and domestic."[13] Daisy Miller would seem on the one hand to represent a woman who defied these conventions and was suitably punished. On the other hand, she fits perfectly into the European notion of the American girl: a shameless flirt and tease who never lives up to her promise. Daisy is, in short, caught between two differing social constructions of the adolescent girl. For Welter, the ambiguity of the narrative and its tragic consequences are grounded in cultural context.

A similar sort of engagement with the American girl is represented in popular culture. Published less than a year before the release of Bogdanovich's film, Erica Jong's *Fear of Flying* (1973) is less a rereading than a complete dismantling of cautionary tales concerning the American girl. The uninhibited, sexually adventuresome, and intellectually daunting heroine of the novel is a Daisy Miller for the 1970s. Isadora Wing recalls her first trip to Europe with her family in a way which invokes Daisy: "I remember myself traveling abroad with my parents as a teenager and always trying to pretend they weren't with me."[14] Her return as an adult, however, turns into a wild sexual romp as if Daisy herself were being exorcised, replaced by a newly liberated woman.

Unlike the academic and the novelist, however, Bogdanovich does not challenge the nineteenth-century mores of James's Daisy or attempt to reinvent her in another context. He asks none of the questions that feminist scholars were posing and does none of the reevaluation which a novelist like Jong was undertaking. He would instead strip his adaptation of cultural context in order to tell the story of two individuals who fail to find one another. Yet those cultural factors addressed by Welter and Jong force their way into the film through the casting of Cybill Shepherd and work to undermine Bogdanovich's strategy.

IV

In 1974 the independent film movement in America was at its height. Bob Rafelson, Hal Ashby, Robert Altman, and others had directed serious and often iconoclast films appealing to what might be called the art house audience which had been attracted in the previous decade to the films of international directors such as Akira Kurosawa, Ingmar Bergman, and Federico Fellini. Bogdanovich himself, especially in his first two features, *Targets* (1967) and *The Last Picture Show*, had been part of this movement. Clustered around the release of Daisy Miller were Altman's *Thieves Like Us* (1974) and *Nashville* (1975); Ashby's *The Last Detail* (1973) and *Shampoo* (1975); and Steven Spielberg's *Sugarland Express* (1974). Each of these films was challenging in its own way. It would be a few years before the box-office mentality ushered in by *Jaws* (1975) and *Star Wars* (1977) would have an impact. Looking back, one might think it odd that the formal achievements of *Daisy Miller* went largely unappreciated. As was mentioned earlier, Bogdanovich's career never recovered from the largely negative reception of *Daisy Miller*. Much of this was Bogdanovich's own doing. His homage to Depression era musicals, *At Long Last Love* (1975), came out the following year and

Figure 10. The title character from *Daisy Miller* is caught between her American heritage and the apparently greater refinement of Italian culture. Here portrayed by Cybill Shepherd in the 1974 Paramount Pictures release.

was deservedly panned. The immediate culprit for his demise, however, was the cultural climate of the times. When he cast Shepherd in the leading role, he offered his audience a particular representation of the American girl, but then naively declined to engage the social implications of that representation. That a few years later he would take up with Dorothy Stratton, a former *Playboy* model, no doubt did nothing to dispel the image of Bogdanovich as one out of touch with the redefinition of gender roles undertaken in the 1970s.

Works consulted

Cross, David, "Framing the 'Sketch': Bogdanovich's Daisy Miller," in John R. Bradley, ed., *Henry James on Stage and Screen* (New York: Palgrave, 2000).

Gerstner, David A., and Janet Staiger, eds. and "Introduction," *Authorship and Film* (New York: Routledge, 2003).

Naremore, James, ed. and "Introduction," *Film Adaptation* (New Brunswick, NJ: Rutgers University Press, 2000).

Wexman, Virginia Wright, ed. and "Introduction," *Film and Authorship* (New Brunswick, NJ: Rutgers University Press, 2003).

NOTES

1. Henry James, *The Portrait of a Lady*, ed. Nicola Bradbury (New York: Oxford University Press, 1995), p. 47.
2. Walter, Benjamin, "The Task of the Translator," trans. Harry Zohn, in Benjamin, *Illuminations: Essays and Reflections*, ed. Hannah Arendt (New York: Schocken, 1968), pp. 71, 73.
3. Brian McFarlane, *Novel to Film: An Introduction to the Theory of Adaptation* (New York: Oxford University Press, 1996), pp. 166–168.
4. Matthew F. Jordan, "Mourning, Nostalgia, and Melancholia: Unlocking the Secrets of Truffaut's *The Green Room*," in Susan M. Griffin, ed., *Henry James Goes to the Movies* (Lexington: University of Kentucky Press, 2002), pp. 84–87.
5. Michael Sragow, "A Sexual Battle," *New York Times*, January 30, 1974, p. AL15.
6. McFarlane, *Novel to Film*, p. 159.
7. Vincent Canby, "Daisy is an Unexpected Triumph," *New York Times*, January 16, 1974, p. AL1+.
8. Sragow., "A Sexual Battle."
9. María DiBattista, *Fast-Talking Dames* (New Haven, CT: Yale University Press, 2001), p. 23.
10. Ibid., pp. 33–34.
11. Henry James, *Daisy Miller and Other Stories* (1922), ed. Jean Gooder (New York: Oxford University Press, 1985), pp. 34–35. Further quotations will be cited parenthetically in the text.

12. Peggy McCormack, "Reexamining Bogdanovich's *Daisy Miller*," in Susan M. Griffin, ed., *Henry James Goes to the Movies* (Lexington: University of Kentucky Press, 2002), pp. 34–47.
13. Barbara Welter, *Dimity Convictions: The American Woman in the Nineteenth Century* (Columbus: Ohio University Press. 1976), pp. 3, 4.
14. Erica Jong, *Fear of Flying* (1973), (New York: Signet, 1996), p. 5.

10 Jane Campion's *The Portrait of a Lady*

Harriet Margolis and Janet Hughes

Henrietta's granddaughter

In 1996 Jane Campion's *The Portrait of a Lady* opened to negative responses, though Campion's star was high because of *The Piano*'s 1993 success. *Portrait* features Nicole Kidman as Isabel Archer, supported by John Malkovich, Viggo Mortensen, and Sir John Gielgud, among others. Kidman could carry a film now; then she was neither a star nor a respected actor. Malkovich was a respected actor associated with manipulative parts such as his role of Gilbert Osmond in *Portrait*. However well-regarded, the rest of *Portrait*'s cast were moving modestly either up or down the stairway to stardom – with the exceptions of Gielgud, whose part is limited, and Mortensen, whose Aragorn was not yet a gleam in Peter Jackson's eye. Inevitably, *Portrait* was marketed as "a film by Jane Campion," "the director of *The Piano*."

So we begin by asserting *The Portrait of a Lady* as a director's film, the work of an *auteur*. *Auteur* films manifest an artistic personality through theme, style, or both; Campion's films prove the concept's value. All her films have played with narrative structure, exhibited a distinctive visual and aural style, and explored power struggles within families and between men and women.[1] Campion's *auteurism* makes her *Portrait* a work of art itself, rather than a poor relation of Henry James's original.

James's status as a great novelist is a given, but who is this New Zealand-born, Australian-trained woman to make a film of one of his greatest novels? It is as if Henrietta Stackpole's granddaughter had set out to tell the story from her point of view. Campion was exposed early to arthouse films that studied female responses to patriarchal societies; even as a student she found herself wanting "to tell an erotic story, particularly from a woman's perspective."[2] We will examine the means by which she converts James's novel to this purpose.

Although James (1843–1916) championed high over low culture, Peter Brooks explains how James's work embodies a trend in nineteenth-century novels toward "excess," "heightened dramatization," "intensity,"

and, of course, "melodrama."[3] The cinema inherited the theatrical tradition of melodrama. Campion, like James, works within the melodramatic
frame, "excess" and "intensity" typifying much of her work. For both of
them, *Portrait* "is at its core an effective melodrama, chillingly equipped
with an unsuspecting victim and sinister schemes and disclosures."[4]

Arthouse filmmakers are part of contemporary high culture, and Jane
Campion is as much an arthouse director as any working today. Yet in
1992 she told an interviewer, "I'm not concerning myself with making a
blockbuster, but I'm not into high art film making either."[5] Although she
says, "[T]here's a part of me that wants to be popular,"[6] she has also said,
"If one of my films becomes very popular, I begin to ask myself questions
about the degree of truth that it contains, and wonder if that truth isn't too
easy to accept!"[7]

It was almost inevitable that James and Campion would rendezvous
on screen. Good economic reasons underpin the adaptation phenomenon: name recognition, public domain status (meaning no copyright
fees), and pre-existing markets for classic novels. However, "classic"
status sets up and hems in expectations, chiefly regarding fidelity. At
one point, Campion says, she and scriptwriter Laura Jones "wondered . . .
if it was even possible to do such an adaptation, until the moment
I realized . . . that we weren't going to shoot *Portrait of a Lady*, but
simply the story of *Portrait of a Lady* interpreted by me, with some of the
original dialogue" (Ciment, "A Voyage," 178) – blasphemy to hardcore
Jamesites, especially the word "story," which James used with disdain.

Philip Horne classifies Campion's film among "faithful" adaptations,
but then details ways in which the film "deviates" from the novel.[8] Along
with the changed ending, the film includes three brief but complete
departures from fidelity to the novel in the form of surreal passages that
contrast with the prevailing realism. We will return to these departures;
for the moment we note that Campion otherwise largely adheres to the
novel's dialogue and plot – it is a "faithful" adaptation in a straightforward sense. Nonetheless, it exemplifies "interpretation through adaptation," offering a reading of James's novel that implicitly critiques it,
bringing to bear frameworks of thought – especially a feminist one – that
developed during the intervening century.

Like Campion, James was interested in the consciousness of young
women faced with choices that determine the course of their lives. Both
have produced works exploring Isabel Archer and the question, "What
will she 'do'?" posed by James in the preface to the 1908 edition.[9] We
find their different answers equally interesting, partly because of their
different ways of reaching those answers: James observes Isabel; Campion

also identifies with her. James insisted that Isabel came to him as a "given," "an acquisition," and that he wanted to write a novel about her, which then propelled him to find other characters, situations, and complications;[10] whereas Campion admits that *The Portrait of a Lady* "is one of her favorite books, partly because she herself feels 'so Isabel Archerish.'"[11]

Pragmatically, Campion says, "I love James' subtle psychological analyses, his manner of weaving his web around his characters, but obviously that's not what you can do in film. My aims were to make the situations physical, develop the sexual elements that were only suggested, give Isabel some fantasies" (Ciment, "A Voyage," 178). Compounding differences in perspective and medium, Campion enjoys irony in a postmodern way, that is, for its own sake – a stance that distances her from a prescriptive feminist understanding of Isabel's position as well as from James's account of that position.

Talking beans

Campion's three conspicuous additions are the opening sequence; a sexual fantasy to which Isabel succumbs; and the surreal representation of Isabel's travels before her marriage. Campion has always been a "stylish" director, using visual style to prod her audience to reevaluate the ordinary. Some of the oddities of framing used in *Sweetie* (1989) can also be found in *The Portrait of a Lady*, though pragmatism sometimes accounts for unusual shot compositions – for example, an Italian exterior shot on the diagonal to avoid anachronistic vehicles and power lines (Ciment, "A Voyage," 184). Campion elaborates variations within the formal constraints of the "portrait" imposed by her source. This interplay between refinement and formality, on the one hand, and loose surrealism on the other, is part of her trademark as an *auteur*.

Surprisingly, Campion's film begins with women in contemporary dress; over a dark screen, a voice talks about kissing. Eventually, we see a group of young Antipodean women posed in a hazy, romantic forest clearing, while the soundtrack continues their unscripted accounts of romantic experiences and aspirations. Accompanied by opening credits, this black-and-white sequence declares itself a preliminary, serving, Campion tells us, "as a link to our era" (Ciment, "A Voyage," 180). Lest we miss the point that Isabel Archer still lives among us in every young woman whose "romantic hopes" will lead to "the process of disenchantment" (Ciment, "A Voyage," 180), the last young woman we see gazes curiously at the camera. The next face is that of Isabel

Archer/Nicole Kidman, also within the sheltering leaves of a tree; the kinship between these two women is apparent. They are open to the experience of life; they look at it and live it with intelligence and feeling.

With the visual transition into a past that might easily, it is implied, be the present, the *story* in James's *The Portrait of a Lady* has begun, and Isabel is already learning of the pain associated with romance. Campion's *interpretation* of James's story has also begun, for the witty banter between Mr. Touchett, Ralph, and Lord Warburton with which James begins disappears in the film, and instead we see Isabel's tears. Throughout the film, Campion emphasizes Isabel's pain, even masochism, in the face of Osmond's sadism; in fact, "the problem," as Campion sees it, "is that Isabel is an easy victim, so much does she want to fall in love" (Ciment, "A Voyage,"181). Campion's films have characteristically focused on a girl's or woman's development – in particular, on her sexual development, and the options available to heterosexual women. As Lizzie Francke notes, Campion "taps into the most perverse parts of the female psyche, unafraid to deal with women who are the undoing of themselves. At the troubled and therefore fascinating centre of her work is the exploration of female masochism."[12]

In keeping with Campion's stated aim – "to make the situations physical, develop the sexual elements that were only suggested, give Isabel some fantasies" (Ciment) – her second conspicuous addition to *The Portrait of a Lady* is an erotic reverie. Isabel conjures up a narcissistic masturbatory fantasy that identifies her suitors with sexual passion in a scene that James could never have written. Prompted by Caspar's gentle touching of her face earlier, Isabel indulges in imaginings. She moves with eyes closed, trance-like, the fringes of her bed's canopy echoing Caspar's touch, before lying down to picture herself the object of her three suitors' physical attentions. Lighting and music help to set the scene, and the music guides us toward its climax. While Caspar kisses her face and Warburton her knee, Ralph watches and tells her that he loves her, which disrupts the fantasy. As the men detach themselves, grow insubstantial, and disappear, Isabel sits up with a startled recognition of her physical weakness when tempted by desire. She has discovered that she does not know herself, and must face what her curiosity and desire have summoned from within her. The slow melody accompanying this scene, which picks up intensity from repetition, also accompanies the scene in which Osmond declares his love; it suggests that Isabel is hypnotically sucked into a world of physical desire, a slightly illicit world that she fears as well as longs for.

The music ties these two scenes together, and repetition of Osmond's declaration – "I am absolutely in love with you" – ties the parasol scene to the film's third departure from realism. The comically accelerated account of Isabel's travels deals deftly with a theme that figures much larger in the novel than in the film: Isabel as the American ingénue abroad in the Old World. This "travelogue" incorporates surreal elements, such as the outrageous talking beans. They morph into swollen lips, catching up the erotic overtones of the earlier reverie. They echo Osmond's declaration of love; and his mesmeric twirling of Isabel's parasol, a potent warning of his influence upon her life, reappears as a graphic element, also suggesting "whirlwind tours," and vertigo. This has a basis in the narrative facts – we see Isabel, overdressed and overheated, revolted by strange food and succumbing to faintness; but it also works metaphorically, referring to her emotional confusion and erotic thrall, and proleptically to her poisonous marriage and "stupefaction" by Osmond.

These surreal irruptions justify a reading of the film in which psychosexual motive is ever present and ever subdued, save for these moments when it bubbles to the surface of Isabel's consciousness. Consider the scene in which overheated young girls faint and are carried off the ballroom floor for their mamas to loosen their clothes and fan them; one of Campion's persistent motifs is the way physical reality threatens to escape the confines of costume and good behavior, especially when impelled by suppressed desire.

Isabel's increasingly elegant but restrictive clothing, and her increasingly elaborate ways of dressing her initially unruly hair, indicate her repression of physical and emotional desire. Campion uses costuming combined with camerawork to track Isabel's journey toward self-knowledge and recovery of the autonomy she forfeited by marrying Osmond. The curly hair returns upon Isabel's return to England, where she no longer represses and hides her emotions; she no longer needs to.

As Isabel becomes trapped in the "cage" of Italian society and her marriage, costume conveys the emotional reality beneath her compliant and proper surface. Here Campion takes her cue from James. Seeing Isabel in Rome after her marriage, Ralph is struck thus: "Poor human-hearted Isabel, what perversity had bitten her? Her light step drew a mass of drapery behind her; her intelligent head sustained a majesty of ornament. The free, keen girl had become quite another person."[13] Campion shows us not just the upshot, but the process; it is managed in parallel with James, but not always identically. She is with James on the marriage – "It was the house of darkness, the house of dumbness, the house of suffocation. Osmond's beautiful mind gave it neither light nor air" (395–396) – and on Europe – "When Isabel saw this rigid system closing about her . . . she seemed to be shut up with an odour of mould and decay" (397); but, typically, she also contrives to hint at a dimension of Isabel's being that interests James little, if at all.

At the point where Isabel's costumes are most restrictive, her rigid posture and hampered gait are emphasized, intercut with images of light and darkness and opening or closing doors, intimating her pride and her imprisonment in wretchedness. But the "mass of drapery" that Ralph noted is hijacked to betoken more than the artificial formality that he deplores. As Isabel's costuming grows more elaborate, the camera follows it avidly, particularly the train of her dress. Flicked by her heels, the pleated ruffles that burst from her ankle-hugging gown respond to the urgency or anger of Isabel's movements, expressing the sentiments she dare not voice before servants or visitors or Osmond's malevolence. A token of constraint, the train is also Isabel's only means of expressing her near-defiance.

The train forms part of a complex of images depicting Rome and European society as a gilded cage in which individuality, especially female individuality (think of the convent's formal garden), is almost without scope. Sometimes lashing like an enraged snake, it functions as an extended visual metaphor for repressed sexual energy in a standard Freudian association. It helps to supply a psychosexual motive for Isabel's behavior – specifically, her choosing to stay with Osmond when she has the chance to do otherwise, and devoted admirers prepared to help her leave him.

Malkovich creates an unnerving, sinister Osmond. When he declares his love, Isabel reacts with fear, plain in her posture, voice, gestures, and widened eyes. The uneasy, dizzy music of the fantasy recurs, the abbreviated Jamesian dialogue dances around meaning, and the bodies enact a counterpoint of circling, advancing, and retreating sadomasochistic desire. Significantly, when Isabel "finds" her temper, she betrays a flash of arousal in reply to Osmond's violence – he grabs her parasol and the hand holding it, placing him in control of the dance, which seems to emanate from the parasol he twirls. The camerawork amplifies the movement, introducing erotic and symbolic undertones along with a fetishistic focus on their feet.

James puts Isabel in a white dress with black ribbons early in the novel, before Lord Warburton proposes (92); in the film Isabel wears this dress when Osmond declares his love, among shadows interspersed with shafts of light. The black-and-white parasol picks up this motif; its spinning speaks of chance and choice, the blurring stripes muddying the distinction between light and darkness. It also hints at loss of control under hypnotic influence. A threat is implied to the innocence proclaimed by Isabel's sprigged muslin gown, with its echo of Botticelli's *Primavera*; and the music taints a merry-go-round innocence with the erotic charge it picked up in its original context. Malkovich makes Osmond's profession of love sound like a threat; to the question, "Why does she fall for him?" we are left with a nonverbal answer. He has dazzled her with a sadistic spell to which her subdued narcissistic masochism involuntarily responds.

The erotic subcurrent runs through the depiction of the Osmonds' marriage. Tiny gestures suggest that Osmond's bullying frightens and arouses Isabel (the one as much as and because of the other); this attraction becomes explicit in the scene where Osmond plants Isabel on a pile of cushions to intimidate her eye to eye, then trips her by stamping on her train. This aggression flies in the face of James's express statement that his cruelty was not physical. Campion's Isabel is aroused by Osmond's violent proximity. She makes as if to kiss him, and her erotic humiliation as Osmond teases then rejects her is the focus, rather than his whispered insults.

Yet even here Campion picks up a cue from James. *The Portrait of a Lady* was originally published in 1881; when James revised it for publication in 1908, his changes tended to make Madame Merle and Osmond blacker, simpler characters in order to explain how the revised, more intellectual Isabel might have been taken in by them. Changes that affect our perception of Osmond can be found, for example, in Chapter 29. In the revised version Osmond loses his "universal" knowledge (which becomes "his knowledge of the right fact") and his "gentle" manners.[14] As for Madame Merle, in 1908 she plays Schubert when Isabel first meets her; in 1881 it is Beethoven; in the film, too, she plays Schubert, traditionally the "smaller" composer. The change subtly deprives Serena Merle of the grandness of vision associated with the "heroic" Beethoven. The film's editing also isolates her response – ("clever creature") – to Mrs. Touchett's news that Isabel is to inherit a fortune, subtly cueing us to distrust her, for the implied cynicism is alien to Isabel's view of life.

Jamesian language, Emersonian vision, and postmodern irony

James is an intrusive narrator; much of *The Portrait of a Lady*'s considerable length consists of commentary on the characters' thoughts and motives, and the plot's events. For example, James tells his readers how to respond to his heroine:

Smile not, however, I venture to repeat, at this simple young lady from Albany, who debated whether she should accept an English peer before he had offered himself, and who was disposed to believe that on the whole she could do better.

She was a person of great good faith, and if there was a great deal of folly in her wisdom, those who judge her severely may have the satisfaction of finding that, later, she became consistently wise only at the cost of an amount of folly which will constitute almost a direct appeal to charity. (96)

The sheer length of such passages, the intrusive narration, and the complex language represent difficulties in adapting the novel.

The text is so verbally dense at least partly because, although the plot focuses on emotional entanglements, *The Portrait of a Lady* is primarily an ideas-driven novel. Human behavior is repeatedly represented as motivated by ideas rather than emotions; Isabel's "quest," Harold Bloom tells us, is "towards her own quite Emersonian vision of aspiration and independence."[15] The novel's concerns are moral, concerning right or wrong behaviour, or wisdom or folly in given circumstances. See, for example, the direct judgment delivered in the quotation above.

Isabel's quest for her "destiny" might be intelligible to audiences used to following heroes on journeys of accomplishment, except that Isabel's goal is not discrete, to be won once and for all. As an Emersonian product, she seeks to live her life's principles daily – to *be* rather than to attain. James represents her achievement at the end as understanding that she must abide by these principles even if, having innocently erred in judgment, she must live with the consequences.

Choices interest Campion, like James, acutely: "For me, *Portrait of a Lady* speaks of the choices that one has to make in life, and tells us also that we can make sense of our destiny – disastrous as it may be, as is Isabel's – if we approach life with love, with honesty and with a will to self-discovery" (Ciment, "A Voyage," 185). Unlike James, Campion works with motives that are more psychological and physical than philosophical. Her Isabel is more physical – someone who can unselfconsciously sniff her boot or dry her hair around Ralph. She is also more emotionally volatile (and here Campion takes her cue from the 1881 *Portrait*).

For example, Campion drastically reduces the conversation in which the Countess Gemini reveals Pansy's parentage. The cuts make the story easier to follow but also change the tenor, externalizing and amplifying emotions in a way that heightens the scene's melodramatic potential. In the novel Isabel reacts with cautious curiosity; she asks many questions, begins to cry only when she reflects on the fact that Pansy unknowingly dislikes her mother, and recovers to converse further. She may be dizzy and disturbed at the interview's end, but nothing like Campion's agonized, sobbing Isabel who quickly becomes too distressed to speak. This simplification renders Isabel's reaction in a way that a modern audience, conditioned by a century of melodramatic cinema, is more likely to find convincing and sympathetic. Through such artistic choices, Campion speaks to her own audience on her own terms.

Where James often covers serious matters in the witty upholstery of his dialogue and commentary, Campion does not have such luxury within the scope of her film. Much of the verbal humor and Emersonian context that saturate the book is lost from the adaptation, as the play of the dialogue is too subtle and written too much for its own sake (and its exploration of what will become at best secondary characters in the film) to be used in an adaptation. Nevertheless, Campion's characters retain a stilted Jamesian turn of phrase, and the excision of snippets of dialogue from their wider contexts often makes their oddity more acute. The viewer is sometimes left uncertain about what exactly the characters mean. What are we to make, for instance, of Isabel's words to the dying Ralph: "Why should there be pain? Pain is not the deepest thing." Campion's selection process subtly disrupts the verbal fabric of James's text, casting doubt upon the characters' accounts of themselves, their motives, and actions. The strangeness of the idiom, exacerbated by fragmentation, suggests some kind of disjunction in the characters' emotional lives – some failure of authenticity or self-awareness. Searches for fidelity in the dialogue only intensify the disjunction, for they increase our consciousness of the actors as performers.

This dislocation and heightened self-consciousness contribute to Campion's particular brand of irony, one at odds with James's, which is specific and purposeful. As Dorothy Van Ghent explains, *The Portrait* sets up intertwining metaphors of the verbal and the visual; the title itself "asks the eye to see," "seeing" becoming "the theme of the developing consciousness," and "the metaphor of doors, as it combines with the metaphor of 'seeing'" takes on different "ironic force," depending on its context.[16] Arnold Kettle emphasizes James's "insistent use of dramatic irony in the construction of the book."[17] Where James bends words to specific ironic purposes, Campion's irony is more open. She has no specific purpose; rather, she is curious about what happens if she shakes one of the trees under which her heroines are so often found. (Her mother has said, "She likes to set things into action and see what happens."[18] Like any irony, Campion's flatters her audience, for she assumes that we can see what she sees, though she allows – forces – us to make of it what we will.

An emotional identification such as Campion's with Isabel does not preclude distancing oneself enough to observe and analyze intellectually. Ralph restrains his emotions and becomes a participant observer because of his illness. Campion could have chosen Ralph to narrate the film in a voiceover, thus solving certain difficulties created by James's narratorial style. Ralph could easily have taken the audience with him, but Campion prefers a more neutral realism that leaves us outside the characters' minds. The effect is twofold: to prioritize the visual, and to create the necessary gap for irony to function.

"An erotic story"?

While Campion's subject has generally been female eroticism, James has a more general and generalizing interest in *The Portrait of a Lady*: the character of the nineteenth-century American abroad. Through this figure he can study what it means to be an American at a time when that character was developing toward maturity, and what it means to be a European, by contrast. The possibilities opened up and curtailed by one's nationality interested James as much as those governed by class and gender.

James is said to have got his inspiration for Isabel from a cousin.[19] Campion brings to Isabel her own experience, colored by her Antipodean point of view. She has observed, with reference to *A Portrait of a Lady*:

coming from Australia or New Zealand now makes one more like Americans going to Europe were then than Americans going to Europe are now . . . we have more of a colonial attitude about ourselves, a more can-do, anything's-possible attitude. I felt so much like Isabel as a young woman, a sense of having extraordinary potential without knowing what the hell to do with it.[20]

Each artist thus cares about Isabel's choices and their consequences. Each artist considers the character's psychology and social circumstances as factors determining her interests and decisions. James focuses on intellectually and socially formed aspects of the psyche, while Campion emphasizes less conscious aspects, especially those connected with physical sexuality. The motives she implicitly attributes to James's characters are primarily psychosexual, with Freudian overtones – appropriately for a text that seems to repress emotional considerations in favor of rational ones in dealing with affairs of the heart – and feminist implications.

The sexual fantasy provides a glimpse into Isabel's semi-conscious psyche; but Campion also deploys visual devices that uphold Isabel's perception of the world, implying that the threat comes from the *outside* rather than emanating from her own fears. So, for instance, the sequence in the British Museum where Henrietta tells Isabel that Caspar Goodwood has come after her has Isabel retreating physically before Henrietta's words and meaningful approach. The shot is curiously framed by a long horizontal slot (formed from out-of-focus antiquities in the foreground). The effect is to enclose the two in a claustrophobic space, from which Isabel's exit is blocked as she fearfully retreats from Henrietta's advance. The frame – the world – rather than either woman's behavior or beliefs is implicitly responsible for the panic Isabel evinces as Campion exposes Isabel's psychological projections on screen.

Campion's Isabel can be verbally assertive but emotionally timid; her gestures, facial expressions, and body language represent her as physically terrified of sex – even in the mild and respectful guise of Lord Warburton's overtures. There are small hints that beneath her initially tomboyish persona there lurks an urgent sexuality, repressed because its power frightens her. This becomes explicit in the sexual fantasy, but elsewhere her gestures of recoiling, or hesitating, paralyzed, before intimations of sexual interest suggest that she interprets such overtures as sexual *threat*.

Our point is to suggest that the starting point for comparing film and novel is the study they make of a specifically young, female character, her options, and her choices. Both novelist and director observe her and consider her actions; that is, they take the role of observer, though Campion also identifies with her.

"What will she 'do'?"

Returning to the essential question about Isabel Archer ("What will she 'do'?"), we can see that James relies on his Emersonian understanding of the world while Campion brings a different perspective to bear in answering it. Campion's Isabel often faces this question with real fear when "doing" involves possible loss of autonomy through subordinating herself in marriage. In this response to the potential threat of romance combined with sexuality, Campion touches on the concerns of the women's romance novel. Some readers may be reluctant to identify James's protagonists in such terms, yet his story – in contrast with his plot – does begin with Isabel in retreat in her Albany home. She is apparently reading, or, as James jocularly puts it, "trudging over the sandy plains of a history of German Thought" (24); more truthfully, she awaits a visit from Goodwood, her suitor. She may have previously encouraged him, but now and throughout the novel she will more or less fear what the man and marriage to him would mean for her experience of life. This "conception of a certain young woman affronting her destiny" (Preface, xii), and her hesitation in the moment, is not unique to James. The theme is common to many women's romance novels from Georgette Heyer to Rita Clay Estrada, from regency romances to short contemporary category romance novels,[21] since they, too, usually present "the journey of an uncommitted, undefined self which sets out to find the right house to live in and the right partner to live with."[22]

Such a protagonist, though, always has something exceptional about her that makes us interested in her destiny. Campion's Isabel cuts across the opposition James sets up between Old World and New, colonial and European, unsophisticated and cultivated, naïve and knowing, good and bad ideas. When Osmond tells her that she has "very bad ideas," Campion's audience has already been primed to think of her as refreshingly spontaneous, commendably her own woman, whereas James requires his reader to see her as an undereducated, inept colonial, who is blundering uncomprehendingly into the complexities of European society. Part of the shift is effected by selection from the novel, but visual cues also mold the viewer's perceptions. We have repeatedly seen Isabel moving quickly and impulsively, her unruly red hair a splash of colorful disorder against the dark, formal interiors of the Touchetts' house. The way her uncle and Ralph watch and react to her encourages us to read her as an injection of spontaneous life into a moribund household. Hostile reactions from other characters, who are depicted as frankly stuffy, confirm this implication and extend it out into the social milieu.

Comparing James's interests with those of women's romance novels is not, in our minds, an insult, nor do we wish to suggest that Campion's film represents the Harlequinization of *The Portrait of a Lady*, for better or worse. Instead, we call attention to the fact that, when James announces "the germ of my idea" for *Portrait*, he rejects what many people might expect to be his starting point – an action or series of actions – in favor of character, specifically, "the character and aspect of a particular engaging young woman" (Preface, vii). He emphasizes that "the centre of the subject" lies "in the young woman's own consciousness," something typical not only of women's romance novels but also, according to Molly Haskell's early contribution to studies of women and film, of the woman's film.[23]

A happy ending – a romantic union with assured prospects – is one characteristic of women's romance novels. Campion's films tend toward open-endedness, a characteristic common to her treatment of irony and choice. In contrast, James ends *The Portrait of a Lady* with two secondary characters discussing Isabel's return to Rome. Campion, via a freeze-frame, leaves Isabel literally suspended in time. Haskell associates four themes with the woman's film, and Campion adopts two of them, self-sacrifice and choice, for *Portrait*: "In the distinguished women's films, the combination of director and star serves the same function as the complex perspective of the novelist: They take the woman out of the plural into the singular, out of defeat and passivity . . . into the radical adventure of the solitary soul, out of the contrivances of puritanical thinking into enlightened self-interest."[24] It is about living life authentically, especially when that means finding "what's love, what's romance, what's the difference."[25]

Campion's Isabel flees Goodwood and flees her reaction to Goodwood. Her choice, very likely, is also to return to Rome, but unlike James, Campion does not close off her options for us. Instead, she provides reasons for us to consider: Will Isabel return because of Pansy? Because of propriety? Fear of Goodwood and losing herself to his sexual allure? Lasting if perverse desire for Osmond? Bloody-mindedness about winning a war of wills with him? Or does she turn back to look because she may finally choose not to return to Rome? In the most open-ended reading possible, we are left considering both Isabel's and Campion's choices, with Isabel intent always on refining herself in order to live a fine life, and Campion always intent on artistic representations of the ways women find their way through life's choices. She could not, like James, end with two secondary characters on screen; and, unlike James, even with the focus directly on Isabel, Campion prefers us to judge for ourselves. From our point of view, the differences between their presentation of Isabel, her milieu, and her choices reflect a century's social changes in the global Anglo-American environment, and in turn the social position of women in most of the English-speaking world.

NOTES

1. See Harriet Margolis, "'A Strange Heritage': From Colonization to Transformation?," in Margolis, ed., *Jane Campion's The Piano* (New York: Cambridge University Press, 2000), especially pp. 3–12.
2. Mary Cantwell, "Jane Campion's Lunatic Woman," *New York Times Magazine*, September 19, 1993, p. 51.
3. Peter Brooks, *The Melodramatic Imagination: Balzac, Henry James, Melodrama, and the Mode of Excess* (New York: Columbia University Press 1985), p. ix.
4. Cynthia Ozick, "What Only Words, Not Film, Can Portray," *New York Times*, January 5 1992, Section 2, p. 1.
5. Miro Bilbrough, "Different Complexions," in Jonathan Dennis and Jan Bieringa, eds., *Film in Aotearoa New Zealand* (Wellington: VUW Press, 1992), p. 101.
6. Rachel Abramowitz, "Jane Campion," *Premiere Magazine* (1996). Rpt. in Virginia Wright Wexman, ed., *Jane Campion Interviews* (Jackson: University Press of Mississippi, 1999), p. 190.
7. Michel Ciment, "A Voyage to Discover Herself," *Positif* (1996). Rpt. in Virginia Wright Wexman, ed., *Jane Campion Interviews* (Jackson: Univerisity Press of Mississippi, 1999), p. 179. Further quotations will be cited parenthetically on the text.

8. Philip Horne, "The James Gang," in Ginette Vincendean, ed., *Film/Literature/Heritage: A Sight and Sound Reader* (London: BFI, 2001), p. 16.
9. Henry James, *The Portrait of a Lady* (1881), 2 vols. (London: Macmillan, 1909), I, p. xx.
10. Laurence Bedwell Holland, "Organizing and Ado," in Harold Bloom, ed., *Henry James's* The Portrait of a Lady (New York: Chelsea House, 1987), pp. 44, 42, 41.
11. Cantwell, "Jane Campion's Lunatic Women," p. 51.
12. Lizzie Francke, "On the Brink," in Ginette Vincendeau, ed., *Film/Literature/Heritage: A Sight and Sound Reader* (London: BFI, 2001), p. 84.
13. Henry James, *The Portrait of a Lady* (1881), (New York: Signet Classics, 1995), p. 363. Further quotations will be cited parenthetically in the text.
14. James, *Portrait* (1908), II, p. 10; (1881), p. 280; Nina Baym, "Revision and Thematic Change in *The Portrait of a Lady*," in Harold Bloom, ed., *Henry James's* The Portrait of a Lady (New York: Chelsea House, 1987), pp. 75–77.
15. Harold Bloom, "Indroduction," in Bloom, ed., *Henry James's* The Portrait of a Lady (New York: Chelsea House, 1987), p. 6.
16. Dorothy Van Ghent, "On *The Portrait of a Lady*," *Studies in* The Portrait of a Lady, Compiler Lyall H. Powers (Columbus, OH: Charles E. Merrill, 1970), pp. 33, 35, 41.
17. Arnold Kettle, "Henry James: The Portrait of a Lady," *Studies in* The Portrait of a Lady. Compiler Lyall H. Powers (Columbus, OH: Charles E. Merrill, 1970), p. 61.
18. Lizzie Francke, "Jane Campion is Called the Best Female Director in the World: What's Female Got to Do with It?" *Guardian* (February 21, 1997). Rpt. in Virginia Wright Wexman, ed., *Jane Campion Interviews* (Jackson: University Press of Mississippi, 1999), p. 207.
19. Holland, "Organizing an Ado," p. 56.
20. Cantwell, "Jane Campion's Lunatic Women," p. 51.
21. See, for example, *Lady of Quality* and *Million Dollar Valentine*. In the latter the protagonists discuss their mutual fear of commitment, which leads to sharing with each other and consequently growing emotionally closer (Rita Clay Estrada, *Million Dollar Valentine* [Chatswood: Harlequin Mills and Boon, 2000], pp. 162–163). Georgette Heyer's lady has achieved a degree of independence that she fears she would lose if she were to marry; again, when she and the hero discuss this fear, it brings them closer (Heyer, *Lady of Quality* (New York: Bantam, 1972), pp. 202–203).
22. Tony Tanner, "The Fearful Self: Henry James's *The Portrait of a Lady*," *Studies in* The Portrait of a Lady Complier Lyall H. Powers (Columbus, OH: Charles E. Merrill, 1970), p. 106.
23. Their language is remarkably similar: "In the woman's film, the woman – *a* woman – is at the center of the universe" (Molly Haskell, *From Reverence to Rape: The Treatment of Women in the Movies* [Harmondsworth, Middlesex: Penguin, 1974], p. 155).
24. Ibid., pp. 162–163.
25. Jane Campion, "*In the Cut*: Behind the Scenes," DVD, uncut director's edition, Columbia Tristar Home Entertainment, 2004.

11   *The Europeans* – and the Americans

Brian McFarlane

One of the crucial differences between the Merchant Ivory film version of *The Europeans* (1979, UK) and Henry James's novel is that the film omits the novel's striking opening chapter. In this chapter James establishes with wonderful exactness the differences between a brother and sister in their approaches to America. This brother and sister – Felix, who earns his living precariously "by going about the world and painting bad portraits"[1] and Eugenia, the Baroness Munster of Silberstadt-Schreckenstein – are "the Europeans" of the title, though they are actually expatriate Americans returning home. The title is thus ironic: they are not so much Europeans as European*ized* and must learn again to be Americans if they are to find their niche in the closely organized world of New England.

This opening chapter establishes with wit and subtlety what this pair of siblings is up to. Eugenia is in retreat from an unsatisfactory marriage: she has been the morganatic wife of a minor German princeling, and she has come to America quite explicitly to seek her fortune. Felix has come seeking entertainment: if the Wentworths, the New England cousins they have come to visit, are rich, so much the better, but this is not a condition of his entertainment. To him, it will be merely "pleasanter" if they are rich (they are), whereas Eugenia can ask rhetorically, "Do you suppose if I had not known they were rich I would ever have come?" (13). On a first viewing, I felt that the film, in many ways excellent both *as* a film and as filmed *James*, lost something by omitting a comparable scene – a resonance of the kind that Peter Bogdanovich's *Daisy Miller* (1974) missed by ignoring the implications of that novella's last sentence, in which Winterbourne complacently returns to Geneva and discreet dalliances. Shortly, though, I shall seek to account for this initial response – and then to undermine it.

It is no part of my intention to praise James Ivory for being generally "faithful" to James or to chastise him for a lapse in fidelity to the antecedent text. In fact, I would like the notion of fidelity to be confined to relationships and to be outlawed from discussions of adaptation from

175

one narrative form to another. (At the same time, I cannot help wondering if there is not endemically a secret yearning for that fidelity that the more high-minded of us are at pains to discredit.) A film will not necessarily be good if it is merely "Jamesian" in spirit ("spirit" – that vague hold-all for sloppy-minded reviewers); equally, it may resonate as Jamesian in moments of purely cinematic invention. That remarkable scene in Bogdanovich's *Daisy Miller* in which Cybill Shepherd sings "Maggie," a sentimental American folk song, in an opulent Roman hotel room, has always seemed to me to go to the core of James's international complexities more directly than anything else in the film, which is so careful in its transpositions from novella to screen. It is a scene created for the film, but it draws together a great deal about the kinds of American guilelessness (innocence or fatuity?) and European sophistication (experience or decadence?) that preoccupy James.

Of course, the film adaptation will mean different things to those who know the novel and those who don't. For the former, it will inevitably be seen in some sort of conjunction with the novel: from a crude "it wasn't like that in the book" approach to more thoughtful consideration of how the film extends the ideas of the novel or which of the novel's interests seem most to have engaged the filmmaker. And however lofty one is about insisting on the autonomy of the film, the viewer who has read the novel will almost certainly have a preference for one or the other, more often than not for the precursor text. Those who know *The Europeans* (1878) will probably wonder at Ivory's decision to start his film in a way different from how James begins his novel; and it would be strange to have no view on the consequences for the ensuing action in the film.

So what does "Jamesian" mean? In attempting to answer such a question, we are thrown back on another: Why do people read James? (One accepts that there are plenty who can't and won't, or in any case don't, and it would be instructive to know what *they* make of the films). Speaking as one of the converted, I would say that it is not, as a rule, because one finds the plots especially enthralling. Indeed, there seems often to be a melodramatic urge at work in James which he fastidiously refuses to give its head, and to have done so might have made for more conventional, what-happens-next novelistic rewards. The irreducible appeal of James seems to me to inhere in the extraordinary subtlety of the authorial mind, as it is evinced in the linguistic precision, in the fineness of the discriminations at work in characterization and relationships, and in the moral dimension that overarches the whole achievement. In the later (and, to some, unrewardingly convoluted) works, that subtlety can seem perilously near etiolation, but in works as accessible as *The Europeans* or as taxing as *The Golden Bowl* (1904) (Merchant Ivory's latest passage of arms with James) there is a coherent grip on the inner and outer worlds of personages and situations that is far less conducive to simple summary than usual.

James is not an author whose works seem to shout "Film me!," so it is surprising how often filmmakers (for screens large and small) have been drawn to just this enterprise. It cannot but make us wonder how much of the peculiar strengths of James, especially perhaps that endlessly ruminative interior analysis whose discernments one so admires, are likely to survive in cinematic equivalents – even supposing the filmmaker has wanted, perhaps foolhardily, to look for these latter. Does this mean that the film will inevitably feel coarser or thinner than the novel? Or does it more properly mean that the filmmaker will have at his disposal cinema-specific means of producing his own subtlety and complexity, qualities so often attributed to James?

James's first brush with cinema was the 1933 Fox film *Berkeley Square* (directed by Frank Lloyd). This was actually based on John Balderstone's play which, in turn, was derived from James's unfinished novel, *The Sense of the Past*, posthumously published in fragment form in 1917.[2] The first credited film adaptation of James appears to have been the long-lost 1947 Hollywood film, *The Lost Moment* (directed by Martin Gabel) the first of many versions of *The Aspern Papers* (1888), which, along with *The Turn of the Screw* (1898), has been one of the most often filmed of all James's works. Strong on atmosphere and enigmatic plotting, these two have appealed to filmmakers in several countries, for television as well as cinemas, but the one definitive treatment has been Jack Clayton's masterpiece, *The Innocents* (1961, UK), a chilling black-and-white evocation of the ambiguities of *The Turn of the Screw*. William Wyler's *The Heiress* (1949, US), based on Ruth and Augustus Goetz's dramatization of *Washington Square* (1880), made from James the powerful melodrama he shied away from, and won several Oscars in the process. Agnieszka Holland's 1997 US version drew directly from the novel and, in settling for what it conceived as period realism, flavored with late twentieth-century feminism, had none of Wyler's potent distillation of a woman growing to hard-won independence of mind. Iain Softley's *The Wings of the Dove* (1902) (1997, UK/US), with ruthless precision, sheared away all that deflected attention from the central trio and made the contrasting *mise-en-scène* of stifling London and duplicitous Venice work exceptionally hard to achieve a film triumph – a triumph that had clearly understood its Jamesian antecedent and was equally determined to make a film derived from but not subservient to James.

Ask many filmgoers, though, whom they most associate with screened James and they are perhaps most likely to reply "Merchant Ivory," the production team that has now filmed three of the novels: *The Europeans*, *The Bostonians* (1886) (1984, UK/US),[3] and *The Golden Bowl* (2000, France/UK/US). The late producer Ismail Merchant and director James Ivory established an enviable track record for continuity of production over forty years, starting with their Indian-based films of the early 1960s, *The Householder* (1963) and *Shakespeare Wallah* (1965), both written by their longstanding collaborator, the novelist Ruth Prawer Jhabvala. They had a coterie following through a series of very attractive arthouse pieces in the 1960s and 1970s, and scored a major commercial success with their adaptation of E. M. Forster's *A Room with a View* (1985). This may now be seen as a watershed in the Merchant Ivory career. There has been a steady diminution in their critical acclaim, until it has become almost a cliché to write of their work, chiefly but not always literary adaptations (James and Forster dominating), as essentially undaring in approach to their literary sources, overtalky and not quite trusting the film medium to create meanings in visual terms. They have been seen – with some justice but also some unfairness – as catering to an unadventurous middlebrow, middle-class sensibility, too deferential to literary values. Andrew Higson sums up the critical divide thus:

They were also extremely influential films, both because they came to define English "heritage" cinema and because they convinced the major distributors that it was worth dealing with niche products that had a chance of becoming crossover mainstream successes. Critical opinion about Merchant Ivory's films has been mixed. For many, their films are wonderfully refined, boast superb performances, and display production values that far supersede what might be expected from such modestly budgeted films. But others dismiss the films as overly nostalgic, middlebrow and reverential, the Laura Ashley of contemporary cinema.[4]

The Europeans comes toward the end of their earlier period when they were moving westward from India (and their "Indian" period includes a masterpiece such as *Autobiography of a Princess*, 1975, technically a British film), but were still likely to produce such idiosyncratic work as the triptych piece *Roseland* (1977, US), *Hullabaloo over Georgie and Bonnie's Pictures* (1978, UK/US), and *Jane Austen in Manhattan* (1980, UK/US). There is really nothing as personal, as off-centre, again after the success of *A Room with a View*. They had found a market for which the spectacle of accomplished actors performing stylishly before listed buildings was almost enough. *The Europeans*, however, comes before the gloss has settled and it remains a film of remarkable freshness, indebted of course to James for a great deal but achieving its own autonomy. Not for the first time have filmmakers, given access to larger budgets and star-heavy casts, lost some of the verve and rigor that made their earlier work a greater pleasure, before they moved from the modest rewards of the arthouse to the uncertain commerce of the multiplex.

The point of this skirmishing approach to the novel/film pair in question is to suggest that more is at stake in the matter of adaptation than merely how the filmmaker has gone about rendering the novelistic in terms of the cinematic. However rigorously a comparison between the two might be conducted, it will give only part of the story of the processes of transposition. Adaptation studies, my own included, have not generally made as much as they might of the intervention of the screenplay and the possibility of the screenwriter's having a distinctive "voice" of his or her own – a real issue in the case of the Merchant Ivory oeuvre in which Jhabvala is a distinguished novelist in her own right and one with a special interest in the impact of one culture on another. Further, the intertextuality that accretes about (ramifies from?) the film of *The Europeans* will also include other Merchant Ivory titles, what is conjured, in terms of style, by their "product name," the kind of audience to which the work seems addressed, the "industrial" aspects of the production (budget and its implications for, say, casting, locations, and shooting schedules), and how hindsight may qualify one's first viewing of the film more than twenty years earlier.

I began this essay by referring to the novel's opening chapter and how Ivory's decision (or Jhabvala's?) to omit this scene in which Eugenia's and Felix's aspirations for America are contrasted. It is possible that I am both right and wrong in my view that Ivory has missed a crucial resonance as a result of this decision. Certainly, Ivory and Jhabvala, by denying us this initial view of Eugenia's bitterly unhappy response to being in America, undermine the power of that sudden access of genuine emotion she feels when she says, in words directly taken from the novel, to her uncle: "I should like to stay here . . . Pray take me in." This is in answer to his simply felt, "You have come very far." Without having seen the earlier restlessness of spirit, the viewer's experience of this moment is almost inevitably diminished. On the other hand, Ivory and his collaborators have chosen to open the film with Gertrude Wentworth's (Lisa Eichhorn) restless dismissal of the solemn Unitarian minister Mr. Brand (Norman Snow), followed by her meeting with Felix (Tim Woodward), as if Felix comes in response to her need for a new impulse in her life – and in search of "entertainment" for himself. Felix is more open to the American experience than Eugenia, and he is the one who will profit from it in every sense. The film aims to accentuate the more positive aspect of American probity working on Europeanized flippancy – and of Europeanized sophistication working wholesomely on American inhibition.

The extratextual matter of the star system perhaps worked against my giving full weight to this possibility: as Eugenia, Lee Remick was virtually the only member of the cast widely known to film audiences (Robin Ellis, as Robert Acton, had played the title role in the BBC series *Poldark*, 1975–77, but had made no impact in the cinema), and this leads us to assume that she will be the centre of narrative interest. There is no question that she is the most charismatic performer in the film, though Remick was never one of those huge stars that affect us like famous brand names. We nevertheless expect to be involved with her more intensely than with anyone else in the film, and it is interesting to consider why Ivory chooses not to start (or finish) his film with her. It is possible to argue that in constructing his film as he does, he intensifies our sense of her as simply passing through the world of the film, a world that is there when she arrives and continues when she is gone. I shall also argue that Ivory has other ways of measuring the distance that Eugenia has traveled during her time in America.

My own theoretical position[5] in regard to adaptation involves distinguishing between what can be *transferred* (essentially, "narrative") and what must be subject to *adaptation proper* (essentially, "narration" or "enunciation"). The former refers to that series of events, large in the sense of influencing the outcome of the narrative or small in the sense of grounding those major events, which are *con*sequentially as well as sequentially organized, in the quotidian actions that are linked merely by sequence. The latter (*adaptation proper*) refers to the medium-specific ways in which either film or novel goes about presenting the transferable matter of the original – that is, supposing the filmmaker *wants* to effect such transfer, and the extent to which he may wish to do so.

It would be tedious here to trawl through *The Europeans* to identify what Roland Barthes categorizes as "cardinal functions," those "real hinge-points of narrative" that initiate the prospect of alternative developments in the plot,[6] and then to scan Ivory's film to see how far *his* hinge-points or "risky" narrative moments correspond with James's. Such a (laborious) process does, though, show a very considerable degree of retention, so that the omission of the "action" of the novel's opening chapter, which might be summarized as "Eugenia and Felix discuss their expectations of America," is the more striking. Their disagreement on this score has the consequence of Eugenia's sending Felix off to inspect the Wentworths and their establishment, and to report back. The film, as we have seen, plunges Felix into the Wentworth world, in both its autumn beauty and its repressions as epitomized in Gertrude's irritable rejection of Mr. Brand's suggestion of church. Felix prepares the way for Eugenia's visit, having clarified for Gertrude, and for us, the nature of their family connection with the Wentworths and the state of Eugenia's marriage. In the following sequences, Eugenia and Felix drive to the Wentworths' house where, as described above, she is "take[n] in."

By this point in the film, a good deal of James's recurring thematic intentions has been made clear, by drawing on contrasts of character and style, of costume and speech, on those "integrational" functions (Barthes's term again)[7] which embed the actions and events in a set of signifiers that relate them to the world in which they take place. Through the ways in which, say, Eugenia and the Wentworth girls dress, move, and speak, or in the contrast of Felix's ease and gaiety with Mr. Wentworth's gravity of demeanor, we are drawn into a very Jamesian encounter of the Old World and the New. By comparison with later James, in, say, *The Ambassadors* (1903) or *The Golden Bowl*, in which this theme still preoccupies him, *The Europeans* is a minor work, yet I do not want to describe it as slight. Kathleen Murphy, in an essay on the film of *Daisy Miller*, has written: "His Americans were brash, uncomplicated, crudely ignorant, or gloriously innocent. He pitted them – sometimes on their own ground, sometimes overseas – against European complexity and wisdom that occasionally ran to decadence."[8] It seems to me that neither James nor Ivory mounts so crude a binarism as this in *The Europeans*, that there are levels of subtlety that preclude the play of such simplistic dichotomies. In these opening scenes alone, we have seen that, whatever innocence or wholesome New World setting Gertrude inhabits, it has not guaranteed her either simplicity or peace of mind. Similarly, however sophisticated Eugenia appears in her locutions and dress, she can be startled into an awareness of how much she needs simple affection and shelter. Gertrude will eventually arrive at a more mature understanding of what she wants from life and will be prepared to throw in her lot with Felix, and Eugenia's "European wisdom" will be vitiated by affectation and duplicity. James and Ivory are as interested in how a different background helps to dictate behavior as in how one individual character responds to another. But these people are not just representatives of the cultures that have formed them; they are also individuals reacting idiosyncratically to the world in which they find themselves.

On a narrative level, that is, on the level of what is "transferable," there is not much sense of difference between the two texts. Two Europeanized Americans, with dissimilar motives, return from a long expatriation to sound out their New England cousins. Felix arrives in Gertrude's life just as it is being at its most oppressive to her; he is drawn to her, and she to him, thus causing the minister Brand to feel rejected and to his ultimately turning for solace to Gertrude's sister Charlotte (Nancy New). Eugenia, interested in a fortune, attracts the attention of yet another cousin, Robert Acton, but he, though returning her regard, becomes aware that she is a woman who will "lie" if necessary, and will not commit to her. Ultimately, Felix, who has come to be entertained, finds in his love for Gertrude the seriousness that his life has been lacking, while Eugenia, who has perhaps mistaken an elegant sophistication for wisdom, loses Acton and returns to Europe. That is what "happens" in both novel and film. In terms, that is, of major cardinal functions, Ivory has chosen to transfer almost all from the novel.

I want now to turn to the matter of where the weight of the film seems to lie in comparison with where it is felt in the novel and it takes me back to the vexed question of the film's changed opening. While the panache of Remick's star performance ensures that the viewer will register Eugenia's personal flair and extravagance of manner as well as the clouds of European refinement she comes trailing, the emotionally charged intelligence of Eichhorn's Gertrude, and the way she is placed in the film's narrative and *mise-en-scène*, make seriously competing claims.

After the credits have been given against contrasting artists' images of European artworks and the "noble savages" of America, and of ships as a shorthand for the distance that is being traversed between the two, the film cuts to a young woman, Gertrude, in the autumn glory of outdoors New England, her cheerfulness cut short by the arrival of Brand. The pressures in her life, her restlessness of spirit, are rendered through her movement and intonations, in the way she wanders away from the house which stands for the values she can no longer embrace uncritically to the woods which offer less clear-cut guidance. The setting is serenely beautiful in cinematographer Larry Pizer's luminous images, and with the old hymn "Shall We Gather at the River?" heard on the soundtrack, the scene is as American as John Ford. However, the mood is neither reverent nor celebratory and, in the wholly filmic terms of interacting aural and visual imagery, Gertrude is established as waiting for an experience that will give her life new direction. As if in answer to her unspoken need, Felix appears, and their first scene together plays off his cosmopolitan ease against her strained ingenuousness.

Some time later, after the visitors have been installed in the Wentworths' guest house, Felix and Gertrude are walking together in the woods, aflame with autumn in a way that makes the Wentworths' inhibitions seem more intense and willful. The contrast of the truly natural with what is nature subdued in Gertrude is made in wholly cinematic terms. It is abetted by her professed yearning to *learn* from Felix along lines hinted at in his assessment of her family: "They don't get the pleasure out of life that they might." When, in the same sequence, Brand tackles Gertrude with having "new interests," adding "You're very much changed," she replies bluntly, "I'm glad to hear it." Brand, and what he has represented, belongs to a past in which she has not fully known herself and she makes clear "I'm not going back." The contrasts in appearance and modes of discourse in Felix and Brand, juxtaposed here, make plain that Brand's influence over Gertrude is finished. The growth of feeling between Gertrude and Felix is tenderly confirmed in the scene in which they run away from the church in the rain and kiss for the first time, and it is played for further sweet-tempered (but not cloying) comedy in the sequence in which Felix asks Wentworth (Wesley Addy) for his daughter's hand. Here Felix's precipitate request is vigorously seconded by Gertrude, then by Brand, and finally by Charlotte, who says firmly, "Father consent!," when Wentworth worries, "Where are our moral grounds?" The sequence considerably contracts James's corresponding scene (Chapter 12), and it can afford to do so, because – and it is a truism to say so – the *mise-en-scène* involving matters of character grouping and actorial differences, of camera placement to enhance contrast and solidarity, of costume and setting, is doing so much of the work of dialogue, let alone of James's intervening discursive prose.

After this buoyant melding of the values, and of what is valuable, in Old World and New, the film, like the novel, turns to the more melancholy business of disposing of Eugenia. If she has "come very far" on the day she arrives at the Wentworths, and to bring her there by carriage and for this to be our first glimpse of her is to emphasize the sense of the wearying journey she has made, two further sequences will show how much further she has "come" in the emotional sense. The first of these is the ball sequence at the Acton house, an invention of the film, an invention that helps to dispel any simplistic notion of New England gloom. My interest in it here is to remark how Eugenia is revealed as arch with Acton on the matter of singing and affected in her vivacity with his ailing mother. In this house, which James describes as "a mixture of the homely and the liberal," Eugenia strikes a series of false notes, and she feels that "she has been observed to be fibbing" (84). The film creates these impressions very vividly as the handsomely dressed Remick moves among the Acton guests, very conscious of her cosmopolitan manner. Then, in a brilliant scene with Mrs. Acton (Helen Stenborg), she prattles affectedly about needing, as a cook, "An old negress in a yellow turban." This remark, made in the novel (57) to Acton, who is astute enough to deal with her, seems more artificial when the film directs it to Mrs. Acton, whose gentleness is at a loss. In Acton's shrewd directness and Mrs. Acton's sweet simplicity, Eugenia has met matches she is unused to confronting.

The film, by making an occasion of the ball, as compared with the novel's briefly noted visit, has the advantage of showing Eugenia in relation to the community she has invaded. (It also provides a focus for the state of play in several of the film's important relationships.)

The other sequence crucial to the film's rendering of how far Eugenia, about to sail for Europe, has continued to travel during her time in America is her farewell to Mrs. Acton, who is dying. This time it is Eugenia who is at a loss, in the face of Mrs. Acton's direct and touching concern for her children's – and Eugenia's – happiness. Eugenia has been faced with a kind of honesty and goodness she can recognize, and it recalls the sudden capitulation to genuine feeling that she registered on first arriving at the Wentworth house. The two scenes with Mrs. Acton tell us a great deal about the failure of Eugenia's American experience, and by implication they reinforce our sense of how Felix has succeeded.

The fact that the film ends with the suitably partnered Brand and Charlotte, walking and reading outdoors in the late autumn, acts with a telling symmetry as we recall how Gertrude, having dismissed Brand, in the same alfresco beauties of a year ago, had gone inside to receive Felix.

Figure 11. *The Europeans* is a costume drama in the heritage film tradition, a nuanced exploration of difficult personal relationships and conflicting social values. A 1979 Merchant/Ivory production.

The film has chosen to stress these relationships of continuity, whereas the novel began with Eugenia's discontent, ends with her departure, and, in a very Jamesian touch, adds, "Robert Acton, after his mother's death, married a particularly nice girl." Eugenia has lost her goal as a result of being too clever, too practiced in dealing with situations, and Remick's assurance stresses this in the film; whereas Felix, by being open in a way that sometimes astonishes his cousins, finds what he wants in Eichhorn's intelligently receptive Gertrude. The "facts" of the story are similar in each text, but Ivory's structuring means that the film may be seen as more romantic than the novel. Nevertheless, I would claim that, like the novel, it is short without being slight, complex without being obscure. It is not a matter of Ivory's having sentimentalized the novel but of his having opted for a different emphasis. In doing so, he is not so much tinkering with James but rather suggesting another way of reading him; he is indebted to the novel, but his film has its own autonomy. If he is indebted, it may be said that he has paid his dues.

NOTES

1. Henry James, *The Europeans* (1878) (Harmondsworth, Middlesex: Penguin, 1964), p. 160. Further quotations are from this edition and will be cited parenthetically in the text.
2. I do not know if James's novel receives any credit on the film. The play was filmed again in Britain as *The House in the Square* (aka *I'll Never Forget You*) in 1951, with no reference to James in its credits. It was directed by Roy Baker.
3. *The Bostonians* was refilmed as *The Californians* (2005).
4. Andrew Higson, "Merchant Ivory," in Brian McFarlane, ed., *The Encyclopedia of British Film* (London: Methuen/BFI, 2003), p. 449
5. See Brian McFarlane, *Novel to Film: An Introduction to the Theory of Adaptation* (Oxford: Oxford University Press, 1996).
6. Roland Barthes, "Introduction to the Structural Analysis of Narratives" (1966), in Barthes, *Image-Music-Text*, trans. Stephen Heath (Glasgow: Fontana/Collins, 1977), p. 93
7. Ibid., p. 92
8. Kathleen Murphy, "An International Episode," in Gerald Peary and Roger Shatzkin, eds., *The Classic American Novel and the Movies* (New York: Ungar, 1977), p. 90.

Stephen C. Brennan

Carrie, the 1952 adaptation of Theodore Dreiser's (1871–1945) *Sister Carrie* (1900) starring Laurence Olivier, Jennifer Jones, and Eddie Albert, has never been judged one of William Wyler's better films. Contemporary critics found its style "surprisingly conventional" and "static,"[1] and Bosley Crowther, film critic of the *New York Times,* dismissed it as "a violently sentimental version of Mr. Dreiser's ironic tale of love and its deterioration."[2] In the ensuing decades, literary critics have echoed Crowther, Carolyn Geduld faulting Wyler for subscribing "to the suburban moral code" and for creating a "bourgeois heroine,"[3] and Lawrence E. Hussman concluding that distortions of *Carrie* "render the film nearly unrecognizable to the novel's admirers."[4]

The "fidelity approach" that these critics take, Brian McFarlane declares, is "a doomed enterprise" because it is simply "unilluminating." Some things can be "*transferred*" from novel to film, but much "necessarily requires *adaptation proper,*" that is, "equivalences in the film medium."[5] Showing a postmodernist bent, Robert Stam argues that a source novel "can generate any number of critical readings and creative misreadings," for it is "a dense informational network, a series of verbal cues that the adapting film text can then take up, amplify, ignore, subvert, or transform."[6] Wyler was a skilled filmmaker who admired Dreiser's work. Even though he ignored some aspects of the novel, including virtually all of its dialogue, he took up much else, sometimes amplifying, sometimes subverting, sometimes transforming it through numerous "equivalences." The result is a creative misreading, a respectable, and respectful, work of art in its own right.

A picture for adults

James L. W. West, III writes that "a culture [as well as an author] can speak a text . . . and . . . the 1900 edition of *Sister Carrie* is as good an example of . . . a collaborative work of art as we are likely to find in twentieth-century American literature."[7] West has in mind the influence on the novel of Dreiser's wife Sara, his close friend Arthur Henry, and the publishers who pressured him to adjust "a superior piece of reportorial realism" to the sensibilities of "the feminine readers who control the destinies of so many novels."[8] Unlike novels, movies have always been recognized as collaborations. The place to start in understanding how *Sister Carrie* became *Carrie* is with Wyler's relation to his collaborators, wanted and unwanted.

The unwanted collaborator was Joseph Breen, enforcer of the infamous Production Code. When, in late 1938, Columbia Pictures sent a film treatment to the Breen office, Breen responded that the story had been submitted "many times by several of our member companies"[9] and simply enclosed a carbon copy of the rejection sent the previous year to Jack Warner of Warner Brothers. The proposed film, Breen had written, was "thoroughly in violation of our Production Code" because Carrie is "an immoral woman" who goes unpunished and because Hurstwood's suicide is, in the words of the Code, "morally objectionable" and "bad theatre." For the film to be made, Carrie must be "morally clean" and engage in only "honest" relations, and Hurstwood must be got rid of "some other way."[10]

Things had changed little by 1948, when Paramount bought the film rights from RKO, which had purchased them from Dreiser in 1940 for $40,000,[11] and signed on Wyler to produce and direct. The writers Wyler selected for the screenplay, Ruth and August Goetz, were clearly concerned about the Production Code. They considered Hurstwood to be the story's "central element" but thought suicide "too comfortable and undramatic a way out for their tortured hero."[12] They also seem to have viewed Hurstwood as a victim of unrequited love, for they faulted the studio's working title, "Carrie Ames," for not conveying the idea that "in every union, 'one is loved, the other does the loving.'" This title may indicate an effort to make Carrie "morally clean" and "honest" by marrying her off to Robert Ames, the handsome young inventor who becomes Carrie's platonic "ideal to contrast men by"[13] in the novel. Such an ending had in fact been contemplated by Famous Pictures in an earlier abortive treatment.[14]

Even before filming began on *Carrie*, however, Wyler was calling the Production Code "ludicrous" and "old fashioned" for its administrators' condemnation of *Detective Story*, the Sidney Kingsley play about abortion that he was going to direct after *Carrie*. Just because children should be protected from certain subjects, he said, that "doesn't mean that it is my responsibility to make pictures for children."[15] What attracted him to *Sister Carrie* was "Dreiser's intense feeling about poverty and social injustice . . . his compassion for human suffering and tolerance for transgression."[16] When he received the Goetzes' treatment in June 1949, he thoroughly critiqued it, offering a number of suggestions for telling the story "more economically" and for correcting "the weakness of the dramatic structure" (quoted in Herman, *Talent for Trouble*, 319). But Wyler also pushed the film away from romantic melodrama toward a more adult, more compassionate and tolerant, picture of transgression and suffering than is usually recognized.

Despite the Production Code, Wyler did film Hurstwood's suicide and considered the result "very effective" and "marvelously played by Larry" (quoted in Herman, *Talent for Trouble*, 330). Unfortunately, when he turned his final cut over to Paramount in March 1951, the company's brass had "nightmares over *Carrie*" (Herman, *Talent for Trouble*, 330) because they were fearful of HUAC, the House Committee on Un-American Activities. As Wyler explained things, the "super-patriots" of the McCarthy era feared that the fall of a "sophisticated, cultured man" into beggary "showed American life in an unflattering light" (quoted in Herman, *Talent for Trouble*, 330). While he was in Rome preparing to film *Roman Holiday* (1953), Wyler received a long cable from Paramount threatening to shelve the film if he did not allow cuts. Even though his contract allowed him final approval, he gave in rather than see the film suppressed. Paramount had *Carrie* reedited and, after a sixteen-month delay, released it in July 1952, "sneaking it out with almost no promotion" (Herman, *Talent for Trouble*, 330), much as Doubleday, Page and Company had done with the novel in 1900.

Alternatives of consequence

Wyler's efforts to tell Dreiser's story with economy and drama meant identifying what McFarlane calls "the 'hinge-points' of narrative," incidents that "open up alternatives of consequence" and constitute the "irreducible bare bones of the narrative."[17] But Dreiser's long novel has fewer hinge-*points* where alternatives open than long periods of gradual drift on the tide of change toward seemingly inevitable turns. In several instances, therefore, Wyler invented characters and events either to make social forces visible or to create dramatic choices.

In relation to the Chicago portion of the novel and the flight of Carrie and Hurstwood to New York, Wyler kept many of the narrative's original hinge-points. In both novel and film:

Carrie meets Drouet on the train to Chicago and accepts the possibility of a future connection.

Forced by bad luck out of her menial job in a sweatshop, the distraught Carrie decides first to accept Drouet's financial aid and then to accept him as her lover.

Trapped in a loveless marriage and charmed by Carrie, Hurstwood begins to woo her.

Carrie, having begun to realize Drouet's emotional lacks, reciprocates Hurstwood's declarations of love on the condition that he make her an honest woman.

Drouet discovers the affair and reveals Hurstwood's marital status to Carrie, who is left alone feeling betrayed and desperate.

Mrs. Hurstwood discovers the affair and threatens Hurstwood with legal action if he does not give Carrie up.

Hurstwood finds his employer's safe open and accidentally locks it while he has $10,000 of his boss's money in his hand.

Hurstwood tells Carrie that Drouet has been hurt, and she, believing him, allows him to usher her aboard a train where he persuades her to go with him to New York.

For the sake of economy, Wyler eliminates Carrie's long search for work after her arrival in Chicago, her introduction to the city's wonders by Drouet and her neighbor Mrs. Hale, much of her wooing by Hurstwood, her first acting success in an amateur production of a popular melodrama, and the stopover in Montreal during which Hurstwood arranges a phoney wedding. Sometimes economy also results in heightened drama. While Dreiser takes several chapters to show the revelation of the affair and its ensuing chaos, Wyler offers a rapid sequence of intense confrontations in Fitzgerald's Restaurant, first between Carrie and Drouet, then between Hurstwood and Julia, and finally between Carrie and Hurstwood.

Wyler's major invention for this portion of the film is Hurstwood's employer, Mr. Fitzgerald, owner of Fitzgerald's Restaurant. In the novel Hurstwood manages "a truly swell saloon" (*SC*, 33) – Fitzgerald and Moy's and his two bosses are merely evoked as one of many determining forces: "They wanted no scandals. A man, to hold his position, must have a dignified manner, a clean record, a respectable home anchorage" (*SC*, 66). In the film Fitzgerald is a pious, judgmental stick in a top hat who lectures Hurstwood on his moral duty ("Count your blessings one by one; then you'll see what the Lord has done"), snitches to Julia Hurstwood about her husband's carryings-on, and finally colludes with her in pressuring Hurstwood to give up the whore who, he says, "soon will sell her favors elsewhere." He would be a villain of melodrama if he were not more than a bit comical. Still, along with Julia, he is an odious objective correlative for what Dreiser condemns as an "arbitrary scale" of morality that demands one thing: "All men should be good, all women virtuous" (*SC*, 68).

The New York portion of the book offers even fewer hinge-points than the Chicago portion, and of them Wyler keeps only these:

Tracked down by a detective, Hurstwood gives back the stolen money.

After losing his job, Hurstwood tries to find work, without luck.

Because Hurstwood cannot support them, Carrie gets a place in a Broadway chorus line.

Carrie leaves Hurstwood to devote herself to an acting career.

Carrie rejects Drouet's efforts to reestablish their relationship.

A desperate beggar, Hurstwood seeks out Carrie, now a Broadway star, for a handout.

Again, Wyler seems to be after both economy and drama. He deletes not only Robert Ames but also Mr. and Mrs. Vance, the young socialites who introduce Carrie to the wonders of New York. Whereas in the novel Hurstwood keeps enough of the stolen money to buy a one-third interest in a modest Warren Street saloon and he and Carrie live for some two years in middle-class comfort, in the film the detective takes all the money, plunging the couple immediately into poverty. A series of brief dramatic epitomes replaces both Hurstwood's gradual "sagging to the grave side" (*SC*, 239) – brought on by age and brooding and culminating in the magnificent chapters on the Brooklyn streetcar strike – and Carrie's somewhat more rapid rise to Broadway stardom. We see Hurstwood being fired from his demeaning job waiting tables in a working-class lunchroom, Hurstwood lost in a sea of younger men battling in an employment office for a chance of a day's menial labor, Hurstwood reduced to tears when his last good suit is spattered with mud, Carrie among a crowd of young women auditioning for a chorus line, a brief montage showing Carrie's rise through images of performers on stage and theater posters.

Even more than in the earlier portions of the film, Wyler felt the need to invent dramatic choices and sudden disasters. Just when things start to get bad, Carrie discovers she is pregnant, the news bringing a ray of hope. But two hammer blows quickly follow. First, Julia Hurstwood arrives out of the blue with her lawyer demanding that Hurstwood give her permission to sell their house. Trying to protect Carrie's feelings and ignorant of Julia's willingness to give him $2,500 from the house, Hurstwood blindly signs away his salvation in exchange for a divorce. Second, Hurstwood comes home one evening soon thereafter to find that Carrie has lost the baby. When, in an effort to console her, he promises that they can have another child in better times ahead, she assaults his manhood: "When? When we're rich? . . . When you're eighty?" The long, slow process in the novel by which Carrie's love turns to disgust is here collapsed into a moment of bitter resentment.

Wyler also turns the desertion of Hurstwood into what appears to be a noble sacrifice. In the novel Carrie is finally so repelled by his physical and mental degeneration and so drawn to her new exciting stage career that she moves in with another chorus girl, leaving only a brief note and

some guilt money. In the film, feeling herself a pariah, she tries to save
Hurstwood by sending him back to the world he knows in the person of
his son, whose return from a European honeymoon is announced in the
papers. Ironically, of course, at the pier Hurstwood cannot work up the
nerve to intrude upon the joyous reunion of the newlyweds and the
bride's wealthy family. He slinks home to find Carrie gone and a note:

> Good-bye George –
> You will be happier with your son –
> I was not good for you.
>   Carrie

With these inventions, Wyler turns a naturalistic tale of characters
adrift in a sea of forces into something more like the tale that
Shakespeare's Horatio promises, one full of "accidental judgments"
and "purposes mistook / Fall'n on the inventors' heads."[18] Given that
Wyler's first choice for Hurstwood was the man who had recently won an
Oscar for *Hamlet*, the analogy may not be accidental.

The nature of emotional greatness

"In the cinema," Stam argues, "the performer . . . brings along a kind of
baggage, a thespian intertext formed by the totality of antecedent
roles."[19] When Olivier and Wyler reunited in 1951 for *Carrie*, Olivier's
baggage included his melancholy Dane, for, he wrote later, "once you've
played Hamlet, the play's thoughts and actions are part of you forever,"
including "the dramatic ebb and flow of Hamlet's moods, his inhibiting
self-realizations and doubts, his pitiful failure to control events."[20] Substitute "Hurstwood's" for "Hamlet's" and you have a pretty accurate
description of his performance in *Carrie*. The problem is that Dreiser's
Hurstwood is a sham aristocrat, an empty suit who merely "looked the
part" of "a very successful and well-known man about town" (*SC*, 33).
Olivier, we always feel, remains the noble prince deprived of his rightful
place. Ironically, then, while his performance has been called "a
haunting reflection of Mr. Dreiser's Hurstwood,"[21] Jones's is in some
ways more directly inspired by Dreiser's text.

Such a claim may seem perverse. After all, Dreiser's Carrie has no strong
emotional ties, not to her family, not to Drouet, not to Hurstwood. "Self
interest" is "her guiding characteristic" (*SC*, 2), "craving for pleasure . . .
the one stay of her nature" (*SC*, 24). Yet, paradoxically, on stage she is
capable of powerful emotion. When Hurstwood discourages her from
trying to get on the stage in New York, Dreiser remarks, "[H]e did not
understand the nature of emotional greatness. He had never learned
that a person might be emotionally – instead of intellectually – great"

(*SC*, 271–272). Earlier in Chicago, during her amateur performance as a damsel in distress in the melodrama *Under the Gaslight*, she utters affecting speeches on the enduring power of a woman's love precisely at the moment she is thinking about leaving Drouet. In "the fascinating make-believe of the moment" (*SC*, 138), her rival lovers see only "their idol, moving about with appealing grace, continuing a power which to them was a revelation" (*SC*, 140). Wyler was thus being attentive to the novel in advising the Goetzes to show Carrie's "growth from the naïve country girl on the train to a mature woman with *emotional greatness*, the fulfillment of the promise that attracted Drouet and Hurstwood, and which will make her a fine actress later" (quoted in Herman, *Talent for Trouble*, 320; italics added).

Still, one might object, Dreiser never intended anything like Wyler's sentimentalized Carrie, a fallen woman so distraught when a neighbor girl refuses an apple from her that she tries to flee to her prelapsarian state at her sister Minnie's. If he wants her, she tells Drouet tearfully, he will have to woo her there "just like I was home with the family." Yet this view of Carrie is not entirely arbitrary. Dreiser himself glorifies the "lovely home atmosphere" that "make[s] strong and just the natures cradled and nourished within it" (*SC*, 63) and attributes to Carrie enough "industry and natural love of order" to give the "cosey" flat she shares with Drouet "an air pleasing in the extreme" (*SC*, 69). Moreover, as Sheldon Grebstein has noted, she is virtually devoid of sexual passion, and "[h]er sexual allure is completely that of the archetypal Victorian heroine, comprised of innocence, purity and helplessness."[22]

If Wyler was not exactly trying to placate Breen, he no doubt had his eye on the turnstile. Movie attendance was dropping precipitously in the early 1950s, and a domesticated Carrie with "emotional greatness" was likely to attract conventionally minded women who bought into messages about what the feminist critic Brandon French terms "the dangers of women's lost femininity and the bounties which awaited women within the boundaries of the traditional female role."[23] To the extent that Carrie fits the popular feminine image, which largely coincides with Dreiser's implicit ideal, she gives audiences an objective correlative for Hurstwood's sense of loss and becomes a worthy beneficiary of his noble sacrifice. Still, if she were merely a prototypical June Cleaver, we might well fault Wyler for missing "the book's underlying anarchy" (Grebstein, "Dreiser's Victorian Vamp," 547).

A double text

French has found in movies of the period a "double text," that is, a surface validation of female domesticity that "simultaneously reflected, unconsciously or otherwise, the malaise of domesticity and the untenably narrow boundaries of the female role." Emerging in these films is the "transitional woman . . . torn between her desire for a conventional, secure lifestyle and her longing for an unconventional, adventurous, largely uncharted course of action."[24] The Carrie Meeber of Dreiser's novel is certainly such a transitional woman, simultaneously a "Victorian Vamp" and "the first modern heroine" (Grebstein, "Dreiser's Victorian Vamp," 551). A similar doubleness is evident in Wyler's Carrie.

One indication of the film's subversiveness is its jaundiced view of marriage. Couples appear happy only in a state of newlywed euphoria – Carrie and Hurstwood in a New York hotel room before the detective arrives, George, Jr., and his bride laughingly embracing her parents at the pier. While Carrie later often seems the supportive wife, we sense the strain in her attempts to cheer up her depressive husband. As for the film's other married couples, Carrie's sister Minnie, like her prototype in the novel, lives in crowded squalor with her penny-pinching, judgmental husband Sven and their infant son, while at the opposite end of the economic spectrum is the almost equally joyless Hurstwood family dominated by Julia, who remains the "pythoness in humour" (*SC*, 160) of the novel.

Only in Mrs. Oransky, Carrie's working-class neighbor in New York invented to replace the frivolous Mrs. Vance, does Wyler seem to provide a positive image of a married woman. Plain-faced and shapeless and speaking in a vaguely East European, probably Russian, accent, Mrs. Oransky appears at first a cliché – the earthy, wholesome peasant. When Carrie shyly confesses her pregnancy, Mrs. Oransky, happily scrubbing her naked son in a wooden tub while Carrie dandles the woman's infant daughter on her knee, calms Carrie's fears about home childbirth and shares her joy at the coming blessed event. Nowhere, however, is there even a mention of a Mr. Oransky; for all we can tell, Mrs. Oransky is on her own. She takes control of matters when Carrie loses the baby, and, more importantly, she becomes the authoritative voice of real life when she implicitly questions the sincerity of Carrie's love. Having made it big on Broadway, Carrie, draped in furs and bearing the gift of a newfangled oil-burning heater, knocks on Mrs. Oransky's door to ask about Hurstwood. To Carrie's surprise, her old friend looks her up and down distrustfully and when offered the heater – an image of artificial warmth – responds, "You sellin' them?" Still doubting that Carrie really wants to find Hurstwood, she directs her to a Mr. Blum, owner of a laundry where Hurstwood used to take his clothes and apparently Hurstwood's only friend. Blum has no information, but he does have advice. If Hurstwood is all right, he tells her, he will not need her. More significantly, if he is not all right "[h]e wouldn't thank you to see him." The man knows the ways of the world, knows that shabby independence beats a gilded cage. Through this Russian immigrant woman and Jewish shopkeeper, Wyler, himself an immigrant Russian Jew, subverts the suburban moral code that presumably informs the film.

In addition, Carrie is not quite the "simple-hearted helpmate" (Hussman, "Squandered Possibilities," 195) she seems to be. For one thing, she is awfully fond of the first-person singular (her name, after all, is Carrie *Mee*ber). "I can do better than Minnie," she boasts to Drouet on the train to Chicago. "I went to school." "I won!" she exclaims when she beats Drouet at cards, and it does not matter that, as Drouet points out, it took Hurstwood's help to do it: "I don't care. I won!" At the moment of her greatest bliss, she is strutting before the mirror of the lavish New York hotel room dressed in her new finery when Hurstwood asks if she is happy. "Happy?" she replies. "Look at me. Look at where we are. I'm Mrs. George Hurstwood of New York City!" After the detective leaves, she is immediately concerned about how she appears in the eyes of others: "Was he laughing at me?" For a woman who has earlier proclaimed, "I love you with all my heart," she seems curiously self-centered. True, she responds a moment later to his stricken look and seems unfazed to learn that they are broke. "I thought something really terrible had happened," she tells Hurstwood with relief. "We'll manage, you'll see," she says dutifully. But this vow may reflect the enthusiasm over her newly attained social status as much as true love. "Why, we're married," she offers as her reason for standing by her man. "I'm your wife."

Indeed, the veneer of selfless devotion breaks down under greater strain. When, after the miscarriage, a bedridden Carrie derides Hurstwood for being an old man who cannot support his family, she, with quiet determination, asserts her will to live: "I can't advise you, George. But I know one thing. I'm still young and I'm going to live – somehow." Without the melodramatics, her speech echoes that of another scarlet woman who marries out of economic necessity and whose chance for happiness ends with the death of a child: "As God is my witness, as God is my witness, they're not going to lick me. I'm going to live through this, and when it's all over I'll never be hungry again . . . If I have to lie, steal, cheat, or kill, as God is my witness I'll never be hungry again." Wyler's Carrie is not the conscious schemer that Scarlett O'Hara is. Yet given that Jones delivers her lines to Vivien Leigh's husband and that Jones was married to David O. Selznick, who produced *Gone With the Wind*, the parallel is likely intended, perhaps partly as a tribute to Dreiser, whose heroine is an obvious literary antecedent of Mitchell's.

Since Carrie resumes her wifely attitude in ensuing scenes, we might dismiss her outburst as hormonal, an expression of postpartum depression. But Dreiser himself makes such *élan vital* a moral quality. On the train to Montreal, once Carrie has surrendered to Hurstwood's pleas, she looks out of the window at the passing scene and, as the narrator explains, "She did not feel herself defeated at all. Neither was she blasted in hope. The great city held much. Possibly she would come out of bondage into freedom – who knows? Perhaps she would be happy. These thoughts raised her above the level of erring. She was saved in that she was hopeful" (*SC*, 204).

Carrie is Dreiser's prime example of the "anticipatory self," which, as Philip Fisher argues, "has as its emotional substance hope, desire, yearning, and a state of prospective being."[25] When Wyler's Carrie chides Hurstwood for dwelling on the old days ("Stop talking about the past! What good is it? Let's take what comes"), she is not uttering something "unthinkable in the novel" (Hussman, "Squandered Possibilities," 195), but expressing that future-looking optimism that Dreiser proclaims is her saving grace.

As Fisher argues, acting is "a convenient cultural symbol" for the anticipatory self.[26] In the novel not only does Carrie become an actress, but she and her lovers are also always on stage in cities transformed imaginatively "into a brilliantly illuminated theater of desire."[27] Although the film barely touches on Carrie's artistic nature, when Hurstwood first calls on her in Drouet's absence, she is reading a play in which Drouet, not she, is going to perform. He tells her she is pretty enough to play the ingénue and offers to read Drouet's part with her. But before he reads a word, he fixes his half-closed eyes on hers hypnotically, until she, grasping his intentions, rises in high dudgeon. Still, she agrees to attend a play with him a few nights later if he will treat her according to her assumed role: "I try to behave as if I were Mrs. Drouet. I will always behave that way." We, of course, know better. To make the point clear, Wyler places a mirror beside the door to catch the reflection of two-faced Carrie as she closes the door behind her new beau.

The play they attend – *Camille* – is significant as well. Much as Carrie's reading of Balzac's *Père Goriot* in the novel invites a comparison between her and Goriot's heartless social-climbing daughters, her connection in the film with Camille, the self-sacrificing prostitute, makes it hard to forget that, as Mrs. Oransky suspects, she is always, at least unconsciously, selling something. Carrie virtually admits as much earlier when she tries to explain her loss of virginity to Hurstwood: "When you're poor it gets all mixed up. You like the people who are good to you." In case we might think of Carrie only in terms of Camille's selflessness,

Wyler emphasizes the ironic parallels between the play and the film. Curious as to why Hurstwood always cries at *Camille*, she asks, "Why didn't he tell her the truth? And then he wouldn't have left her and maybe she wouldn't have died." Those who know the novel know who will leave and who will die and why Hurstwood ought to cry.

"Willie Wyler's medium"

Sometimes Wyler's actors thought him a sadist, for he would shoot take after take until he got exactly what he wanted. "The vicious Wyler just kept on saying 'Lousy,'" Olivier writes of his 1938 experience with *Wuthering Heights*, "and told me to do it again and again, without explanation" (Olivier, *On Acting*, 259). Wyler was among a select group of directors, including Orson Welles and Olivier, who "not only developed new ways for the cinema to be adequate to serious theater, but also developed a kind of discipline in mise-en-scène" that widely influenced the craft.[28] Looking back on *Wuthering Heights* in 1982, Olivier would acknowledge that Wyler "had taught me more than I knew" (Olivier, *On Acting*, 266) and claim that film is "Willie Wyler's medium" (Olivier, *On Acting*, 346). Wyler's "discipline in mise-en-scène," already evident in discussions above, warrants closer attention here as the basis for understanding the film's conclusion.

One thing Olivier may have learned from Wyler is that "[w]hen an actor gets his eyes right on film, he's reached a peak in his professional life" (Olivier, *On Acting*, 298). Writing of Wyler's attention to his actors' eyes in *The Best Years of Our Lives*, André Bazin asserts, "All the dramatic joints are so fine-tuned that the direction of a pair of eyes shifted only a few degrees is not only legible even for the dullest of spectators, but capable of toppling a whole scene" (quoted in Madsen, *William Wyler*, 275). While some early reviewers faulted *Carrie* for its "static" quality, the many extended shots and close-ups with a stationary camera allowed Wyler to exploit both Olivier's and Jones's expressive eyes.

In this, too, he took his cue from the novel, which focuses on eyes as sometimes the conduit of external forces, sometimes an instrument of power. In the opening chapter Carrie, feeling Drouet's sexual interest, is "bold" in returning his gaze: "A clever companion – had she ever had one – would have warned her never to look a man in the eyes so steadily" (*SC*, 5). For the most part, however, her eyes indicate an essential passivity. When she is most open to the vitalizing force of experience, as she is on the train to New York, her mind "succumbs to the flood of objects" (*SC*, 203) as she gazes at the passing scene "with wondering eyes" (*SC*, 204). A moment later, Hurstwood, "looking into her eyes," generates such "magnetism" (*SC*, 205) that she agrees to go with him if he will marry her. Never in the novel does Carrie achieve like mastery with her gaze.

Wyler's Carrie is much bolder and more masterful, and the turn of her eyes clearly signals her feelings. During the card game, her eyes shift more and more toward Hurstwood, until at their farewell she is looking directly away from Drouet toward this fascinating new object of desire. By the time they meet in the park and begin to plan a life together, her eyes are fixed eagerly, almost aggressively, on him while he glances furtively about with guilt over his married state. During their New York days, Hurstwood's decline is marked by an increasing inability to meet her and others' eyes, and her rise by a direct, at times dominating gaze – when Hurstwood snaps at her for spending too much money, when she reveals her pregnancy, when she urges him to be reunited with his son, when Drouet reveals the theft, and especially when she drags Hurstwood off the street into her dressing room near the film's conclusion.

Olivier uses his eyes most effectively during the cab ride with Carrie after the theft. The scene appears to be an equivalent for the famous one in the novel where, over the course of almost three full pages in the Norton edition, Hurstwood "trembles in the balance between duty and desire" (*SC*, 192) before the lock clicks on the safe and he springs into action. In the film the theft occurs much more rapidly and with little evident conflict since Hurstwood intends to return the money. Only later, in the cab, does the psychomachia evince itself. With each question from Carrie about Drouet's fictitious injury, Hurstwood turns to his object of desire and answers distractedly. In the silences his eyes turn away with a haunted look that might express regret over what he has lost, fear of what he faces. "The wavering of a mind under such circumstances," Dreiser writes about the safe scene, "is an almost inexplicable thing" (*SC*, 193). Without the explanatory resources of the novelist, Wyler and Olivier have captured that inexplicability with visual eloquence.

Wyler also adapted from the novel Dreiser's use of purses, money, and hands to signify power relations. For example, Carrie's seduction begins on the train to Chicago when she is "impressed . . . deeply" by the "fat purse" (*SC*, 5) that Drouet pulls from his pocket; it will be complete a few weeks later when he chances on her down on her luck on the wintry streets of Chicago and buys her a meal at a fancy restaurant. Warmed by his genial personality and the hot food, Carrie finds her hand "held . . . fast" by his "larger, warmer hand"; when he slips "two soft, green, handsome ten-dollar bills" into her palm and overcomes her resistance ("He made her take it"), she feels "bound to him by a strange tie of affection" (*SC*, 47). The "handsome" bills and hands are, if not phallic objects in a symbolic rape, certainly signifiers of male dominance.

Carrie achieves independence when she no longer depends on the kindness of strangers – or their embraces and purses. With applause from Broadway audiences come both a feeling of power so strong that she "hugged herself" (*SC*, 314) and a "purse bursting with good green bills of comfortable denominations" (*SC*, 323). Her attractiveness on stage enables her to emasculate male performers, as the "big comedian" learns on the night of her first great triumph: "She killed my hand all right" (*SC*, 326). Dreiser, however, ultimately returns Carrie to her initial passivity. With the 150 dollars she is earning a week "in hand," she discovers money's "impotence" to bring the "affection" (*SC*, 335) she wants. With no specific object of desire before her, she finds that "[u]nconsciously her idle hands were beginning to weary" (*SC*, 336); even giving money seems for once in the novel curiously passive: "Her purse was open to him whose need was greatest" (*SC*, 369).

Wyler links purses, money, and hands with masculine authority in the film's opening shot of Carrie's father pulling bills from his purse to buy Carrie's train ticket to Chicago. As in the novel, Carrie's development is shown in her growing power over her hands and her purse. She becomes vulnerable to Drouet after she is fired from the sweatshop – significantly because her finger has been caught in a sewing machine, the one penetration anticipating the other. When she tries not to take Drouet's money, he forces it on her, first outside his workplace, then in the restaurant that night. When Drouet first embraces and kisses her, she stands frigidly, arms by her side, unable to resist. With the advent of Hurstwood, she becomes increasingly active, returning his embraces and kisses with equal fervor. When she sets off to meet Hurstwood in the park, in a displaced sexual act she stuffs his note in her muff while turning away from Drouet's arms and lips. Although she surrenders to Hurstwood's embrace on the train to New York, she assumes control over the money box in their apartment. To the very end, her hands remain a potent instrument, as Drouet, the "[g]enial egoist" (*SC*, 350) played wonderfully by Albert, makes evident when he returns at the film's end and takes her by the hand. "Not a scar!" he exclaims. He is about to learn that the vulnerable, wounded factory girl is no more.

As we might expect, Hurstwood's hands become increasingly idle in the film. On the afternoon he is invited up to Drouet's apartment for drinks and cards, Hurstwood hovers over Carrie charmingly, manipulating her hands to play the hand of cards that defeats Drouet, who in his intoxication is blind to the existence of a second game that he will also lose. Before he departs, Hurstwood places in Carrie's hand the tickets to *Camille* that will be instrumental in winning her love. As he becomes more and more powerless, his hands reflect his impotence, especially when he takes money from others, the novel's quintessentially feminine gesture: his hands hang limply at his side when Julia confronts him with her knowledge of the affair; he drops the envelope with Fitzgerald's ten thousand dollars and ludicrously closes the safe with his derrière when he stoops clumsily to pick the money up; when his wife and Fitzgerald try to force him to end the affair, he runs from his home with his arms flailing wildly and the envelope grasped unconsciously in one hand; on the evening he returns to find Carrie gone, he fumbles with the door, lets the newspaper slip out of his hands as he rocks in despair, and, after discovering the farewell note, impotently fondles the purse and money left in recompense and the single hairpin forgotten in her drawer.

The dignity of men

In accepting the One World Award for Motion Pictures in June 1950, Wyler called for "morality" in films, not "sexual morality" but "the morality of humanism . . . The dignity of men everywhere should be our great epic theme."[29] Here Wyler clearly intends "men" in the sense of humankind. But in *Carrie* his great epic theme is just as clearly gendered in its ambivalence toward controlling women. "You've had nothing but contempt for me as a man and loathing for me as a husband," Hurstwood spits at Julia as he vows to have true love before he dies. Ironically, he will die rather than face contempt and loathing from the woman he mistakes for his salvation.

This reading of Hurstwood on Wyler's part would seem to have little relation to the character in the novel who, on the night he ends it all, has become but one among the "dumb brutes" (*SC*, 367) waiting in the snow outside a flophouse. Yet when he is reduced to beggary, "a bent, bedraggled, but unbroken pride" (*SC*, 328) keeps Hurstwood from going to Carrie, and when he finally does take her money, he leaves "almost resenting her excessive pity" (*SC*, 352). Even his suicide is not a complete defeat, for it springs from "his one distinct mental decision" (*SC*, 363). It is this struggle for dignity that Wyler takes up and amplifies and that, along with a generosity of spirit and capacity for understanding not found in the novel, gives the film's hero tragic stature.

Wyler prepares for this reading in the scene very near the film's end when Carrie is again associated with theatrical illusion. While being interviewed by a reporter, she is applying her make-up in front of her dressing-room mirror before going on stage in a frothy comedy entitled *Ladies in Waiting*; in her powdered wig, décolletage, gaudy paste jewelry, and beauty mark she looks every bit the courtesan in a Restoration comedy of manners. Just beyond Carrie, similarly clad actresses move in and out of the frame, their images multiplied by mirrors that dominate the room. When Drouet is announced and the reporter leaves, Carrie continues applying her stage make-up while resisting Drouet's advances with cold formality, at one point holding up a hand mirror before her face. In a scene of mass-produced female images – in the surrounding mirrors and in the other actresses – Carrie's authenticity is implicitly challenged.

During his vain attempt to strike a spark, Drouet reveals Hurstwood's theft, offering the trite moral, "You got to pay the fiddler in this world." Although understandably appalled at the revelation, Carrie ignores the cosmic scheme of justice and typically places herself at the center of the drama. "I *ruined* him," she sobs. Then we hear a knock and a voice calling out, "Curtain, Miss Madenda," and with a second tearful "I *ruined* him" she sweeps out through the door as the orchestra strikes up a spirited minuet. In a film whose music is mostly sappy strings, the minuet sounds a note of mockery. And with the intrusion of the curtain call in the midst of her emotional display, it is hard to tell just when Carrie begins acting.

None of this makes Carrie a monster. As Wyler wrote to the Goetzes, if she were stuck "caring for this wreck of a man" she would "be cheated out of a life of her own" (quoted in Herman, *Talent for Trouble*, 320). She never loses our sympathy even as she remains blind to the liberal mixture of self-interest and guilt in her altruism. That critics have missed this complexity may be due in part to what Bazin calls Wyler's "liberal and democratic" directing style: "All Wyler wants is that the spectator can (1) see everything; and (2) choose as he pleases. It's an act of loyalty toward the spectator, an attempt at dramatic honesty" (quoted in Madsen, *William Wyler*, 274). This honesty is most of all apparent when, desperate with hunger, Hurstwood approaches Carrie outside the theater one bitterly cold night and feebly stretches out his hand for money. "I'm here for a handout," he tells her a moment later. "Don't make me go through too much to get it." But that's just what she does.

The Goetzes intended to convey the idea that in relationships "one is loved, the other does the loving." From the moment that Hurstwood steps out of the shadows, Carrie does precious little loving in return for the love she demands. She left him, she now admits, not to save him but to make herself "safe and secure. Now that I am, make it worth something to me. Let me share it with you." The material comfort she offers, though, comes with a very high price tag: "I know you love me. I want that again. Let me have it back." Along with his love, she expects absolution. When she left him, she wails, she was just too young to know better. "Why didn't you make me understand?" she demands tearfully, dropping her head, and the blame, onto his none-too-sturdy shoulder.

Carrie's hands and eyes are as significant as her words. She takes him literally in hand and forces him to meet her gaze, but seems averse to touching his flesh. At one point, she briefly covers his hand with hers, but the glove in her palm protects her against contamination. Instead of handing him money, she drops her purse on the table and pulls out a wad of bills, leaving them for him to pick up himself. Especially humiliating is the moment when she turns on the light in her dressing room and, with a look of horror and her typical emphasis on herself, asks tremblingly, "Did *I* do this? *Did* I?" When she leaves to get more money, she turns in the doorway and looks at him for several seconds, straining to maintain a smile and nattering on about feeding him and buying him new clothes as Wyler cuts to Hurstwood gazing at her unblinkingly. With his barely audible "Thank you, Carrie," her composure gives way and she hurries out of sight to fetch the money.

The whispered "Thank you" seems to belie Mr. Blum's prophecy that Hurstwood would not thank Carrie to see him. The words, however, are partly ironic, for what Wyler shows is Hurstwood seeing Carrie seeing him, her face struggling to mask conflicting emotions, including the "excessive pity" that Dreiser describes along with something akin to disgust. A few moments earlier, Hurstwood has told her to follow her own advice against living in the past: "You still have time, Carrie. Move on now. Find someone to love. It's a great experience." Implicit in this speech is his recognition that he has never been truly loved, for if Carrie must "find someone to love" she has never had that "great experience" with *him*.

This speech represents Hurstwood's effort to assert his masculine will in the face of Carrie's smothering emotionalism, an interpretation supported by the erect index finger he points at her. After Carrie leaves the room, Wyler trusts us to remember all the preceding shots of hands, and money, and purses as he moves the camera in close to show that, unlike the comedian's in the novel, Hurstwood's hand has not been "killed" by Carrie. Selecting from the change in the purse a single quarter, he takes only what he has come for. Then, in a dramatic, though subtle, assertion of potency, he thrusts the bills back inside the open purse with a single extended finger.

In the film's concluding shots, Wyler again offers us a choice. When Hurstwood stands up to leave, he briefly lays his hand on Carrie's glove draped on a chair back and then pauses before a mirror. We may simply feel the pathos in the last vicarious loving caress, or we may also recognize a reversal of power relations in the image of his hand on top of the glove that recently contained hers. We may see in the mirror a brute whose life is not worth living, or, remembering Carrie's earlier fragmentation by that and other mirrors, we may see an image of restored integrity.

Given Paramount's cutting of the scene in which Hurstwood gasses himself in a Bowery flophouse, viewers unfamiliar with the novel are likely to miss his final "distinct mental decision," one that will preclude his ever humiliating himself again and that frees Carrie from the trap that marriage to him would represent. In close-up, Hurstwood's hand purposefully turns off the gas burner that Carrie has lit to make tea – then on, then off, silencing the ominously hissing gas. Wyler then cuts to the man as he opens the door and disappears with his "bent, bedraggled, but unbroken pride" into what Dreiser calls "that kindness which is night" (*SC*, 367). We should be glad to see him go.

Brothers under the skin

Had Dreiser lived to see *Carrie*, he might have reacted with the outrage he felt two decades earlier when he thought Paramount was trying to turn his psychologically complex *An American Tragedy* into "nothing short of a cheap, tawdry, tabloid confession story."[30] Blaming the Jewish executives B. P. Schulberg and Jesse Lasky, he began to express a latent anti-Semitism that would undermine his reputation from the 1930s on.[31] Some readers may find my reading of *Carrie* an effort to make high art out of another trashy Paramount melodrama. Indeed, when I first saw his tearfully maternal Carrie and nobly self-sacrificing Hurstwood, I smugly thought that Wyler had simply missed the point, as Hollywood hacks are wont to do. Closer study has caused me to modify my judgment.[32] If Wyler sometimes misread the novel, he did so creatively, producing a film with considerable psychological complexity and artistry, one that speaks its own culture as Dreiser's novel speaks its. There is even a nice irony in the fact that Wyler was forced into some of the same compromises with convention that Dreiser had been forced into half a century earlier. *Carrie* is not *Sister Carrie*, but the anti-Semitic son of German immigrants and the Russian immigrant Jew are brothers under the skin.

Figure 12. *Carrie* emphasizes the doomed love affair between the mismatched couple played by Laurence Olivier and Jennifer Jones. A 1952 Paramount Pictures release.

NOTES

1. Jan Herman, *A Talent for Trouble: The Life of Hollywood's Most Acclaimed Director, William Wyler* (New York: Putnam's, 1995), p. 328. Further quotations will be cited parenthetically in the text.
2. Bosley Crowther, "The Screen in Review," *New York Times*, July 17, 1952, p. 20; *New York Times Online*, Online, ProQuest Historical Newspapers, accessed November 15, 2004.
3. Carolyn Geduld, "Wyler's Suburban Sister: *Carrie*, 1952," in Gerald Peary and Roger Shatzkin, eds., *The Classic American Novel and the Movies* (New York: Ungar, 1977), pp. 156, 160.
4. Lawrence E. Hussman, "Squandered Possibilities: The Film Versions of Dreiser's Novels," in Miriam Gogol, ed., *Theodore Dreiser: Beyond Naturalism* (New York: New York University Press, 1995), p. 195. Further quotations will be cited parenthetically in the text.
5. Brian McFarlane, *Novel to Film: An Introduction to the Theory of Adaptation* (Oxford: Oxford University Press, 1996), pp. 9, 13.
6. Robert Stam, "Beyond Fidelity: The Dialogics of Adaptation" in James Naremore, ed., *Film Adaptation* (New Brunswick, NJ: Rutgers University Press, 2000), pp. 63, 68.
7. James L. W. West, III, "The *Sister Carrie* We've Come to Know," *Dreiser Studies* 32:2 (2001), p. 40.
8. The quotation is from a rejection letter that Dreiser received from Harper and Brothers in late April 1900. It is presented in full in the Historical Commentary of the Pennsylvania edition, which offers a full account of the novel's composition, revision, publication, and so-called suppression. For the letter, see Theodore Dreiser, *Sister Carrie*, ed. John C. Berkey, Alice M. Winters and James L. W. West, III (Philadelphia: University of Pennsylvania Press, 1981), p. 519.
9. Joseph I. Breen, Letter to Michel Kraike, November 1, 1938, Dreiser Collection, University of Pennsylvania Library, Philadelphia.
10. Joseph I. Breen, Letter to J. L. Warner, October 11, 1937, Dreiser Collection, University of Pennsylvania Library, Philadelphia.
11. Richard Lingeman, *Theodore Dreiser*, 2 vols., *Volume II. An American Journey, 1908–1945* (New York: Putnam's, 1990), p. 423.
12. Thomas Brady, "Hollywood Holds to Average Production Level," *New York Times*, July 30, 1950, p. X5; *New York Times Online*, Online, ProQuest Historical Newspapers, accessed November 15, 2004.
13. The quotation is from Theodore Dreiser, *Sister Carrie*, ed. Donald Pizer, 2nd edn. (New York: Norton, 1991), p. 239. Further quotations from the novel are from this edition and will be cited parenthetically in the text as *SC*.
14. Lingeman, *Theodore Dreiser*, p. 419.
15. Thomas Brady, "Old Order Changes," *New York Times*, July 23, 1950, p. X5; *New York Times Online*, Online, ProQuest Historical Newspapers, accessed November 15 2004.
16. Axel Madsen, *William Wyler* (New York: Crowell, 1973), p. 299. Further quotations will be cited parenthetically in the text.
17. McFarlane, *Novel to Film*, pp. 13, 14.

18. William Shakespeare, *The Tragedy of Hamlet, Prince of Denmark*, *Shakespeare: The Complete Works*, ed. G. B. Harrison (New York: Harcourt, Brace & World, 1952), V.ii. 393, 395.

19. Stam, "Beyond Fidelity," p. 60.

20. Laurence Olivier, *On Acting* (New York: Simon and Schuster, 1986), p. 284. Further quotations will be cited parenthetically in the text.

21. Crowther, "Screen in Review."

22. Sheldon Grebstein, "Dreiser's Victorian Vamp," *Midcontinent American Studies Journal* 4 (1963), pp. 3–12. Rpt. in Theodore Dreiser, *Sister Carrie*, ed. Donald Pizer (New York: Norton, 1970), p. 545. Further quotations will be cited parenthetically in the text.

23. Brandon French, *On the Verge of Revolt: Women in American Films of the Fifties* (New York: Ungar, 1978), pp. xvi–xvii.

24. Ibid., pp. xxi, xxiii–xxiv.

25. Philip Fisher, *Hard Facts: Setting and Form in the American Novel* (New York: Oxford University Press, 1987), p. 159.

26. Ibid.

27. Ellen Moers, *Two Dreisers* (New York: Viking, 1969), p. 101.

28. Dudley Andrew, "Adaptation," in Naremore, ed., *Film Adaptation*, p. 35.

29. William Wyler, "Statement of Principles," *New York Times*, June 18, 1950, p. X5; *New York Times Online*, Online, ProQuest Historical Newspapers, accessed October 10, 2004.

30. Theodore Dreiser, Letter to Jesse L. Lasky, in Dreiser, *Letters of Theodore Dreiser: A Selection*, ed. Robert H. Elias, 3 vols. (Philadelphia: University of Pennsylvania Press, 1959), p. 522.

31. Donald Pizer, "Dreiser and the Jews," *Dreiser Studies* 35:1 (2004), pp. 8–12.

32. This study really began when I watched the film with David B. Jones, a filmmaker and scholar who taught me to see what I was looking at. I owe him many thanks for his patience and insight.

13 Hollywood and *The Sea-Wolf*

Tony Williams

Although *The Sea-Wolf* first appeared as a novel toward the end of 1904, following its serialization in *Century Magazine* at the beginning of the year, it is a work which has strong connections with nineteenth-century maritime narratives whether fiction (*Moby-Dick*, 1865) or fact (*Two Years Before the Mast*, 1840). As in Herman Melville's classic novel, the main character is an obsessive individual who involves others in acts of self-destruction. Furthermore, Jack London's fictional account contains many factual elements paralleling the earlier maritime industrial aspects contained in Richard Henry Dana's nonfictional study. However, *The Sea-Wolf* is also a work anticipating several dominant themes within twentieth-century fiction, involving duality, gender crisis, sociopolitical critique, and an attempt to reconcile opposites that may not be entirely possible.

The novel begins with literary critic Humphrey Van Weyden leaving his philosopher friend Charley Furuseth, a devotee of Nietzsche and Schopenhauer. Although the opening sentence appears irrelevant, it is actually the key to the entire novel: "I scarcely know where to begin, though I sometimes facetiously place the cause of it all to Charley Furuseth's credit."[1] After an accident on San Francisco's Bay Area ferry, Van Weyden finds himself in a nightmare situation where he experiences the consequences of his philosophical meditations. Rescued from drowning, he is taken aboard a sealing schooner, *The Ghost*, captained by the "abysmal brute" figure of Wolf Larsen. Recognizing the over-civilized qualities of his catch, Larsen decides to tutor Van Weyden in his own version of industrial masculinity in a ship that symbolically represents the nineteenth-century aspects of a division of labor which has benefited upper-class figures while oppressing those of the lower classes. To his surprise, Van Weyden discovers Larsen to be a self-educated man espousing a philosophy akin to Furuseth's admired Nietzsche. The captain also follows his own perverse interpretation of Schopenhauer's concept of the "will to live," contemptuously regarding every human being as being victimized by that metaphysical force that consists of attempting to be alive at any cost.

Despite these philosophical connotations, *The Sea-Wolf* also operates as an exciting maritime adventure story anticipating themes within the novels of Joseph Conrad, whom London (1876–1916) admired. Van Weyden finds himself facing his own version of a "heart of darkness" when Larsen decides to educate him in the brutal realities of a civilization he has never seriously thought about. Larsen decides to deliver an un-"sentimental education" to his reluctant new crew member by plunging him into the "lower depths" of a class structure he has never before experienced and making a man of him. Halfway through the novel, Van Weyden begins to benefit from this process and almost becomes Larsen's "secret sharer" in word and deed. Furthermore, both characters in the novel embody tensions within the author, caught between two aspects of a contemporary masculinity he had experienced himself. Larsen represents an atavistic version of those lower-depth life experiences at the bottom of the social pit that London had undergone and depicted in his documentary essay-novel, *The People of the Abyss* (1902). But both author and character were self-educated men who not only understood the social circumstances governing their particular situations, but also feared a femininity that could undermine their masculinity. Larsen's developing physical disability and Van Weyden's developing homoerotic attraction toward the captain represent two examples of a gender crisis that the novel explores. Furthermore, London himself also felt himself torn between a masculine persona that he was at pains to promote and develop, and the feminized idea of writing as being far removed from the manly ideal. This was a tension that also troubled in twentieth-century writers such as Ernest Hemingway. But before Van Weyden succumbs to the brutal world of industrial masculinity, he is saved by the arrival of Maude Brewster.

Maude represents both London's ideal female and the concept of balance he hoped to realize in *The Sea-Wolf*. Also a writer, she offers a heterosexual counterpoint to the perverse figure of Larsen. When the captain attacks her before falling at the onset of one of his debilitating headache attacks, Van Weyden decides that it is time to leave *The Ghost*. They set up home on Endeavor Island, but their platonic and child-like relationship becomes disrupted by the discovery of *The Ghost* whose only inhabitant now is a blinded Larsen, left to die by his crew after his feared brother Death Larsen has finally conquered him. Maude and Van Weyden work together to make *The Ghost* seaworthy as Larsen declines further. While Larsen's Nietzschean individualism moves towards pathetic decay and eventual death, Maude and Humphrey's romantic relationship results in a positive interpretation of Schopenhauer's will to live. Unlike Furuseth and Larsen, they eschew an individualism resulting in negative consequences. They develop a cooperative loving relationship by raising *The Ghost* together, burying the proud Lucifer figure of the dead captain at sea before their eventual rescue by a maritime cutter.

Nevertheless, the relationship between Maude and Van Weyden is the weakest part of the novel. It attempts to reconcile opposites but, as Lee Clark Mitchell observes, the three main characters are all victims of cultural contradictions that the novel cannot easily resolve. Larsen cannot really become Nietzsche's individualist superman because he relies on others to do his will. Furthermore, Maude and Van Weyden may be in danger of relapsing into their former class-behavioral patterns that the novel condemns. As Mitchell writes, "these contradictions suggest why Wolf can never quite realize that there is no way to 'rescue us from ourselves.'" With these final spoken words, the novel becomes a testament to the arbitrary cultural categories it professes to despise. "The unspoken irony of *The Sea-Wolf* is that Van Weyden's arduous voyage of discovery ends by confirming him as the artist he already was, perhaps less effete now but little different from his earlier self, writing a novel of escape that only reaffirms his stake in his culture and its deep self-divisions."[2]

Like all London's works, *The Sea-Wolf* combines both factual and fictional elements. The model for Wolf Larsen was Captain Alexander McClean, who ran the sealing schooner *Carmencita*: he "had a big record as a rough character and was known as the worst man, so far as physical violence was concerned, among the seal hunters. He also had a brother Dan McClean, who was almost as rough a customer as Alex."[3] Dan was obviously the prototype for Death Larsen. London knew of these figures from his days as a sailor off the coast of Japan in 1893. He kept up with the later activities of Alexander McClean from his clipping service and knew about his $1,600 fine for poaching fur seal after his arrest in British Columbia on September 4, 1905, as well as his death a year later. London's comments about the two brothers appeared in the *Chicago Record-Herald* of January 29, 1906 in an article entitled "'Sea Wolf' Drowned; Savage of the Deep." The relationship between Maude and Van Weyden is a fictionalized rendition of the one that existed between London and Charmian Kittredge, with whom he had fallen in love during 1903, leading to his separation and eventual divorce from his first wife, Bessie Maddern.

The novel has deep philosophical and political undertones, not all of which would lend themselves to appropriate cinematic adaptation. For the purposes of literary and film marketing, the product could be promoted as an adventure narrative with the expected romantic undertones. Apart from a few exceptions, this was the general approach governing most cinematic adaptations. It simplified the material for public consumption in the same way that *The Call of the Wild* (1903) became understood as a harmless "dog story" despite its other embodied meanings as a protest against industrial exploitation and the search for different forms of human resilience and resistance.

The first film version appeared in 1907 and appears to have escaped the notice of an author eager to defend any copyright violations of his work. During this time, London was involved with beginning his world cruise on *The Snark* and may have been too busy to pay attention to other matters. *The Sea Wolf* was produced by the New Jersey-based Kalem Company and directed by Sidney Olcott. From surviving information, it would seem that this lost film was the first to emphasize those elements of adventure and romance that became predominant in later adaptations. A mere 655 feet long and probably running no more than fifteen minutes, Olcott's version could make no claims toward comprehensive narrative adaptation. Instead, it followed the practice of contemporary adaptations such as Cecil Hepworth's *Alice in Wonderland* (1903) by choosing familiar scenes from the literary original. However, although contemporary publicity mentioned the film as being based on "Jack London's Great Character," the actual title was "The Sea Wolf's Finish" in a narrative composed of six scenes with "cartoon titles." These were "Law of the Sailor," "Plot to Destroy the Light [house]," "The Plot Succeeds," "Coast Guards to the Rescue," "In the Nick of Time," and "The Sea Wolf's Finish."

From the above description, it is clear that the first film version of London's novel introduces a practice that its successors would follow. It not only removes the hyphen from the novel's original title, but departs significantly from the novel itself. Kalem's publicity for the film refers to the fact that it is based on Wolf Larsen but "without following the book with any exactness." Like future adaptations, it recognizes the dominant role of the title character but inserts him into a romantic adventure involving the Sea Wolf's supposed daughter and "a manly young sailor." The final scene of the film depicts the death of the old Sea Wolf on the deck of his unnamed schooner and the "re-union of the young lovers." This version remained in circulation until 1908. Although its length prohibited any reference to the philosophical and political issues treated in London's novel, it foreshadowed a trend that other versions would follow, namely the repression of political elements and the elevation of adventure, mystery, and romance. This would make for good entertainment in future decades.[4]

The rapid development of the motion picture industry and the possibility of literary works reaching a wider audience led London to take an increasing interest in the new medium. During 1911 Jack and Charmian London began to take an increasing interest in both theatre and film for both story material and commercial reasons. At this time, the film industry began advertising "exclusive" contracts with writers such as Rex Beach, Carolyn Wells, and Richard Harding Davis. So when the former actor Sydney Ayres approached the Londons with an enthusiastic plan for movie adaptations, they eagerly seized the opportunity. A contract was signed with the Balboa Amusement Producing Company in 1913 for the production of several London adaptations, including *The Sea-Wolf*. However, owing to dissatisfaction with an inexperienced Ayres and Balboa, the Londons subsequently turned to the more experienced actor-director Hobart Bosworth and signed a contract with his company, Bosworth Incorporated, for a series of more prestigious adaptations that would begin with *The Sea-Wolf*. A series of complicated legal and commercial problems meant that both versions appeared at the same time with the same title until copyright issues were resolved. Retitled *Cruise of the Hell Ship*, the Balboa version ran for three reels and was directed by Richard Garrick. It featured two actors who would become important in Hollywood cinema. Future director Henry King played Van Weyden while future scenarist Jeannie MacPherson appeared as Maude. The role of Larsen was taken by Lawrence Pathan, who would later play Martin Eden in Bosworth's film of the same name. According to contemporary reports, his performance as Larsen left much to be desired.

The most prestigious version influenced by a movement to make more sophisticated American film narratives stimulated by the release of Italian spectaculars such as *Quo Vadis?* (which had its American debut in 1913) was the Bosworth's. Although now lost, contemporary evidence suggests that had not distribution been problematic, thanks to the unstable nature of states right distribution, Bosworth's version of *The Sea-Wolf* could have had several claims to be regarded as the first American feature film, rather than *The Squaw Man* (1914) or *The Birth of A Nation* (1915).

Premiered on September 30, 1913 at the Los Angeles Athletic Club before an invited audience, but not officially released until December 1913 because of the legal battle with Balboa, this seven-reel version featured Bosworth both directing and playing the title character. Supported by Herbert Rawlinson as Van Weyden and Viola Barry as Maude with prologue and epilogue featuring London himself, this version was acclaimed for its beautiful photography and forever defined Bosworth as silent cinema's Sea Wolf. He would play variations on this role in several Hollywood maritime adventures. Surviving contemporary plot synopses and stills suggest that Bosworth's version was the most faithful of all cinema adaptations, even including the embarrassing Endeavor Island sequences that later versions dropped. However, some variations were attempted. A blinded Larsen makes a final effort to kill Van Weyden before being killed in the process. Also, rather than making *The Ghost* seaworthy, Van Weyden and Maude sail away on a small boat before being discovered by the revenue cutter.

As well as the uncertainty of survival that affected many American silent films, Bosworth's *The Sea-Wolf* also suffered another act of fate. On June 13, 1914 the original negative was lost in a vault fire at Lubin Studios. Apart from the issue of the original film appearing dated as technology developed rapidly during this period, poor duping stocks meant that secondary copies could never match the photographic quality of the original negative.

After the death of London on November 22, 1916, his literary estate, represented by his widow Charmian and sister Eliza, faced not only economic problems but also those connected with cinematic adaptations at the time. More often than not, the heirs fielded offers from inexperienced producers such as Ayres, even as they had to face the fact that Jack London film versions would never become prestige commodities within the Hollywood film industry. They would rather be promoted as adventure narratives, bereft of the author's original philosophic and political concerns that were foreign to the new visual age of mechanical reproduction.

Although Bosworth hoped that he could return to the screen with a new version of *The Sea-Wolf* after touring America with a stage performance of the novel in 1917, Paramount was already planning a new version with William S. Hart in the title role. The eventual film appeared in November 1920 with Noah Beery in the title role. Directed by George Medford and scripted by the English playwright Guy Bolton and Joseph Noel, this version moved farther away from the premises of the novel. It was also the first of two versions to feature the hitherto unseen "Death Larsen," played by James Gordon. In the Medford film Van Weyden (Tom Foreman) and Maud (Mabel Julienne Scott) are already betrothed and end up on *The Ghost* after the novel's ferry-boat accident.[5] Attracted to Maud, Larsen refuses to send them ashore. The captain discovers Maud's attraction to strong men and aims to degrade Van Weyden in her presence, beginning by making him a cabin boy. Despite their betrothal, Maud has refused to marry Van Weyden because she considers him a weakling. After Larsen's attack on Maud and his debilitation by one of his frequent headaches, the couple seize the opportunity to escape and land on a small island. Later, the deserted ship arrives, containing the blinded Larsen. He attempts to attack Van Weyden but dies from one of his headaches. A cruiser finally rescues them and Maud is cured of her longings for a caveman. She finally realizes that she loves Van Weyden.

According to contemporary reviews, this lost film does not appear to have been a box-office success. Even the former Bosworth Incorporated executive Frank Garbutt (now working for Paramount) regarded it as a misstep. *Variety* criticized the production for its low-budget values, poor screenwriting, and stereotyped acting. Since this was the last major studio production of *The Sea-Wolf* during the silent era, it set into motion a pattern whereby London's novels would be regarded as suitable material for low-budget action narratives, but not for expensive artistic literary adaptations. In 1925 the Ralph W. Ince Corporation, headed by the brother of the late Hollywood director Thomas Ince, who wished to achieve similar fame, contacted the Jack London Estate aiming to option three London stories including *The Sea-Wolf*. Its version was released a year later. Ince both directed and appeared in the title role with Theodor Van Eltz (the future Arthur Geiger of *The Big Sleep*, 1946) as Van Weyden and Claire Adams as Maud. The couple first meet in masquerade costume on the Bay Ferry before a collision places them on *The Ghost*. Since Maud wears a sailor suit, the crew mistake her for a boy while Van Weyden's gaudy costume attracts jeers from the sailors. Both are put to work until ship's cook Mugridge discovers Maud's real identity and attempts to assault her. Larsen then places her under his protection. Wearing a more feminine kimono, she attracts the sexual desires of the crew. Larsen then decides to marry her. However, the crew revolt during the ceremony and Larsen is blinded by a seizure. The ship is set on fire. Although another steamer rescues Van Weyden and Maud, Larsen decides to go down with *The Ghost* and perishes in the flames.

The film was not successful. Several contemporary reviews commented adversely upon the poor acting performances, especially Ince's as Larsen, as well as the increasing tendency of romance to overwhelm the political and cultural elements of the novel. As a contemporary review from the Jack London Estate Archives eloquently attests, "This is not the first time that a book in which the feature is the close and intimate study of an extraordinary man's mental processes has been made into a film in which the feature is an ordinary love affair."[6]

Inadequate acting performances and insipid adaptation techniques definitely hindered attempts to make of *The Sea-Wolf* a superior type of cinematic adaptation. However, in 1929, Fox Studios obtained the rights to the 1926 Ince version and planned a new version directed by John Ford and starring Victor McLaglen. This could have been an exciting event at this early period of sound cinema. But the actor's desire to diversify his acting roles led to his withdrawal and that of Ford. The title role eventually went to silent-screen star Milton Sills, who was looking for a successful vehicle to break into sound cinema. Directed by Alfred Santell, the film did attempt to break with previous adaptations by translating London's characters to the pre-Hays Code world of a hard-boiled Depression era. Maud now becomes Jane Keith's prostitute Lorna Marsh and Van Weyden Raymond Hackett's shanghaied landlubber Allen Rand. The story begins in a Japanese port, where Larsen fails to attract Lorna to *The Ghost* because she is infatuated with Rand. However, both are shanghaied, along with three sailors from Death Larsen's steamer. The film then follows London's novel in depicting Rand's apprenticeship to ship's cook Mugridge and his eventual promotion to first mate. After catching a huge number of seals, Larsen decides to celebrate his achievement by knocking out Rand and raping Lorna, but the appearance of Death Larsen's ship thwarts his desire. Rand and Lorna escape in a boat while Mugridge avenges a previous mutilation by blinding Larsen with a poker. After drifting for days, Rand and Lorna find *The Ghost* with Larsen on board. Although he initially attempts to prevent them from leaving by casting off their boat, the dying captain relents by giving them directions to the nearest shore before he dies.

By all accounts, this ninety-minute adaptation was well received. Contemporary reviews commented favorably on Sills's performance and commended Hackett's but criticized Jane Keith's. Unfortunately, the death of Sills from a heart attack immediately after filming resulted in poor distribution since most exhibitors did not want to promote a film featuring a recently deceased star. Thus the property again remained in cinematic limbo until David O. Selznick acquired the rights and sold them to Warner Brothers, which hoped to make a version starring Paul Muni. However, in 1937, the actor stressed his unwillingness to appear in a film version that would differ considerably from the original source. He wished to collaborate on the screenplay and suggested the pedestrian Mervyn LeRoy as the most appropriate director. The studio may have resented Muni's "impertinence," as it continued to develop the novel. One of these developments involved upgrading the role of the rebellious young sailor George Leach, who, while only a minor character in the novel, was seen as an appropriate action hero in contrast to the more intellectual figure of Van Weyden. Warner Brothers offered the role to the star contract player George Raft, but he rejected it as a bit part. It eventually went to John Garfield, who expressed both his enthusiasm for London's works and his willingness to appear in a supporting role as long as the film was worth it – a practice he later followed for Howard Hawks's *Air Force* (1943). Edward G. Robinson eventually played the title character.

Developed by Warner Brothers, the 1941 film version would benefit from the unifying collaboration of a good director, excellent acting performances, creative screenplay, and professional distribution and marketing, which were features absent from most previous productions. Of all versions, it is this production that is the best known and the most imaginatively conceived. Featuring major stars such as Robinson, Garfield, Ida Lupino, Barry Fitzgerald, Alexander Knox, and Howard Da Silva, directed by Michael Curtiz, produced by Hal Wallis, photographed by Sol Polio, with set design by Anton Grot, and music score by Eric Wolfgang Korngold, the film enjoyed the best of professional studio talent. Furthermore, *The Sea-Wolf*'s genesis and reception involved the presence of many talents associated with Hollywood's radical fringe, many of whom would face blacklisting and harassment in the next decade. Ironically, although changes were made to the novel, this very attention resulted in a film that remained true to the radical spirit of the author, whose politics were often ignored or distorted by both film adaptations and future neoconservative literary critics in professional academic societies. The final screenplay was drafted by the radical Robert Rossen, who had worked on Warner Brothers' social consciousness films during the 1930s. Recognizing the political overtones of London's original conception, he adapted the novel as an allegory of 1930s fascism. By depicting the title character as a thinly disguised European dictator reveling in Nietzschean ideas and brutality, Rossen aimed at writing a relevant allegory for his historical period.

Throughout his various screenplay drafts, Rossen aimed at making the novel more contemporary by dropping features that were now hopelessly dated. Van Weyden's and Maude's romantic interlude on Endeavor Island and their literary associations were eliminated. Rossen also made the novel's original hero a secondary character and followed an earlier screenplay draft that turned Leach into a leading character. It appropriately accommodated Garfield's contemporary star persona as Warner Brothers' archetypal Depression era hero. Maud Brewster now became Ida Lupino's Ruth Webster, a woman fleeing from both prison and a life of prostitution. The distinguished Canadian stage actor Knox appeared in his first screen role as Van Weyden, playing the part as an upper-class educated type contrasting with Larsen's brutal sea captain and complementing the more dynamic, action-oriented working-class opposition that Garfield's character offers. Although many of Rossen's speeches ended up on the cutting-room floor, enough features remained in the film to suggest radical dimensions existing both within the novel and in the final screenplay. In many ways, *The Sea Wolf* resembles that type of cinema known as a "premature anti-fascist allegory" that raised the blood pressure of rightist elements in Hollywood as well as the House Committee of Un-American Activities. But its presentation as a costume drama directed by an apolitical studio director such as Curtiz did not attract such unwelcome scrutiny in the future. The film ends with the death of both Van Weyden and Larsen, leaving Leach and Ruth free to sail toward an island representing not the insipid romantic environment of Endeavor Island but a place to "be free . . . to be let alone . . . to live in peace," a place where oppressed people could achieve individual and social freedom away from class and political oppression.

Despite the success of this Warner Brothers adaptation, London's reputation did not develop beyond the adventure narrative format that affected previous film versions. Furthermore, since the studio had acquired the rights to the novel, it decided to use it as much as possible in the future. In 1950 Warner Brothers remade *The Sea Wolf* as a western and never credited the original source material in its publicity. Directed by Peter Godfrey and scripted by William Sackheim, *Barricade* was a seventy-five-minute "B" western starring Dane Clark, whom Warner Brothers often used as a replacement for Garfield, who had left the studio in 1945. This type of adaptation was a common strategy adopted by the studio. For instance, after producing *The Maltese Falcon* in 1931, Warner Brothers remade Dashiell Hammett's classic novel in a new version with different characters, *Satan Met a Lady*, in 1936. Featuring Bette Davis and Warren William, William Dieterle's version followed the basic plot of the novel, while substituting the legendary horn of Roland for Hammett's original bird. The novel gained its definitive film version with John Huston's 1941 classic. Even Hemingway's *To Have and Have Not* (1944) underwent this process. After the 1944 Howard Hawks version, the studio refilmed the property under the different title of *The Breaking Point* in 1950 before Don Siegel's 1957 version *The Gun Runners* starring Audie Murphy. This process continued even when the studio moved into television. Clint Walker's 1950s western series *Cheyenne* also used adaptations of *Angels with Dirty Faces* (1938) and *To Have and Have Not* for certain episodes. *The Sea-Wolf* was also given this treatment.

As in *Satan Met a Lady*, in *Barricade* the characters and locations change, while the plot follows the 1941 film version instead of London's original novel. Van Weyden and Ruth Webster now become Aubrey Milburn and Judith Burns, who are brought to Boss Kruger's gold mine thirty-five miles away from the nearest town. Played by Raymond Massey, this western Wolf Larsen expects Milburn to work for his keep despite his broken ankle. As played by the English actor Robert Douglas, Aubrey retains the upper-class overtones seen in Knox's 1941 film performance, while Ruth Roman's Judith Burns reproduces Lupino's character. As Bob Peters, Clark now becomes another version of Garfield's Leach. But this time he fights Kruger after refusing to work with explosives at the mine. Milburn discovers that the miners are fugitives and criminals, whom Kruger keeps in virtual captivity. He also sees another side of Kruger, who engages him in a debate over power and evil. *Barricade*, moreover, uses the 1941 film version's character of the drunken doctor Louie, changing him into an alcoholic judge whose brother Kruger murdered to keep the mine for himself. Before he dies, the judge reveals that Kruger's nephew Clay had vowed revenge against his uncle.

Like Death Larsen in London's original, Clay is an unseen threat in this film. However, in a plot change diverging from both novel and the 1941 film, Milburn reveals himself to be Clay's lawyer seeking evidence against Kruger. By this time, Peters and Judith have attempted to escape on their own to begin a new life by using one of Kruger's wagons. Unlike the 1941 film, Milburn remains at the mine. When Peters and Judith discover that Kruger had put salt into their water, they return to the mine and find that it has burned down. Clay had attacked the mine and was killed in the gunfight. Milburn is badly injured, while Kruger has survived. A fight begins between Peters and Kruger, but the mine collapses, killing Kruger. The film ends with Peters, Judith, and Milburn leaving the mine and planning to make amends to society. Like Leach and Ruth in the 1941 film version, Peters and Judith are fugitives from the law, but the conclusion suggests that Milburn will defend them when they return to face justice.

Barricade appears to have made little impression at the time, being marketed as a "B" western. As a result, *The Sea-Wolf* once again fell into the category of a low-budget product. In 1958 Allied Artists released *Wolf Larsen*, a project initiated by the actor Sterling Hayden. He wished to play the title role and film the adaptation on his 100-foot schooner, *The Gracie S*, a vessel built in 1893 and thus resembling the type of ship that Larsen might have commanded. Hayden wanted to shoot the film at sea. He disagreed with the usual cinematic portrayal of Wolf Larsen as a maritime gangster, instead believing the captain to be a misunderstood idealist and victim of fate. Hayden seems to have viewed Larsen as a self-projection of his own character and experiences. After gaining critical acclaim in *The Asphalt Jungle* (1950), he had named names before the House Committee of Un-American Activities a year later, after confessing his previous membership of the Communist Party. Although he saved his career, Hayden suffered a great blow to his self-esteem and later apologized for his naming names. He felt an obsessive love for the sea and later wrote several books dealing with this fascination. However, after disagreements with the producer, he withdrew from the project, though he allowed Allied Artists to rent his schooner for a ten-day shooting schedule.

The role now went to Barry Sullivan. Although an accomplished actor, he could not deliver the type of intense performance that Hayden's personal obsessions could have brought to the part. Shot on a low budget by a poverty row studio, *Wolf Larsen* reflected the circumstances of its production. As Van Weyden, Peter Graves delivered his usual bland performance. As a result, the film differed little from the usual adaptation formula except for some minor details. Larsen already knows Van Weyden's class background, the moment he rescues him. The heroine is presented in a more sexual manner and Larsen ends up shot by Henderson, one of his mutinous sailors, during the climax.

To date, *The Legend of the Sea-Wolf* represents the last screen version of the novel to receive international distribution. Directed by Giuseppe Vari in 1975 and featuring Chuck Connors in the title role, the film begins on *The Ghost* after Van Weyden is shanghaied on the Barbary Coast – an episode depicted in flashback. Discovering his victim's class background, the white-bearded captain makes him undergo several humiliations until he gains his sea legs and ascends to the position of first mate, as in the novel. Barbara Bach's heroine remains a marginal figure, while Death Larsen (who makes a brief appearance in this version) is the demonic incarnation of industrial capitalism and is much worse than his brother. Connors's Larsen suffers from debilitating headaches caused by his inability to repress contradictions between an intuitive sense of humanity and the brutality he must exercise to maintain his position as a maritime "captain of industry." Van Weyden and Maud escape from *The Ghost* as in the novel. But, returning, they find Larsen physically debilitated after his brother's takeover of his ship and the desertion of his crew. He later commits suicide by jumping overboard. Larsen's funeral speech, delivered earlier in the film during a burial at sea, echoes over the soundtrack in the final scene: "And the mortal remains shall be consigned to the sea."

Apart from a disappointing 1993 television movie production featuring Charles Bronson as Larsen and Christopher Reeve as Van Weyden, *The Sea-Wolf*'s potential for further adaptations has remained as moribund as *The Ghost*'s condition on Endeavor Island. Owing to the stereotyping of Jack London as a children-and-dog story author and the reticence of the literary and film establishments to take his philosophy and politics seriously, it appears that any future film versions may again fall into the disappointing historical pattern of lost opportunities. Yet the potential still remains for an adaptation to do full justice to the author's intentions in the same way as the 1941 Warner Brothers film did, while incorporating the changes needed to make London's compelling story speak to the current generation as it once spoke to the American public in 1904.

NOTES

1. Jack London, *The Sea-Wolf* (New York: Macmillan, 1904), p. 1. Further quotations will be cited parenthetically in the text.
2. Lee Clark Mitchell. "'And Rescue Us from Ourselves': Becoming Someone in Jack London's *The Sea-Wolf*," *American Literature* 70:2 (1998), p. 333.
3. Jack London, "To the Editor, San Francisco Examiner, June 14, 1905," in London, *The Letters of Jack London*, 3 vols., *Volume One: 1896–1905*, ed. Earle Labor, Robert C. Leitz, III, and I. Milo Shepard (Stanford, CA: Stanford University Press, 1988), p. 492.
4. See Tony Williams, "Another Jack London Film Confirmed," *Jack London Foundation Newsletter* 9:2 (1997), pp. 5–6.
5. The novel's "Maude" often drops the "e" in future screen adaptations.
6. Unsigned review of *The Sea-Wolf*, *The Lady*, n.d., Jack London Estate Archives.

14 An untypical typicality: screening Owen Wister's *The Virginian*

R. Barton Palmer

A contradictory legacy

As a phenomenon, adaptation customarily figures in critical analysis as a series of singular transactions, that is, as instances involving one-to-one relationships between source-texts and their cinematic refashionings. Rarely, a film may adapt several sources, imposing a textual unity (at least of sorts) on a literary multiplicity, as in the case of Robert Altman's film *Short Cuts*, which draws on narrative motifs derived from a number of Raymond Carver short stories.[1] And in at least one special instance, cinematic adaptation is more accurately described as the serial forging of transtextual ties rather than as a unique transformative gesture. Thus adaptation of this kind has multifarious and global effects, with influence to be traced not only in a film that shares the same identity as its source, but also in an emerging series of films that are not "identical," so to speak, but more indirectly related. A literary text, in other words, may give rise to a cinematic genre whose unfolding proceeds for decades.

Such was – and is – the influence on American culture of Owen Wister's *The Virginian* (published in 1902, but in large part composed at the close of the previous century, whose values and traditions it deeply reflects). It is a common enough judgment, as John G. Cawelti remarks, that this novel is "credited with beginning the twentieth-century western craze," establishing itself, if unintentionally, as "the transition between the dime novel and the modern literary and cinematic tradition." Although filmed as itself five times, *The Virginian* has been adapted (perhaps adopted would be the more precise term) in a more general and abstract sense as well, with "its characters and the chief incidents of its plot . . . repeated in countless novels and films."[2] And yet, as some have pointed out, Wister's novel, so responsible for the collective formulation and furtherance of emerging generic conventions, is characterized as well by an insistent antigenericness – not only in its particular inflection of, as Cawelti terms them, "important social and cultural themes," but also in its stylistic and narrative idiosyncrasies.[3] *The Virginian*, then, if important for its contribution to the cinema as a repertoire of culturally resonant formulas, paradoxically finds another kind of significance in its partial rejection of "westernness" more generally for a deep engagement, mediated by the expressive strategies of its author, with its historical moment.

Wister's novel, in other words, has served the cinema as both an indispensable, amalgamating conduit for the transmission of fictional elements derived from highbrow and lowbrow nineteenth-century fiction – and as itself, that is, as an implicit, modernizing critique of the very tradition it helped to establish.

When and where men were men

If, as Lee Clark Mitchell claims, western fiction, in both its novel and cinematic forms, is "preoccupied with the problem of manhood," or what a man *should* be, it is because the genre is also eager to identify and celebrate a landscape that "signals [the] freedom to achieve some truer state of humanity."[4] The western, in short, identifies and celebrates a more authentic, if difficult to achieve, form of maleness, for which readers and viewers are encouraged to yearn, rather as little Joey desires to possess, and perhaps to become, the eponymous hero of George Stevens's hyperclassical *Shane* (1953), a film that not only embodies the western myth but models (fittingly in the person of a starry-eyed child) the emotional attachment to it that viewers are expected to experience. Westerns, of course, deflect the irresistible impossibility of such wish fulfillment into a national past now beyond the clear recall of the present, yet near enough that its vanished plenitude may be savored through a kind of *Weltschmerzig* longing. Western fictions aim to satisfy this desire for a supposedly truer mode of being, which in the fallen era of the present can be experienced only vicariously, through identification with the now-vanished "man of the west." Yet the rearward glance of the genre positions this longed-for past moment as also thankfully unattainable. Shane never does "come back," despite Joey's pleading, and perhaps that is all to the good. The world of earnest sodbusters that he has just saved has no place for him, and, troubled by the discontents of modernity, neither does our own.

Westerns cater to the unfulfillable desire of the industrial and postindustrial American for the pastoral life of constant danger, male camaraderie, and self-fulfilling physical exertion, the existence that is supposed to have characterized this bygone, thoroughly mythlogized era. This was a time when men were men and lived (however implausibly) beyond the reforming and emasculating reach of civilization. Such a view of frontier life is by no means a creation of western fiction, but a powerful national myth (enacting such key American concepts as "individuality" and "freedom") to which that literary tradition lent imaginative shape and cultural power. The most influential late nineteenth-century spokesman for the mythology of the frontier, the historian Frederick Jackson Turner, enthuses that "the self-made man was the Western man's ideal, was the kind of man that all men might become. Out of his wilderness experience, out of the freedom of his opportunities, he fashioned a formula for social regeneration."[5]

Such a reformative descent into the primitiveness of the "wilderness experience," however, is a prospect about which the western is profoundly ambivalent, finding it both enticing and anxiety-producing. Following the narrative and thematic patterns established in the "Leatherstocking" tales of James Fenimore Cooper, the genre does not reject out of hand the blessings of settled culture, especially its promise to substitute the collectively impersonal power of the law for the ethical imperative that every man unhesitatingly and solitarily defend his own honor. Turner, after all, points out that the west is about both the "freedom of opportunities" and the possibility of "regeneration," that is, the renewal of social energies that a reconstituted collective will can effect. This project finds an inevitable connection to national history. For it is the flight from the east that makes possible the restoration of those eastern virtues and strengths lost after the fall into complacent settlement that came with the maturing of the American experiment. In terms of gender politics, the westerner is the American man restored to his natural virility and presumed primal position of dominance. He is self-governing, self-possessed, and self-defining, a "law unto himself," as the cliché so well expresses it.

It matters little, of course, that the particular past that the western invokes has, as Mitchell reminds us, "only the vaguest basis in actual conditions," that it was at best a "negligible history . . . seized upon by writers, who transmuted facts, figures, and movements beyond recognition, projecting mythic possibilities out of prosaic events" (5). But the west of the imagination need only be credited as authentic in order to cast its ideological spell. This moment in time (located vaguely between the end of the Civil War and what Turner termed "the closing of the frontier") must always be conceived as "lost," not fantasized, for, Jane Tompkins points out, "the western is secular, materialist, and antifeminist" and therefore must unfold in a story world whose truth to life, however self-evidently idealized, must also feel in some sense authentic, not the product of either allegory or fabulation.[6] Only in this way can the genre provide a canvas where, among other social issues, gender politics can attain significant representation, where evolving masculinities and femininities can be put into narrative play.

Owen Wister's "Horseman of the Plains"

However grounded in history, westerns connect only vaguely to the forensic aesthetic of literary realism, as the practice of Wister (1860–1938), the most renowned of an earlier generation of western novelists, makes clear. He was deeply affected by his experience of Wyoming in the heyday of the cattle kings, first, in 1885, traveling there on a doctor-mandated rest cure for what was diagnosed as "nervous collapse." Wister chose in his western fiction to ignore, for the most part, much of what he found there: the seediness of the region's jerrybuilt small towns, populated mostly by uninspiringly plain folks, the dirt farmers, merchants, and tradespeople who were in the vanguard of an approaching, degrading civilization. Such "facts" rate only a brief mention in *The Virginian*, his most influential work.[7] In many ways, the actual west was too much like the contemporary urbanizing northeast, the homeland from which Wister found himself in perpetual spiritual and periodic physical retreat. If in his fiction he idealizes the region, exaggerating its importance to the development of the American character, Wister finds himself in good company. Turner, the ostensibly more sober-headed historian, gushes that the "American intellect" owes its "striking characteristics" to the frontier, especially that "dominant individualism, working for good and for evil, and withal that buoyancy and exuberance which comes with freedom."[8]

Only a quite selective and oblique connection with the culture and history of the "real" west is, then, to be found in *The Virginian*, which was confected from short fiction previously published in *Harper's New Monthly Magazine* during the 1890s, a magazine with a significant female readership, which perhaps accounts for some of the book's generic revisionism, of which more below.[9] *The Virginian* is in some sense "about" the infamous Johnson County Cattle War of the early 1890s, but the most direct reference to that conflict between large cattle ranchers and smaller, perhaps less legally scrupulous competitors is to be found in one sparsely detailed sentence on its very last page.[10] So the story's charm is hardly its easily demolished pretense to realism, despite the fact that in the preface Wister claims that his narrative "is of necessity historical . . . [and] presents Wyoming between 1874 and 1890" (6).

Instead, Wister saw a "mythic possibility" in his experiences with the numbingly repetitive mundanity of range life, and the result was that he penned the most popular, and arguably the most influential, of all western novels.[11] The first year of publication brought the sale of 200,000 copies, and *The Virginian* topped that year's bestseller list. Wister and the dramatist Kirk La Shelle not long afterward turned the novel into a play that enjoyed many years of commercially successful production.[12] Based on the novel and the play, five films, the last released in 2000, have done nothing but increase the influence of Wister's engaging tale, as did a long-running (1962–1971) primetime television series based loosely on its characters. By 1968, sales of the book had topped two million, and *The Virginian* remains in print more than a century after its initial appearance, selling a quite respectable six thousand or more copies a year.[13] For several decades *The Virginian* rivaled the phenomenally popular *Uncle Tom's Cabin* and Lew Wallace's *Ben-Hur* as the most-read American novel; all were eclipsed during the 1930s by Margaret Mitchell's *Gone With the Wind* (1936). Unlike Stowe's more topical Christian sentimental narrative and Wallace's religious epic, however, Wister's compelling narrative and charming cowboy hero may be justly credited, along with Cooper's fiction and the nineteenth-century dime novel, with giving rise to one of the most enduring of American popular literary and cinematic forms.[14]

Shepherds with guns

A principal reason for the book's success is its glamorized (if by no means simplified) representation of a certain masculine style, what the critic Forrest G. Robinson identifies as an "amoral" code that "bows down to, depends on, and deeply relishes the authority of force."[15] This is a theme that Wister is hardly hesitant to advertise. The novelist tells prospective readers that his intention is to glorify "the horseman, the cow-puncher, the last romantic figure upon our soil," whose claim to fame is that "whatever he did, *he did with his might*" (7; italics added). Yet the world of the cowboy is a "vanished world," a moment of romance before the inevitable fall into the real time of the present, which according to Wister is "a shapeless state, a condition of men and manners unlovely as that bald moment in the year when winter is gone and spring not come, and the face of Nature is ugly" (6, 7). Importantly, the transformation of this western world and the "condition of men" to which it gave rise is meant to recapitulate national history. Wister reminds his readers that "Wyoming between 1874 and 1890 was a colony as wild as was Virginia one hundred years earlier" (17).

To go west, then, either in the literal sense enacted by the novelist or the vicarious one enjoyed by his readers, is to escape, if only for a time, the inevitable passage of once unsettled America into a society with,

Wister notes ironically, plenty of "Chippendale settees" but not "the same primitive joys and dangers" (6). The comfortable life associated in the present with the east contrasts with the mode of existence of a former, less civilized era, from which danger was never far removed (which was perhaps one of its "joys"). Wister, we might note, defines comfort in terms of both class (the fashionability of antiques among the elite) and also (if metonymically) women, for the "settees" mentioned furnish the sitting rooms where a domesticating feminine presence holds sway and in which "real men" yearning to be free find themselves trapped by convention and duty, obligations they owe to others, not themselves. In the world of Chippendale settees, masculine might counts for nothing. Where women are importantly empowered, men must find other virtues, as Wister acknowledges in *The Virginian*.

Beyond its meaning for what we would now term gender politics, the passing of the west recalls in a larger sense the national fall into a modernity that is defined equally by urban industrializing culture and also, as Wister memorably terms it in his famous essay "The Evolution of the Cow-Puncher," by the advent of those "hordes of encroaching alien vermin, that turn our cities to Babels and our citizenship to a hybrid farce, who degrade our commonwealth from a nation into something half pawn-shop, half broker's office."[16] In such a new world, there is no place for the man dedicated above all else to the preservation of his personal honor. Indeed, the "authority of force" has been lost. Witness the free passage evidently granted to immigrants unwanted by many among the ruling elite to which Wister belonged. Now long past is the moment when social problems could be addressed by the courage and toughmindedness of a man who accepts and enforces a simple code of right and wrong. In the joyfully atavistic fiction of *The Virginian*, the encroaching and alien vermin is solitary (the villainous and non-Anglo-Saxon Trampas).[17] However troublesome, Trampas is finally dispatched with two swiftly delivered and well-placed pistol shots after being soundly defeated and discredited by the Virginian in several battles of wits.

In part, the eponymous cowboy hero of *The Virginian* offers a more acceptable alternative to the "new" Americans for whom Wister manifests such virulent and especially anti-Semitic disdain. The cowboy represents the latest incarnation of a noble, Anglo-Saxon hardiness that can be traced back to that medieval culture so celebrated by late nineteenth- and early twentieth-century Americans, one of whose *idées fixes* was, in the words of the historian Jackson Lears, "the sense that modern life has grown dry and passionless and that one must somehow try to regenerate a lost intensity of feeling."[18] Wister's attempt in "Cow-Puncher" to connect the recent national past to a highly romanticized and essentially literary Middle Ages may now seem strained, but his impulse is very much in keeping with the antimodernism of the era: "No doubt Sir Launcelot bore himself with a grace and breeding of which our unpolished fellow of the cattle trail has only the latent possibility; but in personal daring and in skill as to the horse, the knight and the cowboy are nothing but the same Saxon of different environments" (333). The medieval knight and his own cow-puncher, Wister might have added, are equally fictional, types whose creation in both cases was inspired by an elitist desire for the transcendence of a life devoted, as all lives finally must be, to getting and having.

Unlike medieval romancers, however, Wister glorifies a rural proletariat, not a privileged warrior elite. His "knights" are shepherds with guns, men who do grueling manual labor for hire and whose virtue displays itself in competence, self-possession, and coolness under stress, qualities of the "naturally" endowed rather than of those to the manor born. These men are "made" by the difficult and toughening circumstances of ranch life, constituting an aristocracy whose membership is determined by achievement, not breeding. Such is Wister's Social Darwinist understanding of the workings of democracy or, perhaps better, meritocracy.

The Middle Ages and late nineteenth-century cattle culture are past moments that are equally beyond the reach of what Wister sees as the debased national present, its racial purity defiled, its mongrelized citizens given over to the degrading pursuit of making money. Yet in this present the true Anglo-Saxon (among whose ranks the novelist of course counted himself) senses both displacement and dissatisfaction. While in his view other races may more easily in modern times accommodate themselves to effete pursuits (the French love painting, the Italians sell fruit, the Swedes farm, while the "Teuton is too often a tame, slippered animal"), such weakness does not characterize the Anglo-Saxon, "who is forever homesick for out-of-doors" (331). Men like Wister (and his close friends Frederic Remington and Theodore Roosevelt) found themselves essentially out of place, at least spiritually, in a modern world whose living is mostly done inside. So they seek out the west where, as Turner affirms, "social regeneration" is possible through the adoption (if more symbolic than actual) of the cowboy code. There is every reason to believe, in fact, with the historian G. Edward White, that "the interaction between the idealized traits of Wister's horseman of the plains and the aspirations of Americans at the close of the nineteenth century is particularly significant."[19] The Virginian, we should not forget, finds his historical reflex in the Rough Rider.

The Virginian, however, would not have achieved the amazingly enduring popularity that it enjoys had not Wister offered his readers much more than the bittersweet celebration of a male-dominated past always already receding before the dismal realities of the ethnic melting pot, the debilitating routine of office work, the dreariness of drawing-room evenings, and the uncertainties of developed capitalism, such as those "long empty railroads in the hands of the receiver" that he complains about in "Cow-Puncher" (335). As critics have long recognized, *The Virginian* stages (perhaps even tenuously resolves) the enduring American conflict between the love of a wilderness whose emptiness holds out the promise of unbridled self-definition and the attraction to a civilization whose institutions – law, marriage, and family – might remove the often crushing burden of individuality. In the genre the conflict is figured as a strong contrast between masculine styles, between the virtues required of a physically demanding life (strength, endurance, confidence) and those of settled existence (responsibility, dedication to hard work, ingenuity).

But what Mitchell terms this "problem of manhood" raises the larger question of national self-understanding. Are we an America of rugged individuals whose might counts for everything or a settled society of cooperative, cultured businessmen whose aim is the accumulation of capital? Reflecting the American experience of settlement and the "taming" of the frontier, Wister's story imagines this conflict as in some sense resolved by the passage of time. His deployment of the trope of growth allows him to portray historical change as both the fulfillment of natural destiny and a steady progress away from a state of imagined purity and simplicity. Such growth, collectively and individually, entails both the loss of youth and maturation into the adult world, which *The Virginian* invokes as a sphere of action and values that are identified as eastern, especially full incorporation into the capitalist order and a commitment to married love and family responsibilities. Once again, the novelist's vision matches that of his contemporary, the historian Frederick Jackson Turner, who observes of the west that "gradually this society loses its primitive conditions, and assimilates itself to the type of the older social conditions of the East; but it bears within it enduring and distinguishing survivals of its frontier experience."[20]

In "Cow-Puncher" Wister imagines the cowboys as a hardy race that rose to moral, if not economic prominence, from no solid, biologically homogeneous social roots ("These wild men sprang from the loins of no similar father") and then passed from the national scene without leaving any permanent mark on American culture, for they "begot no sons to continue their hardihood" (341). Such men, while avowedly heteronormal (in the terms of today's identity politics), discovered no feminine or familial order that suited them and so were doomed to inhabit forever, and in spite of themselves, the phallic, sterile narcissism of adolescence: "War they made in plenty, but not love; for the woman they saw was not the woman a man can take into his heart" (341). But if the west cannot produce a woman whose moral worthiness justifies a love that ties and binds, the east can, or so Wister imagines in his novel, which is better described, in fact, as a romance than as a story of, as "Cow-Puncher" terms them, "grim lean men of few topics, and not many words concerning these," in short, the typical taciturn protagonists of western fiction before and since (342). The Virginian's successful pursuit of Molly is central to the ideological project of the novel, for it exemplifies, as the cultural historian Richard Slotkin puts it, the "superior moral character" that brings "the favor of wealthy folk who encourage and employ him . . . and eventually promote him to a 'partnership in the firm'" (175). This plot movement, of course, belongs, properly speaking, more to the *Bildungsroman* (the novel of education) than to adventure narrative.

In fact, as Mitchell points out, measured against the genre it is rightfully credited with significantly furthering if not founding, *The Virginian* seems "scarcely a Western at all," for "the supposedly classic functions of the Western are either absent or vaguely implied" (95). The Virginian defends the right as the western defines it (that is, in terms of property and personal honor). He pursues and lynches rustlers, including his erstwhile friend Steve, who are preying on his employer, and then kills the overreaching Trampas after his honor is insulted. Yet the plot emphasizes the cowboy's wooing of the eastern "schoolmarm" Molly Wood, his youthful high jinks (as described in humorous escapades developed in the regionalist manner of Mark Twain), and his competent handling of a difficult delivery of cattle to market, an episode that illustrates his enviable leadership abilities.

The dime-novel tradition of western fiction, as characterized by Christine Bold, "concentrated primarily on ritualistic adventure," precisely those elements that, while present in *The Virginian*, never receive narrative focus and are evoked obliquely by the flimsiest of metonymies, as a telling detail or two is meant to express a generically conventional whole.[21] Most famous of these is the narrator's "representation" of the hero's climactic gunfight with Trampas:

A wind seemed to blow the sleeve off his arm, and he replied to it, and saw Trampas pitch forward. He saw Trampas raise his arm from the ground and fall again, and lie there this time, still. A little smoke was rising from the pistol on the ground, and he looked at his own, and saw the smoke flowing upward out of it. (313)

The mutual accommodation of male and womanly sensibilities is given much more focus than this violent showdown. We must bear in mind that the stories stitched together were first published in a slick magazine whose readership was substantially female. In fact, the adventure plot as such is entirely absent from these initial sketches; it was evidently fabricated out of whole cloth when Wister, in search of a plot, set out to make a full-length novel out of these self-contained episodes. Yet the archly generic materials like the gunfight, which Wister developed from the dime-novel tradition, are handled with a very light touch. They showcase rather than overwhelm the witty local color descriptions and sprightly conversational exchanges that constitute the bulk of the tale. Tellingly, the novel deals at greater length and in much more detail with the discussion that the Virginian and Molly have about the relative merits of George Eliot and Walter Scott (96–98) than with the duel on which everything, at least in terms of plot, is designed to hang.

If cowboys are, as Wister elsewhere affirms, men "of few topics and not many words," then the Virginian from the outset thoroughly demonstrates his difference from them, for his strength and courage pale in comparison to his considerable verbal abilities, whether he is humiliating Trampas with an elaborate tall tale (and preventing the men in his charge from mutiny) or matching wits with Molly in a debate about the true nature of American democracy (he easily proves his point that "equality is a great bluff. It's easy called", 99). It is hard to imagine any other western hero allowing a woman to instruct him in the niceties of literary tradition, especially after, somewhat snobbishly, she turns down his advances. Even more uncharacteristic of the western hero, perhaps, is the Virginian's commitment to social and economic self-improvement. He tells Molly, "I know what yu' meant . . . by sayin' you're not the wife I'd want. But I am the kind that moves up. I am goin' to be your best scholar" (100).

The westerner goes eastern

The Virginian, after enduring the pain of conforming to the cowboy code that demands he hang his best friend and face down the dangerous Trampas, does "move up" to a social sphere that requires virtues other than rough masculine courage, becoming the business partner of his erstwhile employer, Judge Henry. Yet it is at this very moment, as the hero leaves behind his youth, that the world in which he has proven himself suddenly disappears. The cattle era ends as the big ranchers fall victim to the "equality" (those of lower social rank) who seize control of the courts and government.[22] Other economic opportunities, however, present themselves to those with good luck and the ability to make the most of a main chance: "But the railroad came, and built a branch to that land of the Virginian's where the coal was. By that time he was an important man, with a strong grip on many various enterprises, and able to give his wife all and more than she asked or desired . . . sometimes she declared that his work would kill him. But it does not seem to have done so" (327). In the emerging landscape of complex, unpredictable capital ventures, the one-time cowboy prospers, to the benefit of his beloved Molly, who is able to enjoy the considerable financial fruits of his labor and good business sense.

This finale moves absolutely beyond the struggles that had generated its narrative, in a sense marking them as irrelevant. Yet this is the way in which the novel stitches together a reconciliation of sorts between regional sensibilities, between pastoral and entrepreneurial ways of life, between an unsettled national past and a present dominated by increasingly complex economic relations. In the beginning, Molly comes west after rejecting the effeteness of her native northeast, which cannot provide her with a man who suits her strength and passion. Attracted by the physical beauty and masculine grace of the Virginian but put off by his apparent uncouthness, Molly can admit to being in his power only when, finding her cowboy suitor wounded after an Indian attack, she nurses him back to health. The resourcefulness and resolution she demonstrates in this difficult situation show her mettle as a frontier wife. The western man, in turn, proves able to satisfy the eastern woman only because the strengths and sensibility of the easterner are always already within him; for all his physical skills, it is his good business sense that allows him (and his marriage) to prosper. For this self to emerge, it seems, all that is required is the passing of the cattle era and the hero's once and for all demonstration that he knows "how it must be about a man" (309). On his wedding day he refuses to back down when Trampas insults him in a fashion that no man of honor could ignore. Molly threatens to leave him, but his first loyalty is to his self-respect. In the end, she does marry him despite his rejection of her pleas to forsake the gunfight. Presumably, she comes to accept his argument that he must prove to other men that he values his "nature enough to shield it from their slander" (309). Perhaps it is also his refusal to be ruled by her that she finds so irresistible.

It bears remarking that in rewarding his hero for defending his honor despite the prospect of grievous personal loss (not to mention the risk of his own life), Wister was connecting to a developing principle of American jurisprudence: the rejection of the English common law principle of a "duty to retreat" in the face of physical threat. As Justice

Oliver Wendell Holmes was to declare in a landmark case (*Brown* v. *United States*, 1921), "detached reflection cannot be demanded in the presence of an uplifted knife."[23] In requesting that her husband-to-be ignore Trampas's demand that he leave town or face the fatal consequences, Molly voices an opinion of manly virtue whose preeminence was being challenged. In the closing decade of the nineteenth and the early years of the twentieth century, as Lears suggests, "the educated and affluent felt a persistent need for manly testing . . . the stage was set for a new kind of heroic act with no larger purpose beyond itself."[24]

This is what *The Virginian* offered readers of the time. Wister does not ignore the claims of female sentimentalism and its Christian source, but he does argue for the existential (perhaps natural) limitations of such an ethos. Encouraged by Molly, the bishop attempts to persuade the Virginian from the "walkdown" by an appeal to the "Gospel, that he preached, and believed, and tried to live" (305). Yet the good cleric is unsure of his ground because his "heart was with the Virginian" and to oppose his friend's decision felt to him as though it were "against the whole instinct of human man" (305, 306). Intent on killing his enemy, the Virginian leaves with the clergyman's blessing ringing in his ears (307).

Until recently, critics have emphasized the novel's monologism, its self-promoting ideological success in, as Christine Bold puts it, "resolving the differences between East and West presented in his love story" by creating a western hero "handsome and chivalrous enough (partly because of his Southern origins) to marry an educated Easterner".[25] But because it engages with the contradictions of a complex cultural moment, *The Virginian* is more accurately described, in the words of Stephen Tatum, as "anything but a seamless, monolithic text always and inevitably advancing a dream of empire and of a revitalized white male ethnicity."[26] And these ideological cracks go beyond the book's "positive" view of western settlement (particularly its support of propertied interests) and its deeply racist portrayal of an exclusively Anglo-Saxon race of heroic men. Despite its ostensible reconciliation of regional sensibilities (and the sharply contrasting models of male virtue that they propose), the novel, as Robinson argues, not only "reinforce[s] our sense of the heroic, but also challenge[s] it," extolling "American virtues," while exploring the "dark side of a dominant self image."[27]

The novel's finale emphasizes both the Virginian's imposition of his code of values on Molly *and* his acceptance of domestication at her hands, a legal transformation of his status that means he must make money to support her and their children. Yet Wister also leaves his readers with the hero's powerful musings about the burden of accepting, bearing, and reconciling two different versions of masculinity. Camping with Molly on their honeymoon, and relieved momentarily of all other claims on his selfhood, the Virginian spots an otter cavorting on the sands, and this sight prompts him to muse about two questions: "Where's the use of fretting? What's the gain in being a man?" Yet, except in this unrepeatable moment of relief from the social roles he is called to play, these are questions the Virginian dare not seriously entertain because, as he confesses, "the trouble is, I am responsible" (320). But even though he recognizes that Molly shares with him this desire to be at one with nature ("become the ground, become the water, become the trees, mix with the whole thing"), he also acknowledges that this urge toward the inanimate and primitive cannot be indulged (320–321). The Virginian's uncertainty, however transitory, about a man's life prompts the reader to consider what is gained and lost in his serial conformation to the two versions, hardly uncontradictory, of maleness that the book endorses. In fact, the cowboy's momentary doubts about his life put into question the novel's ostensible ideological project, which depends on the Virginian's ability to adapt to changing circumstances. A productively unstable mix of ideas and values, *The Virginian* raises a number of questions for which subsequent versions of the story, from the stage version to the various screen adaptations, have confected different answers.

The return of history: *The Virginian* (2000)

Because the "domestic" and local color material that constitutes the bulk of *The Virginian* is rather undramatic, the stage version of the novel penned by La Shelle, and to whose final form Wister made important contributions, gives less emphasis to the novel's detailed and nuanced presentation of gender politics and brought much more to the fore its adventure elements, especially the conflict between the Virginian and Trampas. Adhering closely to the stage version of Wister's story are the first four screen adaptations: Cecil B. DeMille (1914), Tom Forman (1923), Victor Fleming (1929), and Stuart Gilmore (1946). There is no little irony in this. As has been noted, Wister sought to distance himself from the adventure tradition of the dime-novel western, yet the first four screen versions of his novel have very much accommodated his novel of sensibilities to the dominant elements of the genre, whose popularity with audiences national and international during the initial five decades of the twentieth century would be difficult to overestimate. Although the publicity trailer for the 1946 Gilmore version terms the property "the all-time best-selling love story of the west," here the hero's engagement in the world of men is the main focus of the narrative as well. Undeniably, all these studio-era films make an important place for Molly, but they are more interested in the hero's relationships with his friend Steve and his enemy Trampas, producing interesting variants of this central triangle. And the history of the cattle era, represented indirectly throughout the novel but of vital importance to its finale, is more or less eliminated, as the "west" of these films is represented as durable (if implicitly past and hence now gone), not evolving toward the easternizing settlement that will destroy it. In four separate productions Wister's fiction was westernized for the screen, with the popular genre arguably exerting more influence on its narrative and dramatic shape than the novelist's largely antigeneric vision of his characters and the world they once inhabited.

Remarkably, perhaps, *The Virginian*, arguably the best-known and most popular, if most untypical, of all western novels, was not filmed again in the three decades after the genre grew to ideological maturity. One can imagine a more realistic version of the novel being screened in a 1950s dominated by the "adult" treatment of psychological and political themes (especially in the films of Anthony Mann, John Ford, and John Sturges); or in a 1960s marked by retrospective celebration of a myth losing its hitherto unchallengeable appeal (especially in the self-reflexive productions of Sergio Leone and Sam Peckinpah's "end of the era" films); or even in a 1970s that offered the deconstructive revision of the history that classic westerns pretended to express, with productions as diverse as Robert Altman's *McCabe & Mrs. Miller* (1971) and *Buffalo Bill and the Indians* (1976), as well as Clint Eastwood's *The Outlaw Josey Wales* (1976), all of which give the lie, after a fashion, to traditional western representations and their hitherto unchallenged basis in fact. With its uneasy and incomplete erasure of cattle culture history; its hesitant, even squeamish endorsement of the westerner's recourse to lawless violence; its preoccupation with gender politics; and its *fin de siècle* retrospectivism, Wister's novel could have been accommodated to any one of these three periods of generic ungenericness, when the western was made to speak much that it had long kept silent about.

Yet potential adaptors may have been discouraged by *The Virginian*'s irrepressible celebration of a growth to maturity, on the part of both the protagonist and his world, that only with great difficulty could be purged of its chauvinism and sexism. Wister's conservatism in these matters, his self-conscious support of establishment values, was perhaps read by prospective adaptors as running too deep during the postwar period of an increasingly liberalized western. It may be, then, that the rightward swing of American society and political life during the late 1990s made Wister's novel a more attractive source-text, with the result that it was brought to the screen again for the first time in nearly a half-century.

Michael Coyne has written of the western that at the end of the twentieth century, "the genre is virtually as outmoded as two-ocean security, each of which had roots in a once dominant ideology predicated on belief in exceptional national destiny," a belief that, clothed in late nineteenth-century racism and *nostalgie*, animates Wister's portrait of the western hero's ruggedness and canny accommodation to changing times. We may grant Coyne's conclusion, that "as a central force in the culture of contemporary American society, the Western is never coming back." Yet as a cultural mythology the western's appeal is strong enough, at least occasionally, to generate a deeply resonant exploration of both the genre's unreflective glorification of the gunfighter (a demythologization undertaken in Clint Eastwood's *Unforgiven* [1992]) or its one-dimensional treatment of the "Indians," hitherto seen as given "naturally" to a Hobbesian savagery. So, with a fine sense of contemporary identity politics, Kevin Costner's *Dances with Wolves* (1990) refigures Native American life with a primitivist ardor, in a film that energetically pursues the depiction of what the now-vanished world of the Lakota Sioux was "really like."[28]

Unlike the ironic hypergenericity that is the central feature of postmodern pastiche, such reinventions of the western as *Unforgiven* and *Dances with Wolves* evidence what the critic Jim Collins has appropriately termed a "new sincerity."[29] By this he means a self-conscious desire to purge the genre of its patent elements of wish-fulfillment or obscurantism in order to reconfigure it as the bearer of larger historical truth. *Unforgiven* achieves its powerfully unconventional effects from a partial defictionalization of western materials, in a move that asks to be read as a commitment to greater realism. The righteous violence that undergirds the genre's resolution of conflict is revealed as brutal, disgusting, and soul-destroying, yet it is not pitted against some more compelling moral principle. Nor is violence despectacularized in *Unforgiven*. In fact, a complexly staged final shoot-out provides customary generic (if inevitably, given the film's pervasive interrogation of violence, somewhat guilty) pleasures.

Something similar can be seen at work in Bill Pullman's version of *The Virginian* (2000). The latest screen version of Wister's novel was produced by Daniel H. Blatt in association with Big Town Productions for cable release on Turner Network Television as part of media mogul Ted Turner's continuing commitment to making and broadcasting conservative Americana films. In this version the novel is to some degree restored to itself (or, to put it differently, dewesternized). It is also accommodated to the gender politics of a new century. Perhaps most striking, the history of the cattle baron era here finds stronger representation in a more ideologically coherent, if somewhat less historically accurate, form.

This "new sincerity" affects all levels of the film's construction, from *mise-en-scène* to dialogue and plot, and it speaks an important truth. In this updated (yet more authentic) version, we are reminded forcefully that Wister's novel has enjoyed a long life of cultural relevance because it expresses a mythology that still powerfully informs widely held notions about the American national character, especially the idea that the self-made man advances because he trusts to his abilities, defers to his betters, and does not forswear the use of force. Yet such a man also acknowledges, and acquiesces to, the moral power that women wield, even as he refuses to surrender his sense of honor to them. It can hardly be an accident that this version's thematic focus on Social Darwinism (whose presence is barely to be felt in previous screen versions) suits the neoconservative doctrine of exceptionalism that is such a prominent element on the political scene in the new American millennium.

Neoconservatism espouses, in a manner Wister would have approved, a philosophy of rugged individualism (and yet, paradoxically, a strong defense of inherited privilege as well). The neoconservative recognizes no duty to retreat in the face of threat and does not look to institutions, especially the legal system, for the mediation or resolution of conflicts. In fact, Pullman and screenwriter Larry Gross make clearer than Wister does the larger political implications of this social mythology by placing Trampas's villainy within a more detailed social context that reflects a revisionist view of the Johnson County Cattle War, which, as recent commentators have emphasized, involved not so much a conflict between ranchers and rustlers in a time of growing economic hardship, as Wister suggests, but instead a bitter rivalry between competitors in the shrinking market place. As Slotkin recounts, "Rather than blame their own faulty operations for the reduction of the herds, managers [of the big ranches] accused the small ranchers of rustling . . . [many of whom] were ex-employees of the big ranchers who had managed to save enough of their meager pay . . . and set up as rivals to their former bosses."[30] This is the social atmosphere that the film invokes.

In the film's reconfiguring of the novel, the intention of the Virginian (Bill Pullman) "to move up" is contrasted with the illegal self-improvement scheme espoused by Trampas (Colm Feore) and the Virginian's erstwhile friend Steve (John Savage). If Steve and Trampas endorse the notion that, in the competition that is life, might makes right, the Virginian follows a softer version of Darwinism, which is that the self-fashioning man on the way up must heed social proprieties, including showing respect for those placed above him in rank. The moral opposition between the Virginian and those who come to oppose his obedience to the law reflects the zero sum struggle over the range and its livestock engaged in by the protagonist's employer, the respectable (but weak) Judge Henry (Harris Yulin), and the unscrupulous (but powerful) Sam Balaam (Dennis Weaver), whose transgressive graspingness attracts both Trampas and Steve to his camp. This competition between different types of landowners is implied but not directly represented in the novel. Only in the film does the survival of Medicine Bow as a law-abiding and righteous community depend on the Virginian's extirpation of the threat that Trampas poses, both to Judge Henry's livelihood and also to the federal government's attempt to bring the law to Wyoming Territory.

In the novel the Virginian kills Trampas in order to preserve his honor; in the other film versions, he is shown both defending himself against Trampas's insults and taking revenge for what happened to Steve. In Pullman's film the Virginian is still much affected by both these motives, but he is also conscious that in ridding the town of Trampas, he is striking a blow against the larger social corruption that has empowered and emboldened the villain. With the pistol still smoking in his hand, the Virginian confronts Balaam and foils the ambush that the scheming rancher had arranged in order to murder the Virginian should he survive the duel. Exposed as a coward and a criminal, Balaam is finished as in any sense a legitimate rival to Judge Henry for dominance over the land and its quadruped riches. None of this is to be found in Wister's novel.

Mavericks and a maiden

The opening sequences of the novel spectacularize the cowboy hero, presenting the Virginian as the object of a double gaze: an image of virility irresistible to the recently arrived dude narrator and the eastern schoolmarm, both of whom fall quickly victim to his self-confident demeanor and physical charms. His is a human presence of moral excellence and beauty produced by, and yet in strong apparent contrast with, the drabness of the social setting (the unimpressive "town" of Medicine Bow, Wyoming) from which he emerges. If this ramshackle frontier whistlestop compares unfavorably with the more settled and refined east, the Virginian's presence suggests a level of cultivation and social attainment whose naturalness deconstructs familiar cultural categories. In this way, the novel develops at the outset the meaning that the west and the westerner will have, for the region's regenerating primitiveness is figured in a powerful masculinity that is initially beyond the full ken (if not the appreciation) of eastern man and woman. The desire that the Virginian arouses magically cures the *ennui* of the neurasthenic narrator and seems to be what is needed to assuage the dissatisfaction of the eastern woman, in flight from the overcivilized men of her native Vermont. The novel's beginning prefigures the nation-building, sectional accommodation of its finale, in which the westerner becomes eastern (more eastern than most easterners in fact, as measured by his economic success and consequent elevation in social rank), without losing his enviable vitality, the energy he derives from "below" in class and regional terms.

In contrast, the opening sequences of Pullman's film pose two problems, propelling the narrative to move toward their solution. What is to become of the formidable Molly Stark (Diane Lane), just arrived unescorted in a Medicine Bow that is a seemingly random collection of jerrybuilt shacks, looking very much as though they had been thrown up the week before? And who is to control this barely settled territory – those who respect property rights or those who believe that might makes right? With our first view of Medicine Bow, a destination arrived at only after long helicopter shots of a stagecoach making its solitary way across verdant and apparently virgin prairie (exteriors were shot in an unsettled region of Alberta), we are far from the conventional setting of the western. In the 1946 Gilmore film, which keeps closer to the novel, Molly arrives on a train filled with passengers. With its much-traversed dirt streets and assorted emporia, dominated by the saloon where all and sundry congregate, Gilmore's version of Medicine Bow exemplifies the classic town of the genre: a setting that anchors the narrative in a west already well on its way to being permanently inhabited.

Pullman's Medicine Bow, in contrast, lacks such solidity: the grass has not been trampled down between the buildings, which are disposed in no discernible pattern and so suggest the absence of secure social relations. Tellingly, there is no "main street." Dressed practically and possessed of a self-confident manner, Molly has come west to take up a position as a schoolteacher, presumably because of her desire to explore what she terms in a letter to her mother "the great unknown," a prospect that both excites and frightens her. Surveying the unimpressive townscape, beyond which is a grand and perhaps terrifying emptiness, she asks an old man if this is "all there is." He nods agreement, then remarks that "the wind blew it all in. Pretty soon it will blow it all away again," an assessment that seems to strike the young woman as reasonable. Civilization has as yet little purchase in Medicine Bow, an impression that is deepened as her appointed cowboy escort drives Molly to the schoolhouse near Judge Henry's ranch. On the trail sprawls a dead cow, its belly ripped open, presumably so that a calf could be pulled from it. In this country, the driver remarks, "too many folks got their eyes on stock don't belong to them."

At issue, we soon learn, are the "mavericks" that roam the open range, calves born that same spring and hence as yet unbranded – of undetermined ownership if they are found not accompanied by their mothers. How to resolve the property rights to the mavericks, and indeed to the land itself and all the profitable stock it nourishes for free? Are these things to be held in common or shared, so that all may benefit? Or are the customary laws of private property to hold sway? The next scene, which is not to be found in the novel, focuses on two men in the employ of Judge Henry who are riding on the open range: Steve and the Virginian, who has just dismounted to examine an unbranded calf as two other riders come up to claim the animal as belonging to their employer, Sam Balaam. No one seems surprised by the implication that they are rustling, suggesting an ongoing dispute between the two ranchers and their men. Affronted by the accusation, Steve remarks that Balaam finds a way to claim all mavericks, especially on the Judge's side of the river, where, as he points out, they now are.

Animals and land are "owned," it seems, but the rights to both are a matter of dispute that will, it seems, not be resolved by lawful authorities, who are neither in evidence nor invoked. A gunfight to settle the matter seems imminent as each side shows a readiness to defend its claim, but is avoided because the Virginian reminds everyone that there are "a host of consequences to consider," thus cunningly finding an impersonal verbal formula to forestall the violence that, so generic conventions make us expect, will determine the right. He refuses to fight, thereby marking his difference from Steve and the two Balaam men, who clearly wish a showdown. Live and let live, the Virginian suggests, and the Balaam men agree. This skirmish is evidently part of a larger struggle between the two landholders for control of the range and its animals. The Balaam men have crossed the river that divides their two ranches, and not for the first time, as Steve reminds his companion, indicating, with evident distaste, that the judge does not wish to confront his rival directly, thus supplying the Virginian's peacemaking efforts with a motive.

In Steve's harsh but accurate evaluation, such weakness means that the judge has met his "measure" in Balaam. So he and the Virginian have good reason to end their employment and reclaim their "freedom," meaning that they should pursue their better chance, wherever that might be. Although he does not dispute the truth of what Steve has said, the Virginian is unwilling to quit the judge's employ: when you side with a man, you side with him, he says, suggesting a loyalty that goes beyond self-interest. Besides, one place is as good as another, so there's no reason to keep moving; here is a place to put down roots. The contrast between the two friends is developed differently in the novel. Charming and childish, Wister's Steve refuses to grow up, and he finds a ready partner in the Virginian, who for a time enjoys a good practical joke; eventually, however, it is Steve's lack of mature judgment that leads to his fatal decision to join the rustlers, a mistake that his more self-controlled friend would never make. Pullman's Steve, however, is no boy given to pranks, but a man who respects only strength and power, neither social position nor, as it turns out, even the law. If he eventually sides with Trampas, it is not because he has been foolishly seduced, as Wister has it, but because the two men share a dislike of authority that does not command respect with a show of strength – and also of any self-restraint that can be seen as cowardly.

The "equality" finds its measure

In the power struggle that the film goes on to trace, Judge Henry reveals himself to be a model of civic virtue, who is authorized for this reason to act as *de facto* governor of the land. Henry treats his men and his wife with kindness and consideration. He plays an important role in civilizing the territory by engaging Molly as schoolmarm. The Judge has apparently achieved prominence because he has taken possession of the natural resources, animal and geographic, that Wyoming provides. But, in a radical departure from Wister, he proves to be a man with an insufficient sense of honor and self-respect, a flaw that allows him to be victimized easily by Balaam, the neighbor who owns less land and fewer animals, but aims to take, by guile and force, those belonging to the judge. Balaam demands the loan of prize horses that he is then loath to return, preferring a swap whose terms he dictates. He is strongly suspected in the chronic sabotage of the judge's property and in the "accidents" that strangely kill his men. But his contest with the judge is by no means public, for Balaam is an ostensibly legitimate property owner. For these insults the judge has at first no answer and enjoins his cowboys to take no action, presumably hoping thereby to gain Balaam's favor. Only when it becomes obvious that someone is stealing from him does he determine to confront his enemies, if only indirectly.

In the novel the judge authorizes the Virginian to track down the rustlers and lynch them, which means that he must hang his best friend Steve, once he is captured and admits his guilt. This difficult moral decision puts the novel's protagonist resolutely on the side of authority and property. If Wister's judge refuses to lead the posse himself and preside over the execution of the captured criminals, he does not shrink from defending the practice of vigilantism at length, taking moral responsibility for what he has ordered to protect his possessions. Much as the Virginian will soon do, he stands against Molly's support for due process (the courts are under the control of men not friendly to the gentry), preferring extralegal violence to restore his honor. The reason is simple: there is an absence, he claims, of a functioning justice system in the territory. In the film, however, the judge shrinks from even discussing what he has set in motion, desiring no report of the specifics of the lynching from the Virginian. Pullman's judge, though, believes more in the law than in vigilantism; his stand against violence is a conventional indication of his weakness.

In an episode not in the novel, he summons and then houses two federal agents who are tasked with rooting out Trampas and the rustlers (a mission that rightly should be his own in the context of the western), but these two men, obviously ignorant of the ways of the country, are easily ambushed and shot down by Trampas. This episode seems designed not only to establish the insufficiency of a law that is not enforced by physical courage and cunning (reinforcing a western theme *par excellence* dear to Wister's heart), but also, and more importantly, to connect the showdown between Trampas and the Virginian to the larger social question of who is to "own" the land and its animals, those who respect authority and social position or those who subscribe instead to the "law" of red tooth and claw. The "equality," those of no breeding who lack moral scruples, find their measure in the Virginian, who restores property to those with a better right to it, which the film establishes indirectly through its contrasting characterizations of Judge Henry and Balaam.

In the film's gallery of masculine types, the Virginian holds a middle position, avoiding the extremes of the morally unrestrained, ultimately self-destructive pursuit of advantage (Trampas), and the self-defeating deference to others, which is nothing less than a failure to assert one's "right" to property (ultimately grounded in force when the law has no power). These two extremes are related. The film clearly suggests that Judge Henry's sort of kindness provokes only the worst in human nature. In contrast to the novel, the film hints at a direct causal connection between Steve's correct perception of Judge Henry's timidity and his decision to shift allegiance to the more nakedly self-assertive Balaam, who promises to be the eventual winner in the battle between the two landowners. The Virginian does the violent work that advantages his employer, not only in lynching the two captured rustlers, but also in extirpating the country of their rival, whose strength has come from illicit "feeding" off his more reticent neighbor.

In the film's opening scenes, the Virginian plays the peacemaker, refusing to allow blood to be shed over the ownership of a lone maverick. But, near the end of the story, when one of Trampas's men presents him with the bloody coats of the two government agents *and* also insults his honor by implying that the Virginian has sent others to do his dirty work for him (a charge that could be made in truth only against Judge Henry), the westerner accepts that a resort to violence is now justified. He must not only restore his personal honor, but also rid the country of the lawlessness that threatens the security of property. If in the novel the cattle kings fall victim to the "equality," in Pullman's film the "equality" is defeated before it can wrest control from those higher in social rank. Such a resolution does not fit the historical facts – the cattlemen lost the Johnson County Cattle War even if they later won the peace, so to speak – but it better suits the film's interest in constructing a hero in the neoconservative mold who believes as much in respect for authority as he does in self-determination. In the film the community is saved by the Virginian's victory. In the novel the death of Trampas does nothing to foil the designs of the small ranchers, who, we are told, outnumber the larger landowners at the ballot box and, ironically enough, defeat them democratically.

With Trampas dead and Balaam defeated, Pullman's Virginian sets out to establish a secure place for himself. The film's Molly, unlike her novelistic counterpart, carries out her threat to abandon her fiancé after he leaves her at the altar. Reestablishing the importance she holds for him, the cowboy must make the long journey back to Vermont in order to effect a reconciliation, but this goes badly at first. The Virginian cannot admit that his decision was wrong, and Molly cannot accept that his sense of personal honor meant, if only for that one moment, that he could refuse to be guided by her moral sensibility. He is about to depart for Wyoming alone when Molly discovers the form that their rapprochement must take. She is allowed to keep what she calls her truth, and he is not asked to abandon his, even though, as she admits, these truths are opposed. While she refuses to endorse the demonstrated social necessity of violence, as well as its central role in her lover's definition of himself, Molly returns to a Medicine Bow delivered to the rule of law by a lawless act. In this way, Pullman finds a new way to establish the reconciliation between regions and genders. The coupling of Molly and the Virginian is now based less on the eastern, feminine surrender to a revitalized western masculinity and more on mutual acceptance and tolerance. However, it is still true that western ways, including extralegal violence, are shown as indispensable in creating the new society, whose vitality suits Molly. In the person of Judge Henry, the well-meaning, peace-loving man who would have lost all to an amoral rival hoping to rise above his assigned station, the film illustrates the feckless idealism of Molly's opposition to the gun. So it is not necessary that in the end she accept the Virginian's viewpoint in order to make Wister's ideological point. The Virginian's displacement of Judge Henry as the authority in Medicine Bow has done that thematic work.

Unlike Shane, for whom no domesticity is possible (the woman who is drawn to him is married to one of the sodbusters, precluding their coupling), this westerner becomes a part of the society he helps to build and then defends. He is not forced to withdraw into the wilderness and the perpetual solitude of which the savage, untamed west is an attractive correlative. Wister's version of the myth, unlike the genre it furthered, promises a renewed and regenerated American domesticity that is compatible with (or, at least, can coexist with) masculine might. His hero does not surrender to the feminizing power of the "Chippendale settee," but instead welcomes the reforming womanly touch in the wilderness that he has redeemed from savagery. He is, simply put, a man's man who will not live without the woman he loves. In Pullman's updated version of the story, Molly loves him in spite of her refusal to accept the code by which he lives. Such mutual respect tellingly redefines the sexism at the heart of the novel. If Molly comes west hoping to make a life for herself, the Virginian, who journeys east to fetch her back, returns her to that vision of herself. This narrative rhyme suggests in part that she has been tamed by the love she bears him, but Molly is also allowed her independence, for she is the one who invents the moral formula by which they are to live. Her willingness to be accommodating matches his, as revealed in the opening scene where his philosophy of "live and let live" forestalls, even if it cannot ultimately prevent, a violent confrontation between competing landowners and their opposed ways of life.

It is true, as Tompkins puts it, that Wister's novel resembles other westerns in that its plot "turns not on struggles to conquer sin but on external conflicts in which men prove their courage to themselves and the world by facing their own annihilation."[31] But (and this is especially true of Pullman's film version) in *The Virginian* the duel to the death must be endured not for its own sake or for what it proves, but so that death's dominance of that too savage world may be ended and the west may be made safe for advancing civilization. In this neoconservative version of a classic tale, the hero makes his world safe for the better sort by putting an end to lawless economic interlopers. Although the judge may be too weak to face his enemy, his loyal foreman is not, and the threat that Balaam has posed to the moral order of the community is ended by *force majeure*, by the violence whose perceived rightness is central to America's understanding of its history.

America, as Coyne and others have declared, may have ended its long romance with the western genre that his novel did so much to shape, but Wister's story, in its untypical typicality, seems capable of continual reinvention. This is an indication, perhaps, of its unfailing usefulness for the neverending project of collective self-definition that is American cultural life. Here is a text, no doubt, that in its multiple and still multiplying forms has imprinted itself most deeply on the national consciousness.

NOTES

1. For an illuminating discussion of adaptations of this kind, see Robert Kolker, "Screening Raymond Carver: Robert Altman's *Short Cuts*," in the companion to this volume, R. Barton Palmer, ed., *Twentieth-Century American Fiction on Screen* (Cambridge: Cambridge University Press, 2006), pp. 186–197.
2. John G. Cawelti, *Adventure, Mystery, and Romance: Formula Stories as Art and Popular Culture* (Chicago: University of Chicago Press, 1976), p. 215.
3. See, for example, the critique of Cawelti's views in Jeffrey Wallmann, *The Western: Parables of the American Dream* (Lubbock: Texas Tech University Press, 1999), pp. 102–103.
4. Lee Clark Mitchell, *Westerns: Making the Man in Fiction and Film* (Chicago: University of Chicago Press, 1996), pp. 7, 5. Further quotations will be cited parenthetically in the text.
5. Frederick Jackson Turner, "The Problem of the West," in Turner, *Rereading Frederick Jackson Turner: "The Significance of the Frontier" and Other Essays* (New York: Henry Holt, 1994), p. 68.
6. Jane Tompkins, *West of Everything: The Inner Life of Westerns* (Oxford: Oxford University Press, 1992), p. 28.
7. Wister was perhaps too much the patrician easterner to refrain utterly from indicting the squalor he found in western settlements, even if it was redeemed in part by a natural beauty that could no longer be found in his native New England. Consider the remarks of the dude narrator (an obvious Wister intratextual reflex) who is just making the acquaintance of a barely civilized Wyoming. Speaking of western towns, he writes: "Scattered wide, they littered the frontier from the Columbia to the Rio Grande, from the Missouri to the Sierras. They lay stark, dotted over a planet of treeless dust, like soiled packs of cards . . . Houses, empty bottles, and garbage, they were forever of the same shapeless pattern. More forlorn they were than stale bones . . . Yet serene above their foulness swam a pure and quiet light, such as the East never sees; they might be bathing in the air of creation's first morning" (*The Virginian* [Oxford: Oxford University Press, 1998], p. 18). Further quotations from the novel will be to this edition and will be cited parenthetically in the text.
  Wister was diagnosed as suffering from "neurasthenia" by the celebrated "nerve doctor" Silas Weir Mitchell, who, as Barbara Will points out, was famous for advocating extended bed rest for nervous women but a form of "self-conquest" for male neurasthenics, who were encouraged to achieve "the continual monitoring and adjustment of nervous energies that produces

'manliness'" (Will, "The Nervous Origins of the American Western," *American Literature* 70 [1998], p. 297). The object, then, is not to encourage the urban man to adopt the will-less personality style of "exact equipoise . . . in which 'straight talk' is equated with clear judgment, moral probity, and certain masculinity," for that would be to negate the value of "strenuous masculine striving" so necessary for economic success in an increasingly competitive business world (pp. 295, 297). The ideal for the eastern neurasthenic, as Will points out, would be the "*temporary* and *repeated* entry of the urban into the rural" (p. 300). Will's analysis of the therapeutic role of "westernness" and the wilderness experience in the cure prescribed for Wister explains the compromised sense of nostalgia that pervades the novel, its longing for a past moment of primitiveness and yet its evident relief that civilization has replaced a society that requires absolute male self-certainty and adherence to a simple, yet unflinchingly demanding code of behavior.

8. Frederick Jackson Turner, "The Significance of the Frontier," in Turner, *Rereading Frederick Jackson Turner*, p. 59.

9. *The Virginian*, then, was not, at least in its formative stages, addressed to a predominantly male readership, as was the dime novel. Instead, as Jeffrey Wallmann points out, "Wister crafted *The Virginian* out of stories sold to slicks whose readers were predominantly female." Thus it can be argued that the novel and Wister's "western" stories "reflect the values of the contemporary middlebrow women who were the bulk of his audience" (*The Western*, pp. 104–105).

10. "Then, in 1892, came the cattle war, when, after putting their men in office and coming to own some of the newspapers, the thieves brought ruin on themselves" (p. 327).

11. In the preface Wister relates how he once read portions of the novel to a "cow-puncher," who tellingly inquired, "Why . . . do you waste your time writing what never happened, when you know so many things that did happen?" Such a challenge to the priority of the mythic imagination over the truth was, he observes, "the highest compliment ever paid me" (pp. 7–8).

12. Collecting substantial royalties in the initial year of the novel's publication, Wister determined, encouraged by the Macmillan editor George P. Brett, to take the novel to Broadway. In 1903, he signed a contract with the producer Kirk La Shelle, who had previously enjoyed much success with the staging of another Western property, *Arizona*. La Shelle did the adaptation of the plot, while Wister occupied himself with penning the dialogue. The Boston opening was not a success, largely, so Wister thought, because La Shelle had prevailed upon him to eliminate the lynching scene. Quickly writing that scene into the play and making other changes (some quite substantial), Wister saved the production from failure. After a number of runs on the road, *The Virginian* opened on Broadway on January 5, 1904. There it played for four months, achieving a modest success; road companies kept the production alive for a full decade, and it was the play that inspired Cecil B. DeMille to make in 1914 the first of what would be, at least to date, five movie versions. For further details, see Darwin Payne, *Owen Wister:*

Chronicler of the West, Gentleman of the East (Dallas: Southern Methodist University Press, 1985), on which the above account is based.

13. Details about the novel's publication history from Stephen Tatum, "Afterword," in Melody Graulich, ed., *Reading* The Virginian *in the New West* (Lincoln: University of Nebraska Press, 2003), pp. 255–272.

14. The Cooperian and dime-novel traditions of the genre are usefully discussed by Christine Bold in *Selling the Wild West: Popular Western Fiction 1860–1960* (Bloomington: Indiana University Press, 1987). Much western fiction, particularly the many books of the incredibly prolific Louis L'Amour, return to the "ritualistic adventure" of the dime novel tradition and put action at the center of the narrative. Such a focus is also characteristic of the western movie (and even, perhaps surprisingly, of the stage version of *The Virginian*, in which time-honored generic elements are much more prominent than they are in the novel).

15. Forrest G. Robinson, *Having it Both Ways: Self-Subversion in Western Popular Classics* (Albuquerque: University of New Mexico Press, 1993), p. 47.

16. Printed as an appendix to *The Virginian*, p. 331. Further quotations will be cited parenthetically in the text.

17. Richard Slotkin points out that this villain's name suggests both "'treason' (from the Spanish) and 'tramp' – the term that had identified the most rootless and 'dangerous' segment of the working class since 1877" (Slotkin, *Gunfighter Nation: The Myth of the Frontier in Twentieth-Century America* [Norman: University of Oklahoma Press, 1992]), p. 179.

18. Jackson Lears, *No Place of Grace: Antimodernism and the Transformation of American Culture 1880–1920* (New York: Pantheon, 1981), p. 142.

19. G. Edward White, *The Eastern Establishment and the Western Experience: The West of Frederic Remington, Theodore Roosevelt, Owen Wister*, 2nd rev. edn (Austin: University of Texas Press, 1989), p. 140.

20. Frederick Jackson Turner, "The Problem of the Frontier," in Turner, *Rereading Frederick Jackson Turner*, p. 62.

21. Bold, *Selling the Wild West*, p. 10.

22. Wister's presentation of this development is influenced decisively by his elitist politics, which blinded him to the ways in which the "cattle kings" he so admired had recklessly created economic conditions that inevitably led to the demise of "free range" cattle raising, forcing a transition to corn feeding and changing the economic model that had made so many rich. For further discussion, see Jeremy Rifkin, *Beyond Beef: The Rise and Fall of Cattle Culture* (New York: Penguin, 1992), and Lewis Atherton, *The Cattle Kings* (Lincoln: University of Nebraska Press, 1961).

23. Quoted in Richard Maxwell Brown, *No Duty to Retreat: Violence and Values in American History and Society* (Norman: University of Oklahoma Press, 1991), p. 34, who discusses this legal change in detail.

24. Lears, *No Place of Grace*, p. 138.

25. Bold, *Selling the Wild West*, p. 43. She is hardly alone in this estimate. Compare John Cawelti's description of the novel's cultural work, which is that it "brings together in harmony a number of conflicting forces or principles in American life . . . Cooper's problematic antithesis between nature

and the claims of civilization was annealed and harmonized" (Cawelti, *Adventure, Mystery, and Romance*, pp. 229–30).

26. Tatum, "Afterword," p. 266.
27. Robinson, *Having it Both Ways*, p. 1.
28. Michael Coyne, *The Crowded Prairie: American National Identity in the Hollywood Western* (London: I. B. Tauris, 1997), pp. 184, 189.
29. Jim Collins, "Genericity in the Nineties: Eclectic Irony and the New Sincerity," in Collins, Hilary Radner, and Ava Preacher Collins, eds., *Film Theory Goes to the Movies* (New York: Routledge, 1993), especially p. 243.
30. Slotkin, *Gunfighter Nation*, p. 172.
31. Tompkins, *West of Everything*, p. 31.

Filmography

When there are several film versions of a single literary text, the filmography lists only those deemed significant.

Ben-Hur (M-G-M, 1925)

Director:	Fred Niblo and others uncredited
Producers:	J. J. Cohn, Charles B. Dillingham, Abraham L. Erlanger, Louis B. Mayer, Florenz Ziegfeld, Jr., Samuel Goldwyn, Irving Thalberg
Screenplay:	Lew Wallace (novel), H. H. Caldwell and Katherine Hilliker (titles), June Mathis (adaptation), Bess Meredyth and Carey Wilson (scenario and continuity)
Art directors:	Horace Jackson, Ferdinand Pinney Earle
Directors of photography:	Karl Struss, Clyde de Vinna, and others
Principal cast:	Ramon Novarro (Judah Ben-Hur), Francis X. Bushman (Messala), May McAvoy (Esther), Betty Bronson (Mary), Claire McDowell (Mother of Ben-Hur), Kathleen Key (Tirzah), Carmel Myers (Iras), Nigel De Brulier (Simonides), Mitchell Lewis (Sheik Ilderim)

Ben-Hur (M-G-M, 1959)

Director:	William Wyler
Producer:	Sam Zimbalist
Screenplay:	Lew Wallace (novel), Karl Tunberg (screenplay), Maxwell Anderson, Christopher Fry, and Gore Vidal (screenplay, all uncredited)
Art director:	William A. Horning, Edward Carfagno
Director of photography:	Robert L. Surtees
Music:	Miklos Rozsa

246

Principal cast: Charlton Heston (Judah Ben-Hur), Jack Hawkins
                  (Quintus Arrius), Haya Harareet (Esther), Stephen
                  Boyd (Messala), Hugh Griffith (Sheik Ilderim), Martha
                  Scott (Miriam), Cathy O'Donnell (Tirzah), Sam Jaffe
                  (Simonides), Finlay Currie (Balthasar/Narrator in
                  pre-credits sequence), Terence Longdon (Drusus),
                  George Relph (Tiberius Caesar), André Morell
                  (Sextus), Frank Thring (Pontius Pilate)

Carrie (Paramount, 1952)

Director: William Wyler
Producers: William Wyler, Lester Koenig
Screenplay: Theodore Dreiser (novel), Ruth and Augustus Goetz
                    (screenplay)
Art directors: Hal Pereira, Roland Anderson
Director of
photography: Victor Milner
Music: David Raskin
Principal cast: Laurence Olivier (George Hurstwood), Jennifer Jones
                    (Carrie Meeber), Miriam Hopkins (Julie Hurstwood),
                    Eddie Albert (Charles Drouet), Basil Ruysdael (Mr.
                    Fitzgerald), Ray Teal (Allen), Barry Kelley (Slawson),
                    Sarah Berner (Mrs. Oransky), William Reynolds
                    (George Hurstwood, Jr.), Mary Murphy (Jessica
                    Hurstwood), Harry Hayden (O'Brien), Charles Halton
                    (factory foreman), Walter Baldwin (Carrie's father),
                    Dorothy Adams (Carrie's mother), Jacqueline de Wit
                    (Carrie's sister Minnie), Harlan Briggs (Joe Brant)

Daisy Miller (Copa del Oro/The Directors Company, 1974)

Director: Peter Bogdanovich
Producer: Peter Bogdanovich
Screenplay: Henry James (story), Frederic Raphael (screenplay)
Art director: Ferdinando Scarfiotti
Director of
photography: Alberto Spagnoli
Music: Classical themes
Principal cast: Cybill Shepherd (Daisy Miller), Barry Brown
                    (Frederick Winterbourne), Cloris Leachman
                    (Mrs. Ezra Miller), Mildred Natwick (Mrs. Costello),
                    Eileen Brennan (Mrs. Walker), Duilio Del Prete

(Mr. Giovanelli), James McMurtry (Randolph
C. Miller), Nicholas Jones (Charles), George Morfogen
(Eugenio), Jean-Pascal Bongard (hotel receptionist
Vevey) Albert Messmer (tutor)

The Europeans (Merchant Ivory Productions, 1979)

Director:	James Ivory
Producers:	Ismail Merchant, Connie Kaiserman
Screenplay:	Henry James (novel), Ruth Prawer Jhabvala (screenplay)
Art director:	Jeremiah Rusconi
Director of photography:	Larry Pizer
Music:	Richard Robbins, Vic Flick
Principal cast:	Lee Remick (Eugenia Young), Robin Ellis (Robert Acton), Wesley Addy (Mr. Wentworth), Tim Choate (Clifford), Lisa Eichorn (Gertrude), Kristin Griffith (Lizzie Acton), Nancy New (Charlotte), Norman Snow (Mr. Brand), Helen Stenborg (Mrs. Acton), Tim Woodward (Felix Young), Gedda Petry (Augustine)

The Last of the Mohicans (Edward Small Productions [Reliance Pictures], 1936)

Director:	George B. Seitz
Producer:	Edward Small
Screenplay:	James Fenimore Cooper (novel), John I. Balderston, Philip Dunne, Daniel Moore, and Paul Perez (all adaptation)
Art director:	John DuCasse Schulze
Director of photography:	Robert Planck
Music:	Roy Webb
Principal cast:	Randolph Scott (Hawkeye), Binnie Barnes (Alice Munro), Henry Wilcoxon (Major Duncan Heyward), Bruce Cabot (Magua), Heather Angel (Cora Munro), Philip Reed (Uncas), Robert Barrat (Chingachgook), Hugh Buckler (Colonel Munro), Willard Robertson (Captain Winthrop), Lumsden Hare (General Abercrambie), Frank McGlynn, Sr. (David Gamut), Will Stanton (Jenkins), William V. Mong (Sacham).

Little Women (RKO, 1933)

Director: George Cukor
Producer: Merian C. Cooper
Screenplay: Louisa May Alcott (novel), Sarah Y. Mason and Victor
                     Heerman (screenplay)
Art director: Van Nest Polglase
Director of
photography: Henry Gerrard
Music: Max Steiner
Principal cast: Katharine Hepburn (Josephine "Jo" March), Joan
                     Bennett (Amy March), Paul Lukas (Professor Baer),
                     Edna May Oliver (Aunt Martha March), Jean Parker
                     (Elizabeth "Beth" March), Frances Dee (Margaret
                     "Meg" March/Brooke), Henry Stephenson (James
                     Laurence), Douglass Montgomery (Theodore "Laurie"
                     Laurence), John Lodge (John Brooke), Spring Byington
                     (Marmee March), Samuel S. Hinds (Mr. March),
                     Mabel Colcord (Hannah), Marion Ballou (Mrs. Kirke),
                     Nydia Westman (Mamie), Harry Beresford (Dr. Bangs)

Moby Dick (Moulin Productions/United Artists, 1956)

Director: John Huston
Producer: John Huston
Screenplay: Herman Melville (novel), Ray Bradbury and John
                     Huston (screenplay), Norman Corwin (screenplay,
                     uncredited)
Art Director: Ralph W. Brinton
Director of
photography: Oswald Morris
Music: Philip Sainton
Principal cast: Gregory Peck (Captain Ahab), Richard Basehart
                     (Ishmael), Leo Genn (Starbuck), James Robertson
                     Justice (Captain Boomer), Harry Andrews (Stubb),
                     Orson Welles (Father Mapple), Bernard Miles
                     (Manxman), Noel Purcell (ship's carpenter), Edric
                     Connor (Daggoo), Mervyn Johns (Peleg), Joseph
                     Tomelty (innkeeper), Francis De Wolff (Captain
                     Gardiner), Philip Stainton (Bildad), Royal Dano
                     (Elijah), Seamus Kelly (Flask), Frederick Ledebur
                     (Queequeg)

Murders in the Rue Morgue (American International Pictures, 1971)

Director:	Gordon Hessler
Producer:	Louis M. Heyward
Screenplay:	Edgar Allan Poe (story), Christopher Wicking and Henry Slesar (screenplay)
Art director:	José Luis Galicia
Director of photography:	Manuel Berengier
Music:	Waldo de Los Rios
Principal cast:	Jason Robards (Cesar Charron), Herbert Lom (René Marot), Christine Kaufmann (Madeleine Charron), Adolfo Celi (Inspector Vidocq), Maria Perschy (Genevre), Michael Dunn (Pierre Triboulet), Lilli Palmer (Mrs. Charron), Peter Arne (Aubert), Rosalind Elliot (Gabrielle), Marshall Jones (Luigi Orsini), María Martin (Madam Adolphe), Ruth Plattes (Orsini's assistant)

The Portrait of a Lady (Polygram/Propaganda Films, 1996)

Director:	Jane Campion
Producers:	Monty Montgomery, Steve Golin
Screenplay:	Henry James (novel), Laura Jones (screenplay)
Art directors:	Janet Patterson, Mark Raggett
Director of photography:	Stuart Dryburgh
Music:	Wojciech Kilar
Principal cast:	Nicole Kidman (Isabel Archer), John Malkovich (Gilbert Osmond), Barbara Hershey (Madame Serena Merle), Mary-Louise Parker (Henrietta Stackpole), Martin Donovan (Ralph Touchett), Shelley Winters (Mrs. Touchett), Richard E. Grant (Lord Warburton), Shelley Duvall (Countess Gemini), Christian Bale (Edward Rosier), Viggo Mortensen (Caspar Goodwood), Valentina Cervi (Pansy Osmond), John Gielgud (Mr. Touchett), Roger Ashton-Griffiths (Bob Bantling), Catherine Zago (Mother Superior), Alessandra Vanzi (Nun #2), Amy Lindsay (Miss Molyneux #1), Katherine Anne Porter (Miss Molyneux #2)

The Red Badge of Courage (M-G-M, 1951)

Director:	John Huston
Producer:	Gottfried Reinhardt
Screenplay:	Stephen Crane (novel), Albert Band, and John Huston (adaptation)
Art director:	Cedric Gibbons, Hans Peters
Director of photography:	Harold Rosson
Music:	Bronislau Kaper
Principal cast:	Andy Devine (The Cheerful Soldier), Robert Easton (Thompson), Douglas Dick (The Lieutenant), Tim Durant (The General), Arthur Hunnicutt (Bill Porter), Royal Dano (The Tattered Soldier), John Dierkes (Jim Conklin, The Tall Soldier), Bill Mauldin (Tom Wilson, The Loud Soldier), Audie Murphy (Henry Fleming, The Youth)

The Scarlet Letter (Allied Stars and others, 1995)

Director:	Roland Joffé
Producers:	Roland Joffé, Andrew G. Vajna
Screenplay:	Nathaniel Hawthorne (novel), Douglas Day Stewart (screenplay)
Art director:	Roy Walker
Director of photography:	Alex Thomson
Music:	John Barry
Principal cast:	Demi Moore (Hester Prynne), Gary Oldman (Reverend Arthur Dimmesdale), Robert Duvall (Roger Chillingworth), Lisa Joliffe-Andoh (Mituba), Edward Hardwicke (Governor John Bellingham), Robert Prosky (Horace Stonehall), Roy Dotrice (Reverend Thomas Cheever), Joan Plowright (Harriet Hibbons), Malcolm Storry (Major Dunsmuir), James Bearden (Goodman Mortimer), Larissa Laskin (Goody Mortimer), Amy Wright (Goody Gotwick), George Aguilar (Johnny Sassamon), Tim Woodward (Brewster Stonehall), Joan Gregson (Elizabeth Cheever), Dana Ivey (Meredith Stonehall), Diane Salinger (Margaret Bellingham), Jocelyn Cunningham (Mary Rollings)

The Sea-Wolf (Warner Brothers, 1941)

Director:	Michael Curtiz
Producers:	Henry Blanke (associate producer), Hal B. Wallis, Jack L. Warner (producers, uncredited)
Screenplay:	Jack London (novel), Robert Rossen (screenplay)
Art director:	Anton Grot
Director of photography:	Sol Polito
Music:	Joseph E. Howard, Erich Wolfgang Korngold
Principal cast:	Edward G. Robinson (Wolf Larsen), Ida Lupino (Ruth Brewster), John Garfield (George Leach), Alexander Knox (Humphrey Van Weyden), Gene Lockhart (Dr. Louis J. Prescott), Barry Fitzgerald (Cooky), Stanley Ridges (Johnson), David Bruce (Young Sailor), Frances McDonald (Svenson), Howard Da Silva (Harrison), Frank Lackteen (Smoke)

Uncle Tom's Cabin (Universal Pictures, 1927)

Director:	Harry A. Pollard
Producers:	Carl Laemmle, Harry A. Pollard
Screenplay:	Harriet Beecher Stowe (novel), Walter Anthony (titles), Harry Pollard, Harvey F. Thew, and A. P. Younger (screenplay)
Art director:	Edward J. Montaigne
Directors of photography:	Jacob Krull, Charles J. Stumar
Music:	Erno Rapee, Hugo Risenfeld
Principal cast:	James B. Lowe (Uncle Tom), Virginia Grey (Eva), George Siegmann (Simon Legree), Margarita Fischer (Eliza), Eulalie Jensen (Cassie), Arthur Edmund Carewe (George Harris, a slave), Adolph Milar (Haley), Jack Mower (Mr. Shelby), Vivien Oaklan (Mrs. Shelby), J. Gordon Rusell (Tom Loker), Skipper Zelliff (Edward Harris, slaveowner), Lassie Lou Ahern (Little Harris), Mona Ray (Topsy), Aileen Manning (Miss Ophelia), John Roche (St. Clare), Lucien Littlefield (Lawyer Marks)

The Virginian (Turner Network Television, 2000)

Director:	Bill Pullman
Producers:	Daniel H. Blatt, Ruth Fainberg, Grace Gilroy, Gary M. Goodman, Bill Pullman, Lynn Raynor
Screenplay:	Owen Wister (novel), Larry Gross (teleplay)
Art director:	Tracey Baryski
Director of photography:	Peter Winstorff
Music:	Nathan Barr
Principal cast:	Bill Pullman (The Virginian), Diane Lane (Molly Stark), John Savage (Steve), Harris Yulin (Judge Henry), Colm Feore (Trampas), James Drury (Rider), Gary Farmer (Buster), Brent Strait (Griffin), Sheila Moore (Mrs. Henry), Philip Granger (Ben), Dennis Weaver (Sam Balaam), Dawn Greenhalgh (Molly's Mother), Norman Edge (Thorsen), James Rattai (Nebrasky), Mark Anderako (Mr. Ogden), Maureen Rooney (Mrs. Ogden), Billy Merasty (Lee Talltrees)

Index